James Z. George

James Z. George

Mississippi's Great Commoner

Timothy B. Smith

University Press of Mississippi / Jackson

www.upress.state.ms.us

The University Press of Mississippi is a member of
the Association of American University Presses.

Copyright © 2012 by University Press of Mississippi
All rights reserved
Manufactured in the United States of America

First printing 2012

∞

Library of Congress Cataloging-in-Publication Data

Smith, Timothy B., 1974–
James Z. George : Mississippi's great commoner / Timothy B. Smith.
p. cm.
Includes bibliographical references and index.
ISBN 978-1-61703-231-8 (cloth : alk. paper) — ISBN 978-1-61703-232-5
(ebook) 1. George, James Z. (James Zachariah), 1826–1897. 2. Mississippi—Politics and government—1865–1950. 3. United States—Politics and government—1865–1900. 4. Legislators—United States—Biography. 5. United States. Congress. Senate—Biography. I. Title.
E664.G34S65 2012
328.73092—dc23
[B]   2011024062

British Library Cataloging-in-Publication Data available

To
Leah Grace

Contents

ix   Preface

3   **CHAPTER 1** "A Struggle with Unfriendly Circumstances": Childhood, 1826–1846

11   **CHAPTER 2** "Young without Position or Wealth": Manhood, 1846–1850

19   **CHAPTER 3** "Ambitious in My Profession": Maturity, 1850–1856

26   **CHAPTER 4** "The Aim of My Official Labors": Wealth, 1856–1860

36   **CHAPTER 5** "This Movement of Secession": Changes, 1860–1861

44   **CHAPTER 6** "The Duties of My Office": Captain, 1861–1862

52   **CHAPTER 7** "My Far-Distant Prison Home": Johnson's Island, 1862

58   **CHAPTER 8** "I Report to Gov. Pettus": State Brigadier General, 1862–1863

68   **CHAPTER 9** "With Gallantry Discarding Caution": Confederate Colonel, 1863

76   **CHAPTER 10** "My Prison Home": Johnson's Island, Again, 1863–1865

85	**CHAPTER 11** "One of the Ablest Lawyers in the State": Reconstruction, 1865–1873
95	**CHAPTER 12** "Surrounded with Difficulties Unprecedented": Politics, 1873–1875
102	**CHAPTER 13** "The Glorious and Decisive Victory": Redemption, 1875
114	**CHAPTER 14** "Eliminating the Last Vestige of Republican Domination": Rewards, 1876–1881
123	**CHAPTER 15** "I Have to Go to the Capitol Now to Do Some Work": First Senate Term, 1881–1886
135	**CHAPTER 16** "The Demands on Me Are Incessant": Second Senate Term, 1886–1890
146	**CHAPTER 17** "The Central Figure of the Convention": Constitutional Convention, 1890
155	**CHAPTER 18** "I Will Correct Them at the Proper Time": Defense, 1890–1891
163	**CHAPTER 19** "Seems to Be Worn Out": Third Senate Term, 1892–1897
176	**CHAPTER 20** "Death Came Very Peacefully": Death, 1897
186	Conclusion
189	Notes
227	Bibliography
243	Index

Preface

"When the Mississippi school boy is asked who is called the 'Great Commoner' of public life in his State he will unhesitatingly answer James Z. George." So wrote Mississippi's premier historian, Dunbar Rowland, in 1901. That certainly may have been the case then. After all, George was a Civil War veteran, Reconstruction redeemer, chief justice of the Mississippi Supreme Court, and Mississippi's longest-serving U.S. senator to that time. He was a very well known figure in nineteenth- as well as early-twentieth-century Mississippi. But that is not the case today. He is mysteriously unknown in today's modern Mississippi.[1]

J. Z. George historiography has taken the same route of decline over the years. In the late nineteenth and early twentieth centuries, academics of the Dunning school viewed him as a hero of white Mississippians, and that was the only story told. Few blacks wrote academic works during that period. Over time, however, George's image began to decline, and he is seen as a racist villain in much of today's academic treatment. Of course, the time period from which he is viewed makes much of the difference. Even in the 1870s white Democrats saw him as a hero, and black and white Republicans viewed him as a rogue. As the decades passed and many of George's racial views went out of use during and after the civil rights movement, he has almost totally been written off as a villain. He has also seemingly been forgotten.

Much of the lack of knowledge about one of Mississippi's most prominent statesmen results from the fact that he has never had a full biography written about him. Several writers have mentioned him in passing in works dealing with the Civil War, Reconstruction, or Gilded Age politics. He has been the topic of several articles. The most complete works on his life are four small master's theses, all done decades ago—one each at the University of Mississippi, Mississippi State University, the University of Alabama, and Louisiana State University. While these theses are in no way complete, they are fodder for the George biographer, providing clues to sources and ideas. The oldest of them also serve another purpose: they are the only real link to George besides the primary sources he left. For instance, the theses completed in the 1930s contain a good deal of family information gleaned from George's sons and daughters, information that is not available anywhere else. Today, no one is alive who knew the senator.

Part of the reason no biography has been written about George is what has long been considered to be a lack of sources. The Mississippi Department of Archives and History has a collection of George's papers, but they are not extensive, and there are large gaps in the coverage of his life. Apparently most of George's official papers were destroyed by fire when his son's law office burned in 1904.[2]

In truth, the perceived lack of sources is not really that at all. Fortunately, most of the existing George papers are letters to his wife, and these provide a much fuller picture of the man than official papers ever could have. Likewise the family has, in private possession at Cotesworth, his home in Carrollton, Mississippi, fully as large a collection of George letters as there are in the Mississippi Department of Archives and History. These letters, never utilized by historians, fill in many of the gaps in his papers in Jackson. A search for George letters in other collections across the country also turned up a vast assortment of his writings. Published records such as Civil War reports, *Congressional Record* debates, and newspapers only add to the wealth of material. Thus it has been a pleasant surprise to find so many rich sources for reconstructing George's life, and the only major challenge has been to read his awful handwriting. He once wrote his wife in jest, "I wonder if you even take the trouble to read my letters through with my very illegible choreography. You must have patience, indeed, to attempt to decipher all I write." It literally takes deciphering, but once the code is broken (he never crossed his *t*'s, for instance), his writings provided a vast portrait of the man.[3]

The existence of so much intimate correspondence, and the lack of official state papers, definitely affected how this biography developed. As more and more items turned up, it became possible to tailor the biography more toward an examination of the man himself rather than a life-and-times treatment. The overall goal has been to present George amid the backdrop of the times. Thus this biography is not an exhaustive examination, for instance, of his legal career, spelling out and quantifying every single case he ever argued, if that would even be possible. It is not a thorough narrative of his military exploits or his every battle action. It is not a comprehensive examination of his judicial career in which every case he ruled on is enumerated. It is not a listing of every piece of land he ever owned. It is not even a detailed examination of his work in the U.S. Senate, what bills he offered, his every debate, or his every step in the capitol. Rather, this biography, while including the context of each of those items, focuses on the man amid the work, not necessarily the work the man did.

The picture that emerges of J. Z. George, or Jim as he was known to his friends around his home in Carrollton, is that of a man who led a complex, intriguing, and entertaining life. Several dominant traits appeared early in his existence, and they reoccurred over and over throughout his days. He was extremely impatient, especially with those who did not agree with him; he even threatened to resign from his positions more than once when matters did not suit him. He was extremely commonplace, even amid the high society of Washington, D.C.; he never let his surroundings or requirements change who he was. He was extremely curt; many individuals, even his own family, remarked about his terse and brusque personality. He was particularly reliant on his wife; he dropped into a morbid melancholy, perhaps even depression, when away from her for long stretches, yet time and again he forced his separation from her. Most important, he was fiercely independent; his life was a life of constantly questioning authority, whether it be his unsympathetic stepfather, his commanding officers in the military, his political party, or his national government. George always seemed to be in the midst of rebelling against authority. Other less combative personal attributes emerged as well, however, such as his ambitiousness, his strong work ethic, his commitment to right as he saw it, and his immense intellect, which, by all accounts, was admitted even by his enemies.[4]

All those conflicting personal traits not surprisingly produced a complex individual who was a maverick in his day. There have been numerous rebellious politicians throughout history. George was certainly not the first nor was he the last, but he certainly was one. On the most basic level, George could be relied on not to side with party or group just because he was a member and was supposed to conform. His life was literally filled with episodes of his going against his party's stance, just because he did not agree. To George, doing what he thought was right trumped doing what was expected of him. On several occasions he did so even at the peril of losing his position, but he did so anyway. He seemed always to be the loyal opposition, even to those allegedly on his side.

Certainly George's complex life, although lived over a hundred years ago, still has relevance even today. While many of his actions and exploits are items of the past, there are many other attributes of George's life that still affect society. Obviously, the most important area in which George's life and actions still reverberate is in the realm of race relations. There is no doubt that George was a white supremacist, and that he took actions to maintain white supremacy in Mississippi. After all, he lived in a day in which white supremacy was the normal way for almost all whites to function. George's actions came at a time when large questions on race and racism were being asked and answered, even by a federal government that by today's standards can only be labeled as racist. While we today in no way condone or approve of those attitudes and actions, we do need to write objectively and openly about men such as George if we are to understand our heritage and history. Only by seeking to understand the actions and ideas of men such as George within the racist context of his times can we learn from our past and hopefully avoid similar mistakes in the future.

Thus writing a biography of George hopefully neither glorifies him and his actions nor vilifies him for acting as he did in the society in which he lived 150 years ago. Rather this book seeks to explain what he did, why he did it, and the results of his actions in an accurate and forthright manner that will hopefully do justice to the past as well as point toward the future. My intent is to see the issues as he saw them and try to explain why he took such actions and why he thought it was the right thing to do.

To be sure, it was mostly George's stances on race that made him a force in Mississippi and national politics. One recent historian, Stephen Cresswell, has termed him "Mississippi's most important Democratic leader in the late nineteenth century." He was of course more responsible than any other man in shaping segregated and black disenfranchised Mississippi politics for at least a century. But his effect went far beyond Mississippi; other Southern states copied his plan of redemption and later disenfranchisement. George was definitely a force in the late 1800s. He thus deserves a modern, academic examination of his life.[5]

◆ ◆ ◆

Many wonderful people have aided in the preparation of this biography. Their support, insight, and comments have all greatly strengthened the work. Any remaining weaknesses are strictly my own.

Archivists and staff members at numerous repositories were extremely helpful and pleasant. Janie Morris at Duke University; Patrick Kerwin at the Library of Congress; Barbara Ilie at the University of North Carolina; Germain J. Bienvenu at Louisiana State University; Mike Ballard, Betty Self, and Ryan Semmes at Mississippi State University; Nan Card at the Rutherford B. Hayes Presidential Center; Cindy Lawler at the University of Southern Mississippi; Jennifer Ford and John Wall at the University of Mississippi; Don Ritchie and Heather Moore at the U.S. Senate Historical Office; Jane Newton and Janet Hencley at the Monroe County, Georgia, courthouse; and the staff at the Tennessee State Library and Archives, National Archives and Records Administration, Georgia Department of Archives and History, Carrollton #36 Free and Accepted Masons, and the Leflore County Courthouse all greatly aided in the research. Steve and Sam Guyton graciously made available letters from their family's collection.

The staff at two of Mississippi's finest institutions were extremely helpful. The Mississippi Department of Archives and History deserves special mention. Hank Holmes, Anne Webster, Clinton Bagley, Jean Hudspeth, Joyce Dixon-Lawson, Grady Howell, and De'Niecechsi Layton endured my monthly visits cheerfully, and entertainingly facilitated my extensive research there. They went over and above the call of duty on several occasions. I enjoyed their help and expertise so much in researching and writing a previous volume on Mississippi that their friendliness went a long way in helping me select another Mississippi topic for my next project.

The staff at the Mississippi Supreme Court building's state library, particularly Clara Joorfetz and Liz Thompson, were helpful beyond all expectations. The Mississippi State Library is a vast but relatively unknown treasure of Mississippi sources. The friendliness of the staff matches the quality of the material.

Working with the University Press of Mississippi, especially with Craig Gill, has again been a pleasure. Copyeditor Robert Burchfield also aided the manuscript with a keen eye.

The people around Carrollton, Mississippi, J. Z. George's hometown as well as my own, were encouraging and helpful. Jenniffer Stephenson at the public library; Wilton Neal at the tax assessor's office; Bessie Pearce, Debbie McClain, Stanley "Sugar" Mullins, and Shonna McGehee at the Carroll County Courthouse; Snooky Lee and Bernard Taylor at the Carrollton Baptist Church; and Susie James all aided in the research. Attorneys Kenny Downs and Danette Roland aided in understanding the legal aspects of George's career.

The family of J. Z. George has also been a very helpful and eager source of aid. George and his wife had nine children who lived to adulthood, so the number of George's descendents now is untold, and there is no way I could have met and talked with each. I do hope that the publication of this volume will bring to the surface more interest in him, however, and hopefully even additional sources on his life that may be owned by the family.

Although I met and talked with several descendents, three of George's great-grandchildren need special mention. Larry E. Noble unfortunately died several years ago, but he performed a massive amount of research on two aspects of George's career, greatly aiding me. First, he transcribed all of George's prisoner of war letters, which was no doubt a painstaking task given George's atrocious handwriting. Even Mr. Noble could not decipher all of his writing, but I was fortunately able to determine a little more of it (after unlocking the code to his penmanship) while comparing documents. Second, he performed a lot of research into George's early Georgia life.

Gloria Kellum, recently retired vice chancellor for University Relations at the University of Mississippi, was an early and enthusiastic supporter in the process. She helped secure sources and contact family members, and her encouragement throughout the process has been a great boost. She is now in the first stages of leading the venture to preserve Cotesworth as a cultural and historical center, and is doing wonders in the effort.

By far the greatest help rendered by the family came from Katherine Williams, who still owns Cotesworth. She gave me complete access to everything at Cotesworth, including original and never-before-used family letters (which she has graciously allowed the Mississippi Department of Archives and History to copy), records, Bibles, photos, and George's massive library. She even drove me around the plantation on her farm machinery. I can honestly say this biography would not be nearly as complete without her help. I could not have asked for a more kind or helpful welcome.

Academic friends and coworkers have also aided in the process, including two anonymous readers for the University Press of Mississippi. My mentor and friend John F. Marszalek read the entire manuscript and made many valuable corrections and recommendations. Richard Damms read and edited a draft chapter years ago as a graduate school research paper. My friend Thomas Adams Upchurch, a scholar of Reconstruction and Gilded Age politics, read portions of the manuscript and made many useful suggestions. A Mississippi treasure, David Sansing, professor emeritus at the University of Mississippi, provided encouragement and discussed numerous issues with me. Colleagues at my academic home, the University of Tennessee at Martin, Deidra Beene, Sandy King, Sarah Conrad, and my department chair, David Coffey, are always helpful in every way.

My family remains my major inspiration. I hope the frequency with which I mention them in my writings does not become repetitive or commonplace, and I hope that they understand my love and appreciation for them.

My father once again performed yeoman work on this volume. As he did on the previously published Mississippi Civil War home front book, he regularly accompanied me to the archives in Jackson, Mississippi, and once again mined sources with expertise. He is really becoming an expert at newspaper research on a microfilm machine. Since he lives in Carrollton, he performed much extra research on this volume, spending numerous hours in libraries, courthouses, and county offices there and in Greenwood.

My father and mother were also willing hosts during our monthly research trips to Carrollton and Jackson. The fact that we brought their two granddaughters with us no doubt made them much more receptive to our visits. My in-laws, Bennie and Barbara Castleman, are totally supportive as well.

My wife Kelly's research trips to the mall in Jackson during my research trips to the archives no doubt helped fuel her interest in the project. She is always very supportive of all my endeavors, although she has just about heard enough stories about the senator, recently informing me that "its time to bury J. Z. George again." For your love and patience, I love you Kelly.

My two daughters are my special little angels. Mary Kate, who had a previous volume dedicated to her, helps daddy in more ways than she knows, mostly by keeping my mind based in reality and the twenty-first century rather than always in the nineteenth. Her frequent visits to daddy's home office are particularly special to me.

This volume is dedicated to my newest little angel, Leah Grace. God could not have blessed me any more than he has with my girls. I hope one day when they read these words they will realize just how much I love them.

James Z. George

CHAPTER 1

"A Struggle with Unfriendly Circumstances"

Childhood, 1826–1846

It was a scene not unlike many others that fall day in 1828, combining elements of fear, sadness, hope, happiness, and reunion. The estate sale of Joseph George had brought in a large crowd. Some of these people, such as the widow and other reunited family members, wore heavy hearts as neighbors and probably some strangers eagerly went through the deceased's belongings. Joseph had died several months earlier, in June, and the hardship had only increased for the widow, Mary, and her family. Making matters worse for her, since he died unexpectedly with no will, according to Georgia law she could not even inherit the items in the sale. She had to buy them back herself.[1]

The sale probably had its biggest effect on Joseph George's only child. A mere twenty months old, young James had been born in October 1826. It is not recorded whether the young toddler was at the sale, although a good guess would have been yes. In any case, the actions of that day, and the larger context of his father's death, would prove to be the major issues of the young boy's life.[2]

Losing his father so early in life had a dramatic effect on James Z. George. Yet the inheritance he received from his father, and later from his grandfather as well, set the boy up for at least a respectable start in life. One of the most persistent myths about J. Z. George is that he rose from a common, poor heritage to reach the heights of success in his state—the American Dream. Many labeled his life as a rags-to-riches story; one Mississippi historian even commented, "the taunt that he did not come from the aristocratic classes was a political jibe of his opponents." However, nothing could be farther from the truth. George, to be sure, faced enormous challenges in his childhood and teenage years, but not because he descended from poor ancestors. In fact, his direct lineage included governors, slave owners, and wealthy forefathers, and he started his adult life fairly well endowed as a result.[3]

George's grandfather on his father's side, James George, was a Revolutionary War veteran from North Carolina who married Mary Adair, the granddaughter of the governor of Kentucky, John Adair. Thus George's great-great-grandfather was governor of the commonwealth between the years 1820 and 1824. James George was a wealthy landowner who farmed land in Georgia, first in Warren County, and then in Columbia and Jones counties. By 1826, the year his grandson was born, James George owned twenty-two slaves, over the magic number of twenty that historians allot to the elite planter class. He owned some 800 acres in both Jones and Monroe counties in central Georgia, and that number would grow through the years. The family also grew, as the Georges had nine children, one of whom was Joseph, who became the father of J. Z. George. Joseph was born in Warren County, Georgia, in 1805.[4]

George's maternal grandparents, Zachariah and Mary Chambliss, were not nearly as well off as the Georges, although they were by no means poor. The most slaves ever recorded for Zachariah was eleven in 1860. The Chamblisses were native to South Carolina, but made a westward trek, owning land in Columbia, Baldwin, and then Monroe counties in Georgia. They had eleven children in all, including Mary, named for her mother, who was born in 1806 in Baldwin County. Thus both of George's grandmothers as well as his mother were named Mary. It is no surprise that he would name one of his own daughters Mary as well.[5]

By the mid-1820s the Georges and Chamblisses lived on adjoining land near Ebenezer Church in Monroe County, about three or four miles east of Forsyth, Georgia. Obviously, they all knew each other, and their sons courted each other's daughters. Such was the case with young Joseph Warren George, who wooed and wed Mary Chambliss in December 1825. Ten months later, on October 20, 1826, the young Monroe County newlyweds had their first and only child, naming him James Zachariah George after his two grandfathers.[6]

Joseph George and his bride were young, Joseph just beginning to farm the land of both families. He owned a couple hundred acres on which he grew cotton and corn, and he owned a few slaves. It was in that context of a young and emerging family that James Zachariah George entered the world. Had matters moved more auspiciously there is every indication that Joseph George would have gone on to own more and more land and numerous slaves, just like his father and brothers, and many other families in the area. Joseph and Mary would have had other children, and young George would have grown up in the same environment in which his father had been raised. George was born into a wealthy family, although his young father at the time of his birth was just beginning his land ownership and had yet to make a name and fortune for himself.[7]

Unfortunately, Joseph George never had a chance to make his wealth. He died on June 8, 1828, just twenty months after his son was born. The baby was now fatherless, his mother a widow. One of George's friends later in life described this time as "a struggle with unfriendly circumstances."[8]

Since the young boy could not see to his own affairs, his uncle, Edmund S. Chambliss, Mary's brother, became his legal guardian until the boy came of age. Chambliss, his brother, and another man put up a $1,500 guardianship bond for young James in 1829, and Chambliss oversaw a growing estate in the boy's name. While baby James lived with his mother, Chambliss made most of the financial decisions. He was close enough to see to the baby if need be, living as he did in the southern part of Monroe County at Russellville. Chambliss himself was a fairly wealthy man, eventually owning fourteen slaves and several hundred acres of land.[9]

Although Mary and young James had a guardian for his estate, they still needed care and a livelihood, which was hard for a young woman and baby at the time. The most obvious way for Mary to gain a livelihood and residence, as well as a father figure for her fatherless child, was to remarry. And so she did, to a man who lived near the Georges and Chamblisses in Monroe County. The Durham family had come west like the others from North Carolina. One of Matthew and Fannie Durham's sons was Seaborn, who had been born in 1796. Seaborn Durham and Mary George married in 1830, he becoming the young boy's stepfather. Seaborn was beginning to make a name for himself, even buying some of the George family land. He owned ten slaves in 1830.[10]

Although Seaborn Durham would never become rich, he now had a stepson who had inherited a substantial sum that went into an estate until he reached maturity. Mary and Seaborn, once he married James's mother, became the executors of Joseph's estate, which provided a moderate sum to young James for use in the present as well as the future, thus aiding the sometimes cash-strapped Durham in raising the child. The entire estate was worth a few hundred dollars, and James received some of that along with three slaves (a woman and her two children), and around 200 acres of land. James's legal guardian, his uncle Chambliss, later sold half of the land to Seaborn Durham and rented out James's slaves, all of which brought more money into the young boy's estate. The annual rental fees for his slaves brought in a particularly steady sum.¹¹

By far, the most inheritance young James received was at the death of his paternal grandfather, James George, in 1832. Although James's paternal grandmother would live into the 1860s, his grandfather was the property owner and owned well over 1,000 acres and scores of slaves with an estate valued at $80,000. Part of that inheritance would go to James, as the only descendent of one of the sons, and it reached a sum totaling nearly $4,000. As a minor, however, James would not receive it until he came of age.¹²

Because James was a minor, Chambliss also oversaw this inheritance until James reached manhood, which would legally come in 1847 at age twenty-one. Chambliss put the young lad's inheritance to work in the meantime, using the slaves and the land James had inherited and making money in the process, some years nearly $2,000. Some of the proceeds were used for James's medical as well as educational benefit, as well as for other items.¹³

Already with his life in an upheaval, another major change came for young James in 1834. Seaborn and his new wife, their children, and his eight-year-old stepson, James, all moved to Mississippi. Several events came together to lead to this significant move. There was an economic recession in Georgia in that year. Also Seaborn's father had died a few months earlier, removing from the scene the patriarch that all the Durham sons had followed. The family thus scattered. New land was being opened in Mississippi after the removal of the Choctaw and Chickasaw Indians. Thus Seaborn, Mary, and the children, including James, all made the move westward and settled near Shuqualak in Noxubee County.¹⁴

Little is known of the Durhams' stay in Noxubee County, much less the activities of eight-year-old James. The family lived on what was known as the "Ratliff Place" some four miles east of Shuqualak. But life in Noxubee County did not work out for Seaborn Durham, so he decided to move farther west, into the newly organized territory in the old Native American tribal lands. He next moved to Carroll County in 1836, where James grew to manhood and set deep roots; despite sojourns in the state as well as national capitals, James George would make Carroll County his home for the rest of his life.¹⁵

Carroll County had been organized in 1833, just three years before Durham moved Mary and young James into its limits. The county was extremely large in that day, 908 square miles and requiring two county seats, one in Carrollton for the northern part and another in Vaiden for the southern portion. The county took form out of land ceded to the state by the Choctaws in the Treaty of Dancing Rabbit Creek of 1830, which was part of Andrew Jackson's removal policy. One of the major Choctaw chiefs was Greenwood Leflore, who did not follow his tribe westward in removal even after signing the treaty that required such a move. Instead, he remained on his palatial plantation in Carroll County, Malmaison. The Choctaws removed him from power because of his actions, but he lived a grand life in Carroll County, owning many slaves and making a fortune.[16]

Seaborn Durham, with Mary and James in tow, first settled near Vaiden in the southern part of the county, at a small hamlet called Shongalo. There Seaborn bought a few hundred acres, set up his household, and began to farm with his nine slaves. His numerous children, including James, all worked in the fields as well. Apparently Durham had little use for schooling, preferring that his children learn to work the land with their hands. One George family researcher has even described Durham as a "negatively good man." And by 1840 James had no choice but to submit to Durham's ideas because that year the stepfather successfully petitioned a Carroll County court for guardianship of young James. Obviously, George's uncle in Georgia could not properly see to him in Mississippi, so James came under Durham's official care, which meant working in the fields. But James very quickly learned he did not desire an agricultural vocation, at least not one in which he had to toil himself. The idea of making his bright and quick mind work for him thus took an early hold on young James.[17]

Another myth is that J. Z. George had little education as a boy and that he was essentially a self-taught and self-made man. Certainly he studied at night after working through the day; one contemporary described him "studying at night by firelight." Later, a U.S. senator described the studious boy: "Books were constant companions. They were not only read, but studied and digested." In actuality George had a good bit of formal schooling as a child as well, both in Georgia and in Mississippi. Records from George's estate before he came of age indicate his guardians paid several dollars in tuition for him at various times, and at other times paid "Board," which could have been tuition for a boarding school. Once in Carroll County, George attended Hughes's school at Shongalo, a large two-story building with the bottom floor used for boys and the top floor for girls. He apparently also attended school at nearby Middleton for a time. Amid his fieldwork, the young boy learned to read and write, and to do so quite well. Family lore, as well as some contemporary newspapers, states that George even learned Latin in school and taught himself some Greek.[18]

What other little information available about George as a boy describes him as being like almost any other Carroll County lad of the time. One newspaper later described him, with some exaggeration, as "a linsey, woolsey, home-spun boy, [who] worked in the cotton and corn fields of Carroll County. He had no great family influence, no generous patron, no money—nothing but indomitable energy, a warm, true and generous heart, a high soul, a strong body and an honorable ambition; with this stock in trade he began the business of life." Another described him as a "sturdy, heavy-set boy" who had a crush on one Mary Wilson. A friend described some of his boyhood work as "trudging over the dirt roads while he drove the team that hauled his mother's cotton the long, dreary way from Carroll to the head of navigation at Yazoo for shipment." He took the nickname "Old Trace Chains," and was apparently hailed as the "acknowledged champion" when it came to "whip poppers."[19]

While plowing in the fields one day in his midteens, however, George decided he had had enough. He stopped plowing and boldly went and told his stepfather he was leaving to further his education. Durham obviously hated to see the strong young man leave, but did not stop him either; George's mother supported the decision. Perhaps Seaborn and Mary could already see the intellect that was obvious in the young boy, as well as his willingness to question authority.[20]

Without the molding influence of a loving father, George grew up as the quintessential stepson, never holding the same esteem as Durham's biological children. Much of George's rebellion and partiality for questioning authority probably dates back to his rearing in these conditions. And the rowdiness inherent in such cases soon came out. In October 1845, for instance, a Carroll County court indicted George on charges of assault and battery. He pleaded guilty and paid a $5 fine. And Durham apparently did not make much of an effort to foster a relationship with the boy, but rather took advantage of the situation. As George's guardian in Mississippi, Durham had access to much of the boy's assets and estate. By 1843 Seaborn Durham owed George's estate some $3,800; the debt had risen to over $4,500 three years later. And Durham frequently made decisions about George's possessions, such as selling, hiring, and buying slaves. No wonder the boy questioned his stepfather's authority.[21]

George's decision to leave the fields would later have more of an effect on him than he perhaps immediately thought because it propelled him into some of the highest offices in the land, but it also, more immediately and more domestically, put George in contact with the man who would become his mentor in life, lawyer William Cothran. George left Shongalo in the mid-1840s and moved to Carrollton, the county seat of the northern half of Carroll County. There Cothran accepted George into his circle and began to teach the young man the law.

William Cothran had been born in Tennessee but came to Carrollton in the mid-1830s, becoming one of the town's lawyers in 1837. In 1838 he built a law office on the north side of the court square in Carrollton, from which he represented all sorts of citizens. In 1839 he married a local woman named Francis M. Young, one of the sisters of the Young family who had earlier moved to Carrollton from middle Tennessee. When the bright young George arrived, Cothran obviously saw potential in him and took him on as an apprentice.[22]

Cothran not only supplied George with training in the field of law, but he also provided the company of a young woman who quickly won George's heart. Cothran's sister-in-law was Elizabeth Brooks Young, born in middle Tennessee on August 10, 1827, and the granddaughter of Colonel William Martin, who had served under Andrew Jackson and in the South Carolina and Georgia legislatures. Elizabeth had moved with her parents, Thomas and Sarah Young, to Carrollton at age nine, in 1836. There her sister met and married Cothran, who later introduced his sister-in-law to his new protégé, James Z. George. Apparently, the two started to converse by letter in January 1846.[23]

But the young George was not yet ready to marry. He was still not of age, being only nineteen years old in 1845. He also did not have much money at the time to start a family, acquire a house, and provide the necessities of life. In addition, he had no hope of obtaining a job in the law until he reached a majority age, which in that day was twenty-one. When he reached that age, however, several things would happen. He would be allowed to practice law, with a license of course, which would provide money for his family. He would also gain access to the substantial amount of the estate left him not only by his father but also, more important, by his grandfather in Georgia. He would also get the money Seaborn Durham owed him. Once he acquired the estate and a living, he could support a wife and children, which would naturally follow.[24]

But George was unwilling to wait that long. George's local representative in the state legislature in 1846, Benjamin Kennedy, petitioned to have George's minority status removed, making him a fully functioning citizen of the state. Such a move would allow him to begin a law practice as well as garner for himself the estate held in his name. The state legislature acted on the request, with the legislation entitled "An act to remove the civil disabilities of James Z. George, minor of Carroll County" going before both the state House of Representatives and Senate in February 1846. The House passed the bill on February 13, with the Senate following five days later. The governor signed the bill on February 20, 1846. George was only nineteen years old, yet he was no longer a minor.[25]

George thus had his start. He had the authority from the legislature to take his inheritance, which amounted to several thousand dollars; to become licensed and begin practicing law; and to marry Elizabeth Young. He also forced Seaborn Durham to pay him the money owed him from his guardianship, which amounted to $4,591.96, plus 8 percent annual interest. George's new friend William Cothran represented the young man in the court case against Durham. Even better, George had the training from Cothran to enter his chosen profession, with an invitation to become a partner with him once licensed. Now it was up to him to make a success out of what others had invested in him.[26]

CHAPTER 2

"Young without Position or Wealth"

Manhood, 1846–1850

Just because James Z. George was no longer a minor, that did not mean he was yet a man. Nevertheless, he had an advantageous start to his life as an adult. He had a small fortune at his disposal, which if invested carefully could give him a tremendous start toward a life of wealth. He also had the mentorship of William Cothran and the eye of his sister-in-law, Elizabeth, whom he called Bettie. But before George could make any headway in his legal, personal, or material affairs, he was diverted.

The delay was not of George's own making. Rather, he became intimately involved, much like the entire nation, in the war against Mexico that erupted in 1846. George put his law practice and his courtship of Bettie on hold to go and fight for his nation. Obviously, George had a vested interest in the outcome, as did most Southerners. The war provided the opportunity to take California and perhaps other lands from Mexico, thus allowing the expansion of slavery, which the Southerner George desired so he could one day own many slaves and become prosperous. It was also an opportunity for George to advance his personal position. It would, if he survived, allow him a chance at military glory, which the ambitious young man desired. Thus George went to war.[1]

The Mexican War, as it is known in the United States, developed ostensibly over a boundary dispute in Texas, but it had much larger causes. One of President James K. Polk's goals upon assuming office was the acquisition of California, which belonged to Mexico. In addition, Mexico had never recognized the independence of Texas or its annexation to the United States. At the least, Mexico disputed America's claim of the Rio Grande as the border between the two nations. Polk was adamant about that and sent Zachary Taylor and a portion of the U.S. Army to hold the contested land.[2]

A minor skirmish in which a Mexican force crossed the river and attacked an American patrol was fashioned into a full-scale invasion and a catalyst for war. Although many Americans believed Polk had used a minor episode to start a war to acquire California, Congress went along with his desire in May 1846 and declared war. States all across the Union began to mobilize volunteers for the war effort. Mississippi was allotted one regiment in the first national call for troops (it eventually sent a second upon another call), and one of the companies came from Carroll County. The assertive George was right in the middle of it.[3]

Local Carroll County leader Bainbridge D. Howard began to organize a company at Carrollton, and he became its captain once the unit formed. Daniel R. Russell, who would later be a colonel in the Civil War, was the company's first lieutenant. George signed on as a private. Although his status in later life afforded him more responsibility, at the time George was a mere nineteen-year-old boy, unmarried, and without a real occupation. The role of private was appropriate. Private George and his company called themselves the "Carroll County Volunteers."[4]

This company left Carrollton in June 1846, marching to Greenwood, where they took a Yazoo River steamboat to Vicksburg. Unfortunately George was sick at the time and later had to travel by buggy to Greenwood to catch up with his command. Arriving at Yazoo City, some of George's spunk appeared, illustrating his lifelong penchant for questioning authority. He seated himself at the landing while others loaded the boat in preparation for casting off. A Yazoo County company's captain, John Sharp, inquired why George was not helping load the boat and told the young boy to get to work. Remaining seated, George somewhat foolishly asked the captain if that was a request or a command. Sharp responded that at the time it was a request, but when he returned it would be a command. Sharp rode off, apparently to find George's captain or another officer of higher rank. When Sharp returned, George was busy loading the boat.[5]

At Vicksburg, the company was officially mustered into service for twelve months, becoming Company D of the First Mississippi Infantry. They elected as their colonel U.S. representative Jefferson Davis, who pulled political strings to get his men armed with rifled weapons. Once the arms arrived later in the summer, the name stuck, with the regiment becoming known as the "Mississippi Rifles," while the weapon itself would become known as the "Mississippi Rifle."[6]

George officially mustered into the army on June 6 at Vicksburg. His military records show him rising no higher than a private, although the local Carrollton paper listed him as a third corporal. Whatever his rank, the regiment remained encamped at "Camp Independence" near Vicksburg until July, when the men boarded steamboats for the trip down to New Orleans. At Vicksburg, George celebrated the Fourth of July; "proper honor was paid to the National flag," remembered one member of the regiment. He also noted that the boys were getting bored in camp: "they cannot bear the idea of remaining inactive." There was also the problem of pay at Vicksburg. "Our boys are complaining bitterly about the tardiness of Uncle Sam's pay master," a soldier noted, remarking that the men had "run through all their funds." "I think after the inhabitants of the vicinity have drained the purses of the regiment they will be anxious for it to leave," another soldier wrote home.[7]

Unfortunately, too, some sickness developed in the regiment, becoming epidemic as time passed and as the men moved into hotter climates. Future Confederate general Carnot Posey, a member of the regiment, wrote that even at Vicksburg, "there are several in the regiment who are very sick." Nevertheless, George and the unit moved on. At New Orleans, where Colonel Davis joined them after his trip from Washington, D.C., the men boarded the *Massachusetts* and *New York* to set sail for Texas, which they reached in late July. "We pitched out tents on the beach near the gulf," one member of the regiment recalled while at Brazos Santiago, but soon the regiment moved on to the mouth of the Rio Grande. Colonel Davis drilled George and the men continually.[8]

The tropical weather made the men even sicker. Hundreds became ill and were discharged. One member of the regiment recorded in his diary, "There are a great many cases of sickness today in camp and one death." He also noted that "strict military discipline has been rigidly enforced," obviously to help keep the sickness down. Then there were other problems such as the terrain on which they camped. One Mississippi soldier described it as "one continual sand plain without any timber at all, not even so much as a bush." Even George's captain, Howard, was so sick that he could not lead the company inland when it began to move with General Taylor in September.[9]

One bit of good news arrived, though, helping raise morale. The regiment would get the new rifles Davis had ordered, on August 21. One member of the regiment recorded, "we delivered up our muskets and drew the finest quality of rifles with percussion locks." Finely armed, the Mississippians believed they were ready for anything the Mexicans could throw at them. It was a good thing the rifles arrived in late August, because Taylor was ready to move by early September. George and the other members of the regiment sailed up the Rio Grande to Camargo by August 31. The unit, though ravaged by illness, was augmented by more recruits before it had to go into combat.[10]

By late September Taylor had marched inland far enough to attack the Mexican city of Monterrey. George, Davis, and the rest of the Mississippians, brigaded with a Tennessee regiment under Mississippian John A. Quitman, engaged in the assault on September 21, with the regiment making an attack on the eastern side of town and capturing a major citadel known as La Teneria. One Mississippian was not bashful about his regiment's action: "The Mississippi regiment distinguished themselves by the most signal bravery," he wrote in his diary.[11]

Although George left no record of his actions during the battle, Daniel R. Russell did. Russell was in command of the company because Captain Howard was sick and absent from the regiment. Russell reported having forty-two men, one of which was George, in line on September 21. The Carroll County boys, the third company in line from the right, were sheltered behind cover at the beginning of the battle, but when Davis ordered the advance to the left, they quickly began to receive fire from the Mexicans. Russell described how the battle soon degenerated into chaos as the movement to the left was made. George and the Carroll County company ran at "double quick time," but by the time they reached the line within 150 yards of the fort they were to assault, the left companies of the regiment had already started firing and advancing. "By the time my command arrived within 50 or 60 yards of that line, order had disappeared and the movement of the companies in front of me was a rush upon the line," Russell remembered.[12]

Colonel Davis appeared and asked Russell, "Why do not the men get nearer the Fort" and "Why waste ammunition at such a distance?" Indeed, George and the other privates were firing rapidly. Russell reported, "The attempt was made to make the firing regular but it was futile for every man loaded and fired with the utmost rapidity." Russell noted that "the shot, as I suppose grape, and from small arms fell thick upon us." At Davis's urging, Russell moved George and the Carroll County boys some forty to sixty yards closer to the fort, and then they were ordered to charge, Russell hearing the order "above the din of battle." "We took the fort in twenty minutes," Russell wrote home, "and proceeded to a second citadel, which the enemy evacuated." The Carroll County boys crossed a knee-deep creek, but were soon recalled, with Russell describing Colonel Davis as "cursing bitterly" at the recall command.[13]

Several of the Carroll County boys were killed or wounded, but George escaped the ordeal without any damage. Two days later, on September 23, George saw a little more action as "Col. Davis called out from the fort a portion of the regiment," Russell reported, "my company among others, for a sally on the town." He described the action as "interesting fight[ing]— every house a fort, every street fortified." The all-day effort saw a lot of street fighting. Russell wrote that "we crawled on roofs of houses, and with the true rifle curled the yellow scoundrels from the house-tops, whenever they rose to shoot." Only twenty-three of the Carroll County company, George included, participated in the urban fight.[14]

Although little was accomplished on this second day of the battle, the Mexican army withdrew southward two days later. "The Carroll boys have put their mark on Monter[r]ey," Russell wrote home, and commented that "a more gallant set of men than we have, God never chose to send into battle." Although little is known of George's participation, beyond the fact that he was engaged in the fighting both days, one Mississippian in Mexico later described George's efforts. Reuben Davis, colonel of the Second Mississippi Infantry, described George's soldierly qualities in his memoirs. "One distinguished private I may be permitted to mention," Davis wrote. "He was of solid parts, and possessed the firm will and steady reason of the man who may have to wait for his opportunities, but who never misses them when they come. Of such a character, the cool courage of a good soldier is rarely lacking, and George was not only a brave, but in many respects a most lovable man."[15]

It was fortunate George escaped Monterrey unhurt, because that would be the only battle he would see. While at Monterrey and then at Camp Allen, George became ill, apparently with dysentery, and had to be discharged like so many others in the regiment. He was sent home on October 13.[16]

The ambitious George hated to leave his comrades and his hopes for glory, but he could not remain in Mexico and hope to live. Indeed, the regiment, without him, went on to other exploits, most notably the famous action at Buena Vista in February 1847, where Jefferson Davis was wounded and the Mississippians helped save the day. But George was not returning to Carrollton as a failure. He had participated in one of the battles in Mexico and had been honorably discharged through no fault of his own. He was always extremely proud of his Mexican War service. And it was not as if he had nothing to return home for. He had a bright future ahead of him, with a pending marriage as well as a budding law profession. George had "seen the elephant," as combat would be known, and had performed adequately if not gloriously. It was now time for him to move on to his professional and domestic affairs.[17]

May 1847 was a big month for George. Within one week he both married and took out his law license. Becoming a full-fledged lawyer meant a steady income, and George had a head start when Cothran took him into his office on Washington Street, just across from the Carroll County courthouse. Some questioned Cothran's wisdom, saying "a capital ox driver was spoiled to make a poor lawyer." Immediately, though, George began to work cases. Much of his early work was in Carrollton, arguing all kinds of cases. Later, George expanded into other local counties as well as to more regional and state venues. From early on George was a success as a lawyer.[18]

George also married Bettie in May 1847, although he was still anything but wealthy and prominent. In fact, she married him despite her parents' wishes. Years later George wrote about their wedding, "when I was young without position or wealth." Even later he elaborated in a letter marking the anniversary of his first correspondence to her in January 1846: "There I was—a boy—you a young lady just budding into woman-hood." He wrote of how his "age and prospects in life" were not enviable, and that the "half formed intention [of marriage] [w]as foolish." Yet he took out the marriage license, which cost him $200, payable to the governor, Albert Gallatin Brown. At this early stage in his career, however, George needed a cosigner of the bond for the license, and his friend Robert Graham did so. Three days later, on May 27, 1847, George and Bettie married, with the service being conducted by minister John A. Neal.[19]

By all accounts George had married his equal if not his better. He knew as much. "I wonder sometimes," he wrote Bettie after several years of marriage, "how I ever became possessed of such a prize. 'Tis said that marriage is a lottery. If so, I have drawn the highest prize. I fear you have drawn a blank. If I should ever attain to respectability in my profession, I know it will be through your influence. I was a loose and wreckless craft without ballast or rudder floating at the will of winds and gales on the sea of life, you brought [me] into port."[20]

George and Bettie were indeed a loving pair. He adored her, almost too much, he said: "I love you more than all else beside," he wrote, continuing,

"I fear that my love almost approached idolatry." She was almost in awe of his intellectual abilities. Yet they had their differences, even from the start. One concerned religion. She was an avid church member who was faithful to the local Baptist church, having joined the Carrollton Baptist Church in October 1849. George came from a family of Baptists as far back as his Georgia roots, but he was not religious, especially in his younger days. Her dedication to religion and his indifference was always a point of contention, as was his participation in what religious people called vices, such as drinking and smoking tobacco.[21]

The two newlyweds had other issues to deal with as well. George was absolutely dedicated to his family and seemed to develop a deep melancholy when away from them conducting trials. His desire for wealth and success, which often necessitated his absence from home, continually was in conflict with his desire to be at home with his wife and children. On the other hand, Bettie often exhibited a deep jealousy. She continually warned her husband, especially when he was away from home, about associating with young women, even in a social atmosphere. Even when he was at home taking care of the family, Bettie did not want him thinking of another woman. In fairness to George, despite his frequent apologies for his "mental and moral imperfections," there is not any evidence or even a hint of contemplation that he was ever unfaithful to her.[22]

Despite the issues, the Georges began to build on their marriage in several ways. In 1848 they had the first addition to their family. Francis Leonore (Fannie) was born on March 25, 1848. Another daughter came along two years later, on September 17, 1850, this one named Emma. In between the birth of his two daughters, George bought his first piece of property, a $1,000, 120 by 470 foot lot with a house on Washington Street in Carrollton. He also paid $800 for a large piece of land around Vaiden in the southern part of the county, presumably near his mother and Seaborn Durham. George clearly desired to get back into the agricultural business, because he also began to acquire slaves to work his increasing acreage. By 1850 he owned twelve slaves, most of them working on the land he owned near Shongalo.[23]

In 1850 George's landholdings were substantial for a twenty-three-year-old. He owned several hundred acres, including some 160 acres of farmland, which was valued at around $400. He also owned farming implements, two horses, a mule, three cows, and four oxen, among other cattle. He likewise owned thirty sheep and fifty hogs, all of his livestock amounting to a value of over $600. On his farm the slaves grew cotton, wheat, corn, oats, rice, peas, hay, and sweet potatoes. In addition, George's real estate in town was valued at $4,800.[24]

In addition to acquiring modest wealth, George had also begun to give back to those who had aided him earlier. His friend and mentor, William Cothran, had lost his wife in 1842, and their infant daughter, named Frances Elizabeth Cothran, died in early 1843. Cothran was obviously devastated, and James and Bettie took him in to live with them. Cothran remained a fixture in the Georges' lives for many years, and George and his wife named their firstborn daughter Frances after her deceased aunt and cousin.[25]

By 1850 George had become a man, having passed through several rites of passage. He had fought in and survived the war with Mexico, which made him a respected veteran if not a military hero. He had also begun his chosen profession by joining his mentor in partnership. He likewise put his inheritance to work for him by purchasing land and slaves, which was exactly what would have been expected of him considering his childhood and family lineage. He was moving toward fulfilling his ambition to become a wealthy Southern aristocrat. Yet it was perhaps his growing family that pleased him most. Obviously, George was starting his young life successfully, having made good, sound decisions. Through marriage, fatherhood, soldiering, lawyering, and planting, George had established a firm foundation for himself and his family. During the 1850s, he would begin building on that foundation.

CHAPTER 3

"Ambitious in My Profession"

Maturity, 1850–1856

The decade of the 1850s would see the emergence of James Z. George, ironically even while his nation was crumbling around him. Although compromise in 1850 had stalled any breakup of the Union over California, slavery, or states' rights, event after event ultimately caused the nation itself to totter and crumble. Events such as the Kansas-Nebraska Act, the Dred Scott decision, John Brown's raid on Harper's Ferry, and even the caning of a Northern senator by a Southerner on the floor of the U.S. Senate caused major rifts in the already controversial relationship between North and South. The essential disagreement was over slavery—its legitimacy, its expansion, and its future.[1]

Little is known of George's views on these major issues, primarily because he was still a local, although emerging, lawyer in Carroll County and thus did not receive much press coverage. His sentiments can well be understood, however. He avidly supported slavery, so a guess as to his views on these national events is not hard to make.

But after his family, first and foremost in George's mind was his law career, which he obviously saw as financing the necessities of life as well as a start on the wealth and status he desired. Little is known about how many cases he argued in county courts because records are few and not very detailed, but it is clear that George made a good living in his practice. George also trained other lawyers, much as Cothran had trained him. One was William Martin Walton, a graduate of the University of Virginia and later an officer in the Confederacy. Unfortunately, in 1856 George had to separate from his mentor, William Cothran, who had been elected to represent Carroll County in the Mississippi Senate and was soon to become the circuit judge of the Tenth District as well as grand master of Mississippi Masons in 1858. George wrote Bettie that the legislature had created a new court district and that Cothran would get it. "This will leave me without a partner," George wrote. He carried on his cases alone until he partnered later in 1856 with Tennessee native Robert W. Williamson, who also practiced law in Carrollton.²

Demonstrating his growing legal reputation, George began in the 1850s to argue cases in front of Mississippi's highest court (supreme court) in Jackson, known then as the High Court of Errors and Appeals. Located in the capitol building in Jackson, this court was made up of three members. George argued his first case before the court in 1850, making only one appearance that year. For the next decade, though, he would average around five or six cases a year, with the most being nine in 1858. In total, between 1850 and 1860 George argued at least thirty-nine cases before the supreme court. In contrast, George's first partner, William Cothran, had only fourteen appearances in front of the court from his licensing in Carrollton in 1837 to 1860, although the last four years were spent as a judge and not a trial lawyer. Cothran and George worked together on at least two cases before the high court, both in 1852 and both of which they won.³

The budding lawyer won his first case, *Aldridge v. Grider*, in front of the state's highest court. In January 1850 George defended the decision of the lower Carroll County circuit court involving the sale of a horse, which turned up lame after the sale. The county court had ruled in favor of the seller, who sued to get his money from the buyer, who charged the horse was lame and would not pay. The high court agreed with the lower court, giving George his first victory on the big stage.⁴

In another case, in 1856, George wrote Bettie that he faced a difficult opponent, whom he described as the "best lawyer in the State—Fulton Anderson." George did not back down, though. "I naturally desire to be well versed in the law of this case and if I cannot win . . . at least I desire not to lose any reputation that I now have." He went on to say, "I doubt not I shall be able to present my side credibly. I shall do my best anyhow." Paired with Yalobusha County Attorney Francis Marion Aldridge, George tried to get the case overturned from a Yalobusha County court. The facts themselves were very much against George and Aldridge, but they had a quirky technicality on their side regarding a bit of evidence offered in a different court. But the high court did not think this detail warranted overturning the decision, so George lost his case, *Crowder v. Nelson*, against Anderson.⁵

The independent George was not always on the debating side of court. A Carroll County grand jury indicted him in December 1855 for betting on a recent election. He pleaded guilty and paid a $20 fine. He also appeared in one case in which he was personally sued. George and several other men of Carrollton had signed as "sureties" on the bond of Carroll County

Sheriff W. P. Boles. The sheriff collected county poor and special taxes in 1850, but died before paying them into the state treasury. The state then sued the sureties, asking that the county board of police obtain the funds from the men who had signed for the sheriff. The county court ruled in favor of the state, and George and the others appealed to the state's highest court. In the decision handed down in December 1855, the high court affirmed the county court decision and required George and the others to be responsible for the $2,180 in question. George appealed for a reargument, but he never got his chance.[6]

During all the legal wrangling, George kept the safekeeping and protection of his family at the forefront of his mind. After complaining to Bettie in a letter from Jackson, where he argued in front of the high court, that he did not like being away from home, he wrote that he had to "resign all thought of self and to . . . secure for you and them a comfortable independence and a reasonable provision against the accidents of life." His ambition was no doubt a factor as well because he wanted the finer things of life. One wonders if Bettie was so desirous of material possessions that she consented to his frequent absence, but without any contemporary letters from her it is impossible to tell. No doubt George wanted to acquire his wealth and keep her as the traditional mistress at home, but he tortured himself to do so. And his absence and corresponding gloom became a pattern throughout his life.[7]

With a wife and two little girls, George was able to provide for his family by the early 1850s, but more children were soon on the way. Starting in 1848 James and Bettie had a child every two years for over a decade; George in fact remarked of "those necessary biennial occasions when a new stranger arrives amongst us." Kate came along on August 2, 1852, with another daughter, Mary, named for his mother and two grandmothers, born on August 12, 1854. During one of Bettie's pregnancies, in 1852, she and the children left Carrollton probably for better care and rest with family, leaving George alone to work. "You cannot imagine the dreariness and lonesomeness I feel, wherever I may be, since you left home," he wrote, and consoled her that "I know what a terrible and dangerous trial you are obliged to go through and I know that I ought to be with you." Still, his work would allow only a quick meeting, and George admitted, "I shall feel great anxiety until I hear that you are safely delivered and our child is not deformed or disproportional."[8]

George's dependence on his wife grew through the years. He rarely seemed satisfied when he was away from Bettie. "I have tried the solitude of study," he wrote her while she was away during her pregnancy, "which I want so much when you are at home, but I fail." He went on to say, "I feel confident that I shall not enjoy myself again until your return," and noted, "I am ashamed of my selfishness when I demand so great a sacrifice on your part." Illustrating the fact that he was still early in his career and had not yet become wealthy, he wrote, "If I had the money I would come up after you but that is out of the question in my present situation." He had to make do with a daguerreotype, which only "inflames my desire," he said, and "merely reminds me of charms which I cannot enjoy."[9]

George seemed to also have issues other than missing his wife. Many acquaintances remarked early in his life on his gruff and transparent personality, and George himself knew it to be one of his faults. He once wrote Bettie, "My naturally irascible temper sometimes gets the better of my good sense and makes me seem wanting in affection." He assured her that "this is momentary only for Heaven knows and I hope you know that I love you with an affection and . . . devotion that knows no other idol." He later promised that "I will not for a whole year . . . do or say one single thing that will not meet your approbation."[10]

Mixed with these personal issues was a healthy ambition, which sometimes bordered on greed. "I am a proud, ambitious man who would sooner 'brook the infernal devil' than that one man in Rome should be ahead of me," he wrote Bettie. Over his lifetime George spent a great deal of time away from home working in various professions, but he always rationalized it by saying he was obtaining wealth and possessions for Bettie and the children. "If I am ambitious in my profession it is because you can share with me the honors and rewards of success," he wrote. "If I desire wealth it is that I may more fully administer with gratification of your tastes and wishes." George also desired a wealthy lifestyle for his children. In one letter he wrote, "I desire to accumulate a fortune so that my children shall have the chance at least of marrying the best men in the community. I am certain they will all be richly endowed with all the natural gifts and grace which go to make up the character of elegant and lovely women." Obviously, he also desired status and standing for himself, speaking of the "respectability of my family." He admonished, however, that until they were independently wealthy, "we must be patient and submit quietly and uncomplainingly to the fate that has befallen us."[11]

By 1854 George had begun to diversify his investments in order to attain that wealth. In addition to the land and slaves he owned in Georgia, where he traveled at least once in 1852 to see after his property and visit family, George invested in more land and slaves in Mississippi. He cosigned for a friend for a substantial tract northeast of Carrollton in 1850, but he began to speculate in more land as the decade wore on. In 1853 and 1854 he bought several more lots in Carrollton as well as a more substantial tract in 1856 west of town. By 1860 George would own several hundred acres in Carroll County plus what he held in Georgia. He also frequently bought and sold slaves, and served as legal counsel in the sale of others. By 1860 George would reach and far surpass the magic number of twenty slaves, making him in the eyes of later historians one of the elite planter class. He was also a stockholder in the Mississippi Central Railroad, which ran through nearby Winona.[12]

George was also becoming involved in politics in the early 1850s. As a die-hard Democrat who had supported President Polk and the war in Mexico in the 1840s, George became more and more interested in the nation's political climate and elections. He once gathered letters of introduction to luminaries in Washington, D.C., in preparation for a trip there, one letter stating, "Mr. G. is a gentleman of character and a prominent member of the Democratic Party." He also corresponded and met with some of the highest Democrats in the state, such as Governor John J. McRae and William S. Barry, who asked for his support in an election in 1855. Later in the decade he attended the state Democratic convention.[13]

George also took on more political responsibility, small duties at first and then larger ones, showing some of his growing reputation as well as his powerful friends. In 1853 the Carroll County Board of Police (forerunner of today's board of supervisors in each Mississippi county) hired George as "Overseer of the 1st Dist. of the Carrollton and Grenada Road," placing several laborers under his supervision. It is not known whether George took this position in an effort to acquire more funds or as a political move to gain entrance into the political appointee world. Nevertheless, he stayed busy overseeing the roadwork north of Carrollton even amid his other duties of family and law.[14]

Also during 1853, and perhaps as a result of his activity on the Grenada Road, George leased a large tract of land with a substantial dwelling on that road about two miles north of Carrollton. The dwelling had been built around 1840 as an inn on the stage road. There is no evidence that George and his family ever moved into the former inn; the next year, possibly because he was short of money, George gave up the lease to another individual. Later, the owner of the estate sold the plantation outright. George and his family thus continued to reside on Washington Street in Carrollton.[15]

George also garnered a higher political position in 1853. With the nudging of former governor Albert Gallatin Brown and High Court of Errors and Appeals chief justice Cotesworth Pinckney Smith, the Mississippi Senate made George the engrossing clerk of that body. Taking that position required him to be away from home during the Jackson meeting of the state legislature every two years and during sessions specially called by the governor. George was uncomfortable being away from home so much, but he continued to rationalize his guilt with the desire to provide adequately for his family.[16]

George did not remain long in his Senate position. In 1854 the state legislature appointed him, at the tender age of twenty-seven, as recorder of the state's High Court of Errors and Appeals. It was a prestigious position, but it also required George to be in Jackson during terms of the court's meeting, which were twice a year every winter and summer. But he would be there some of the time anyway, arguing cases before the court. At least his nearness to the court would better facilitate a growing caseload before that body.[17]

In 1850 the state legislature had altered the process by which the court reporter was appointed. The new law required election to the position by a joint session of the House and Senate. The first reporter thus elected was J. F. Cushman, but he was not reelected in the next term, although he was nominated. On January 13, 1854, a joint session of the legislature allowed nominations, one of which was Cushman to continue in his job. Fortunately for George, Cushman was not popular, and several members were not satisfied with his published volumes of cases. Representative W. B. Helm of Carroll County nominated George, while other members nominated other lawyers, including future attorney general Thomas J. Wharton. On the first ballot, George received the most votes, but not the necessary majority. Cushman ran a close second. A second ballot saw George increase his lead while Cushman lost ground. George won on the third ballot. "Mr. George having received a majority of all the votes cast, was declared by the President to be duly and constitutionally elected Reporter of the decisions of the High Court of Errors and Appeals for the term prescribed by law," the legislative journal read.[18]

The job carried a term of four years and was essentially what it said—reporter of the cases of the high court. The 1850 legislation spelled out what was required, which was basically to compile all the cases the court heard in a given year. The legislature was obviously wary of the cost, and gave the reporter quite a lot of latitude as to what cases to include, in essence saying he should include only those deemed most important. The members of the court itself also had the duty and authority to review the manuscript before it went to press to see if anything was missing or needed to be removed. The 1850 law also severely limited George on how he might publish the volumes: "to be done at a price not exceeding four dollars per copy, of each volume, and each page shall contain not less than forty-eight lines, averaging not less than fourteen words to the line, printed on the type now prescribed by law." Despite such curious and detailed regulations, George's major duty was to compile and publish the cases heard each year.[19]

George's new job would have a major effect on his life. It would obviously take him away from Bettie and the children, but he saw that as the price he had to pay to support and provide nice things for them. Also, it would make George a known commodity in both legal and political circles in Jackson and the state. Everything centered around the statehouse in Jackson, and George would have a front row seat from his new office inside the capitol.

CHAPTER 4

"The Aim of My Official Labors"

Wealth, 1856–1860

"I am now seated in my office in the 3d story of the Capitol, enjoying the comfort of a blazing fire," George wrote Bettie upon entering the office of court reporter in December 1855. For the next several years he spent his winters and some summers in Jackson while the court was in session, despite the loneliness of being away from home. As he would be in the capital for only a couple of months each time, however, it was not feasible to move the entire family for so short a period. Thus he continued to torture himself with his absence away from home and family. But he did his job well, and all could see he took his duties seriously and entered each term with a passion. In fact, he was so well regarded that when his term expired, George was unanimously reelected as recorder in 1859 by acclamation. On November 11, 1859, H. T. Ellett, who had nominated and supported Wharton back in 1854, nominated George again, and there were no other nominations.[1]

In his years as recorder, George compiled ten years' worth of high court decisions, and they would later be regarded as the best volumes in the series. But George's first volume, the thirtieth in the series, was not the start he desired. It did not appear until 1857, though it covered the cases from December 1855 to April 1856. In the preface to the volume, he wrote candidly:

> When I was elected to the office of Reporter to the high Court of Errors and Appeals of this State, I determined to put a note at the end of each case containing a short reference to, and concise statement of, the previous decisions of the Court on the same subject matter.... After having entered upon the discharge of the duties of the office, however, finding the labor much greater than was anticipated, and the compensation

much less, I saw that the original design could not be carried out without a greater sacrifice of time than could be conveniently spared from my professional labors. This, I hope, will be a sufficient apology to those of my friends to whom I had announced my determination, for the failure to consummate it.

He also wrote that "the present volume, I fear, contains many errors, which have, unavoidably, resulted from two causes." One was the printing of the volume in Philadelphia, Pennsylvania, or "at a distance of a thousand miles from my personal presence." The second was that "my late law partner retired from the bar to a seat on the bench, just at the commencement of my labors, thus doubling the demands of clients on my time and attention." Then George added that this would be his last apology; "to secure their [colleagues'] approbation, is the highest honor I covet—to merit it, the aim of my official labors."[2]

The next volumes were much better. Working with the T. and J. W. Johnson and Company in Philadelphia, each year, George published two volumes in 1858, two in 1859, three in 1860, and one in 1861. George's reports were so thorough, in fact, that a later colleague in the Senate, Edward C. Walthall, commented, "when their completeness and the rapidity with which they were prepared and published in the midst of other engagements are considered, it was a remarkable achievement." He also noted that in examining the volumes, "it would be inferred that their preparation was the author's sole employment, when in fact they were issued amid the exactions of a varied and extensive practice, which took him much from home, and when private interests claimed much of his attention."[3]

In compiling the records, George worked hard to get his labor in Jackson done as swiftly but as accurately as possible, knowing that when he finished his manuscript as well as the cases he was trying, he could return home to Bettie and the children. Often, however, the direct route by stage over the 100 miles from Jackson to Carrollton was not passable, particularly in the winter. On one such trip he reported, "We were much exposed on Tuesday night to rain wind and water, but I believe I have suffered no ill consequences from it." In the worst times, which were frequent during the winter, George had to go by way of Vicksburg, taking a steamboat up the Yazoo River to Greenwood and thence to Carrollton.[4]

George thus worked hard in Jackson. "I am considerable exhausted from my week's labor," he wrote Bettie in January 1855, "and feel a great indisposition to continue my labor longer." A year later he wrote, "I shall have a very laborious time of it I have no doubt." But George was able to get his friends in the legislature to alter the law allowing him to carry the court records home with him to do the work of compiling. That way he could, as he told Bettie, "be able to be with you all the whole year except about two months in the winter."[5]

The family man was clearly miserable 100 miles away from his wife and children in Jackson, though, and his letters were alternatingly full of pitiful fits of depression ("I thought that you would at least take time to write me a letter every other day") and ardent statements of love ("If I had a thousand hearts you would easily fill all of them"). "My mind of course when not engaged on business instantly reverts to home and home folks," he wrote, adding, "O what a joyous time I could have this evening if I were at home with my dear wife and sweet little children!" The cold and dreary weather of winter did not help his mood. He spent several Christmases away from Bettie and the children, writing in 1855, "For myself I shall spend the day in looking into the Record for argument in the High Court."[6]

Despite such feelings, George gained many friendships and much experience in Jackson. He continued to argue cases before the very court for which he served as reporter. He admitted to Bettie that there were "some [cases] of which I fear I shall lose, but I shall do my duty." In one particular case, he did his job but obviously had reservations: "I hope to be able to save his life, although he acted very badly." Watching the justices as reporter and as a lawyer allowed him to become a better litigator. Likewise, George made a great friend of the court's chief justice, Cotesworth Pinckney Smith. In fact, George was so impressed with Smith that he later named his mansion as well as a child after him.[7]

One thing that George did not gain in Jackson was a healthy social life. All his life he seemed to be a recluse, never enjoying the social aspects of his various careers. "I find myself at great fault when in company to furnish the little small talk," he wrote Bettie, "which is as necessary in the social world as small change is in the everyday business of life." He much preferred to be alone studying in his room. He informed Bettie that he switched boardinghouses one winter: "I am much more comfortable now than before and besides I am much more quiet and have better opportunity for work." George thus never became very involved in city society. "I find the great men down here are not so very great after all," he wrote Bettie. "They grow small as you approach them," and noted, "'Tis distance lends enchantment to the view." He jokingly wrote, "Under that rule no doubt I appear a pretty considerable man to you when I am from home."

All jokes aside, George basically did not feel the need for or desire the acceptance of the socialites of Jackson. He did not even attend the inauguration of Governor John McRae, a fellow Democrat, in January 1856. "Tonight is the time for the governor's inauguration and I have determined to spend it in writing to you instead of mixing with the throng of beauty and fashion who will congregate there," he wrote. "When I am not at work I prefer to be alone," he mused. In telling her of another ball to which he had been invited, George wrote, "but [I] would not go because you were not here to go with me." He did say that William Cothran went, and that it "was the first frolicking the Maj. has been guilty of." He also declined an invitation to a party at the Bowman House in 1858, "having no desire to mix in such crowds." Obviously, George needed just one person for acceptance, his wife.[8]

Another reason for George's lack of socializing in Jackson could have been Bettie's jealousy. She admonished him often about not keeping company with the women of Jackson, and George reassured her every chance he had that he did not keep their company. "Every lady knows that I am married and I always tell them that I have got four girls," he wrote, "[so] you need not be uneasy on the subject of my gallantries with the young ladies." But whether intentional or not, he could not help but describe them and the few he met while there, no doubt increasing Bettie's concern over him being away so far for so long. He once told her there were "seven or eight" women at his boardinghouse, but that "with not one of whom I have become acquainted. I have neither the leisure nor desire to cultivate them." He jokingly added, "as the Mormons have not taken the country yet I am not at liberty to have but one wife. If I had the privilege I would not increase the number. If your husband could not be satisfied with one wife he would be hard indeed to please." He also wrote, "As to the girls, I have not made the acquaintance of but one." He assured Bettie that "she . . . says she knows you must be a very interesting woman, or else I would not talk so much about you." George also described other women, such as "Mrs. Mat MacAfee [who] says that she knows that I am a model Husband when at home because I don't forget my wife when absent." He dined with Governor John J. McRae in 1856, describing his wife as "an interminable talker." He also noted that the widower Cothran "has not mixed any with the girls."[9]

But the main reason George did not mix with the public was because he worked so hard. "I have been most closely confined to my room on business," he wrote Bettie, and noted that "all the time I waste in that way adds to the length of my stay here." And he could see several years of this work in the future: "Though whether in office or not I shall if successful in my profession be here every winter as much and as long as I have work down here." Eventually, he began to see a difference in his practice before the court and his work for the court as reporter. The work of reporter became boring very quickly. "If I have to remain here to do the work," he wrote Bettie, "I think I shall resign. I begin to fear there is very little money in it and as for the honor, that is nothing compared with the loss of your society by absence from home." His law practice was a different matter, though. "I hope to make a good deal of money in the High Court," he wrote Bettie. "The practice in it suits me in as much as I am not here annoyed by clients or witnesses."[10]

Despite his workaholism, there were a few times when George attended functions, such as balls or parties thrown by the elite. Whether he did so out of duty or a desire to cultivate his image with the powers that be is not known, but it was probably both. He wrote Bettie of attending a dinner with Governor McRae in 1855, but admitted that he had trouble with the "small talk of the day of which, you know, I have but a small store." The dinner fare included turkey and duck, as well as "six different kinds of wine and ale," he reported. George did imbibe, although he told Bettie it was "very moderate," but that was enough to bring "its usual consequences—a headache—which rendering me quite unfit for society, so I was glad when I could return." He was not truly comfortable, he said, until he returned to his room and could relax. "My retirement to my room is as solitary as the seclusion of a hermit in his cell," a relieved George wrote Bettie after returning from the party.[11]

One of the few major events George attended was "the party given by Col. Davis on account of his election to the Senate" in 1856. "There are a great many gentlemen and fine looking ladies in attendance," he wrote, although he told Bettie, "If I see a fine looking lady I am immediately reminded of you." Naturally, George left when the speeches began. "I have no desire for speech making or speech hearing," he wrote, saying, "I left in order to write to you." All in all, George described the event as "a most bilious affair, as they say here."[12]

Surely Bettie did not worry about George's reclusivness, but she most likely worried about his other activities, such as not attending church while in Jackson. Despite Bettie's dedication to the Baptist church in Carrollton, George remained a nonmember and rarely attended. "I understand that Parson Clinton is preaching at the Baptist Church to-day. I shall not go out," he wrote Bettie. "I don't think that my head or heart would be much improved by anything he would be likely to say."[13]

George's annual absences were as hard on the family at home as they were on him. He deplored being away from Bettie and the children at Christmas, during which the legislature and courts were typically in session, writing, "I hope you have had a pleasant and happy Christmas of it. I know I would have had if I had been at home." In fact, George threatened to resign his office, a trait that would follow him throughout his life when he was unhappy. He was not altogether convinced that Bettie was doing so well herself, though, writing in 1856, "I am rejoiced to see you are taking things so philosophically. I am half inclined though to believe that a good deal of it is feigned for the purpose of keeping my spirits up." She may have been acting, because it was obvious George needed her support; he was continually begging for letters from home. "I shall consider myself very badly treated unless you write me every other day," he wrote from Jackson. He later wrote, "The fact is that I cannot bear this long and continued absence from home. I must see my wife and children often and I will do it."[14]

Yet George knew his wife wondered at his fervent desire to be at home, considering that when he was in Carrollton, he spent much of his time in town or practicing law. "I know you laugh at my frequent allusion in every letter to my desire to be at home once more," he wrote, "and you say to yourself, 'Well when he does come home I'll see how much real value [is] in these earnest protestations of his on the subject. I'll see if he don't stay down in town all-day and go there sometimes at night. If he does, the fit he is in now won't last long." George wrote, "I know that is the way you think and talk about my letters, but I am going to behave so well when I get home that you won't be able to be drawing any unfavorable comparison between my theory and practice." He finished with, "Well, Bet, I am in a fine humor tonight."[15]

Bettie's letters, as well as those from the children, lifted his spirits greatly, "filled as they are with expressions of the most devoted love and affection," he wrote. He told her that he "read them over and over again and again until I could almost repeat every word in there." But when he did not receive a letter, it tended to push him into gloom. On one occasion, Cothran told him at supper that he had a letter in his box. George wrote that he "swallowed a hurried meal" and went to the post office, only to find it closed. Not willing to give up and wait until morning, he searched for the postmaster, but could only find a worker under him who had no key. Thus dejected, he returned to his room, which looked out over the street toward the post office. "I went to my window ... a dozen times," he wrote, "to see if there was a light there, before I went to bed, but was as often disappointed." He spent a long night knowing "there was a letter from my dear wife within 50 yards of me which I could not peruse until morning." The next morning, "without waiting to dress," he went to the office and got the letter, but found it was not even from Bettie. "I won't say what I did," he wrote her, but he did say, "I never was so much disappointed in my life." That the mail route from Carrollton and Lexington to Jackson was occasionally closed due to bad weather also caused him great pain.[16]

At times George's seclusion and lack of letters from Bettie had a truly depressing effect on him. He wrote in January 1858 that he had been thinking about how badly he had treated her. "I have thought over some things that I have done or said which I think ought not to have been said or done," he wrote. "That I am frequently irritable I know," he admitted, and he continued, "I have been stern and unforgiving." He apologized, saying his behavior for years had been "highly improper and inexcusable." He tried to explain himself: "I am a proud ambitious man. . . . The same high standards which I have put up for myself in the intellectual world I have fixed for you in the same sphere." But, he wrote, "I have sometimes forgotten that although you were my wife you were [also] human." Despite calling her attention to some things that she did that "would irritate in Heaven," such as correcting him in public, he promised to do much better in the future.[17]

Even from a distance, however, George continued to direct family operations and prod Bettie into becoming a refined and intelligent mistress. He often showed a desire for the niceties of life. "I intend to have . . . my wife nicely dressed," he wrote her in 1855, and continued, "I am going to make money enough for that." In 1858 he wrote that he wanted his wife and children to "use every opportunity of mental and moral culture." But he had a hard time balancing work and his desire to provide nice things with his desire to be at home. He sometimes had little patience with his family's lack of understanding about his frequent absence. "Tell the children that I shall come home as soon as I can and not to cry about it," he wrote. When Bettie informed him that the children were asking about his absence and suggested he write them, he spelled out exactly what was happening, on their level. He told them he did not like being away from home, but that he had to be in order to provide the "pretty dresses and nice little play things and plenty of good things to eat." He wrote, "Well it takes money to buy all these things and your father has no money except what he can make, by practicing law." He went on to describe how people "get into difficulties, they shoot and stab one another," and that they "have their rights tried and settled by the Judge and Jury," which, he said, necessitated "a lawyer to speak for their side." "To get a lawyer to speak for them," he wrote, "they must pay him, or at least promise to do so." He also told them to be sweet and to mind their mother. "This will make her happy and she will then not think so much about father's being away."[18]

George also lectured Bettie about her writing, encouraging her in "expressing your ideas on paper." "I have a great desire that my wife shall write well," he prodded, but then added some humility, perhaps thinking he had gone overboard. "I regret that my own letters do not furnish you a model in this respect," he wrote, "since you already write much better letters than I can." Whether he meant in syntax or actual handwriting is not known; his handwriting was atrocious, and he knew it. He once wrote of her "deciphering my letters." Nevertheless, he continued, saying, "I am satisfied that I shall never attain any considerable degree of excellence in any other department of literature." Still, he cautioned her to "let your thoughts flow naturally," before ending, "But enough of this."[19]

When he detected in her letters a tendency to be down on herself, he was always quick to build her up. "You seem to think that there is a great mental disparity between us and that difference is against you and that this idea is ever present to my mind," he wrote in 1858. "On this subject permit me to say that I am not conscious of any superiority mental or otherwise existing." He also rejected her concern that "I will become accustomed to absence." He told her he was tempted to "abandon the ambitious race for professional distinction," but his seriousness is doubtful.[20]

He also offered Bettie history lessons in his letters, such as when he wrote on January 8, 1857. "This is the glorious 8th of January," he wrote, "the anniversary of the victory of the American arms over the British forces at New Orleans." He used the occasion to remind Bettie to be thankful she was safe; the battle, he said, should "be of great interest to your sex since it saved the women of that devoted city from the ruthless violence of the soldiery whose watchword was 'Beauty and Booty.'"[21]

George was able of course to spend some time at home. As the 1850s passed he sired more children, and joked of Bettie "present[ing] me with the 5th daughter instead of the first son." Fortunately for George, she broke the string of daughters: the first boy after four girls was born on August 16, 1856, and they named him Alfred Hudson. Another son came two years later on July 24, 1858. James and Bettie named him William Cothran George, after James's mentor and brother-in-law.[22]

At times, problems surfaced with the children, such as an ailment of daughter Emma. "I wish you would at once procure a pair of stiff shoes to be made for Emma[;] let them reach above her ankles and fit closely—steel ribs." Although the exact problem is unknown, it was a major concern for George. "I am really uneasy about it," he wrote. "Make her wear them continually even if she can't walk." The child seemed to remain sickly, because a few years later he wrote, "be sure to keep a strict watch over Emma this cold winter. I feel uneasy about her every time I leave home. I sometimes think when I leave that it may be the last time I ever shall see her." But he ended the letter, as he did most, with "Kiss all of them for me."[23]

George's monetary situation was improving as well. Earlier in his career George told Bettie that he had to come to Jackson "for meat and bread for my family." He also had to caution her about money, saying, "A little economy for a year or so and a little more hard work on my part will straighten everything out." As the decade passed his law practice and his farming assets began to bring larger dividends. His accounts in the local store showed the vast assortment of niceties he bought on a regular basis, including dishes, knives, calico, and other items. The vast majority of items were normal in nature, though, including shoes, eggs, socks, and diapers. Every few days George also purchased a plug of tobacco. Obviously, he chewed it often.[24]

By 1860 George had amassed a good reputation as a lawyer and recorder, with a large family and a growing fortune in land and slaves. His reelection as court reporter without any opposition illustrated his standing among members of the legislature, and Bettie and his growing hoard of children, six in all by the end of the 1850s, were a source of enjoyment as well as a spur for him. By 1860 he owned some 500 acres of land valued at $25,000. Working all that land were sixty-five slaves. But George was also willing to help others, such as taking in little Mollie Grubbs, whom George referred to as "the poor orphan." During one of his absences, George told Bettie to send Mollie to school "whether our own children can go or not."[25]

Obviously, George had done well in the decade or so between his passage into manhood and the beginning of the Civil War. It was fortunate for him that he was so successful in the 1850s because the next decade would not be so prosperous for him or the nation. Looming clouds of war and destruction appeared on the horizon, no doubt causing George to wonder if all he had worked so hard for would last. Like most other Southern Democrats, George was aghast at the election of Abraham Lincoln in November 1860. To George and countless other slave-owning families in the South, Lincoln's election signaled an end to any power the South had left within the federal government. With South Carolina continuing its long history of threatening secession, Mississippi also began the process of leaving the nation. George had some major decisions to make.

CHAPTER 5

"This Movement of Secession"

Changes, 1860–1861

As he had for many years, J. Z. George returned to the state capitol in Jackson in January 1861, but this time things were different. He was not going to attend the supreme court hearings, to argue his own cases, or to work on his court reports in his office in the statehouse. This time George was attending Mississippi's secession convention. On his and the other delegates' shoulders rested the fate of Mississippi, at least for decades into the future. At the young age of thirty-four, he had worked hard to build his wealth; now, to him and many other Mississippians, it seemed that all was in jeopardy.

The tumultuous events of secession were not the only recent upheavals for George, however. The new decade had begun in terrible fashion when, in 1860, Bettie gave birth to their seventh child, another boy whom they named James Z. George Jr. Little James continued the streak of a child every other year in even years. James Jr. was born on February 22, 1860, but he lived only ten months, dying on December 20. James and Bettie had him buried beside his grandmother, Bettie's mother, who had died in 1859, in the new Evergreen Cemetery just outside Carrollton. They felt the loss terribly.[1]

This personal tragedy was similar to a corresponding crisis on the national front. After the call of the governor and legislature to hold elections for the secession convention in December 1860, candidates throughout the state broke down into one of two basic camps, the "separate state secessionists" and the "cooperationists." But neither term meant the same thing throughout the state, with the cooperationists meaning cooperation with other slave states in secession in some parts while meaning cooperation within the Union in others. Generally, most counties did not instruct their delegates to vote any certain way on secession.[2]

In Carroll County, George was an early and well-known candidate for the convention. His growing status both in the plantation community and the legal arenas in Carrolton on the local level and Jackson on the state level made him a candidate with name recognition. George favored secession and went into the canvassing process with that mentality well known. But he faced opposition from the cooperationists within Carroll County.³

Soon a compromise within the county developed that assured George a seat at the state convention without a formal or heated race. Most counties left it to the voters to decide who would be the delegates out of a list of nominees from both sides. A few counties that were awarded two delegates worked out a bipartisan compromise in which both sides would be represented equally. Such was the case in Carroll County. The only ticket presented to the voters was one with William Booth representing the cooperationists and George representing the secessionists. Eight hundred and sixty people voted for what has been termed the "coalition ticket" of Booth and George, with no votes going to either side alone. Unfortunately, less than half of the participants in the 1860 presidential election bothered to vote in the convention canvass.⁴

Newspapers are rare from that period, and few details of the canvassing and election process have survived, so there is no way of knowing about any speeches George may have given as a candidate. But once the election took place on December 20, 1860, and George was assured of a seat, he began making preparations to go to Jackson. George's enthusiasm for his new duty was no doubt tempered by the death of his little boy that same election day. Nevertheless, George and Booth, although holding differing views, both made their way to Jackson in early January to take part in the historic event.⁵

Governor John J. Pettus was the chief secessionist in the state, having called the state to "go down into Egypt while Herod reigns in Judea." There were many other fire-eaters in line behind Pettus, including L. Q. C. Lamar of Oxford, Wiley P. Harris of Jackson, William S. Barry of Columbus, and James Z. George of Carrollton. In all, there were 100 delegates, most of them bent on secession even before the convention began. George certainly was.⁶

The only debate was whether to immediately secede or to await events and act later. There was also a small Unionist group of old Whigs led by men such as Jacob S. Yerger, Walker Brooke, and James L. Alcorn. This group also had differences of opinion as to which course to take. Finally, there was a small group of independent delegates who listed themselves as "A Mississippian," "Opposed to Universal Suffrage," "Extremely and Intensely Southern," and "Disunionist per se." The independent-minded Democrat George listed himself as a Baptist and "Southern."⁷

What one delegate described as "the ablest, the finest, and the most opulent men in the State" met on January 7 at the statehouse in Jackson. George was present for the opening rituals, which included a roll call of the counties, with each delegate making his way to the front of the chamber and registering his name when called. No doubt George felt enthused and excited when the clerk called out "James Z. George" and he made his way forward. Later, the delegates participated in organizing the convention, which included electing officers, appointing committees, and working out the logistics of the convention. But the first major issue was to hammer out the actual ordinance of secession. L. Q. C. Lamar offered a motion that a committee be appointed to "prepare and report as speedily as possible, an ordinance providing for the withdrawal of the State of Mississippi from the present Federal Union, with a view to the establishment of a new Confederacy, to be composed of the seceding states." The president, William S. Barry, soon did so, appointing a committee of fifteen. As would be expected, the committee was filled with secessionists. Lamar was the head of the committee, having actually come to Jackson with an ordinance of secession already written. The state's foremost lawyer, Wiley P. Harris, was also on the committee, as was George, who had already made a name for himself within the bar of the state. There were a few token Unionists as well.[8]

George was regarded as one of the leading men of the convention, demonstrated by several younger members who seemed almost in awe of the men with whom they served. Thomas H. Woods wrote:

> The Mississippi Secession Convention was adorned, inspired, and largely controlled by its lawyer members. Judge Wiley P. Harris, then and until his death the recognized and unchallenged leader of the bar in Mississippi, was pre-eminently influential in the work of that epoch-making assembly, and his voice was regarded as the voice of an oracle. . . . Beside Judge Harris, there were Lamar, George, Brooke, Marshall, Yerger, . . . Barry, . . . Alcorn, with many another,—all accounted luminaries of the first magnitude in the legal firmament.

One member of the convention, George's future son-in-law William R. Barksdale, wrote after making a speech, "I do not expect to speak any more during the sitting of this convention. There is as much danger of a man speaking too much as too little. Some men in the Convention have already lost their influence and do not even get the respectful attention of the house while speaking because they have spoken so much." But when

Harris, Lamar, Alcorn, or George spoke, which George often did, the convention listened.[9]

George was a major supporter of the secession ordinance, working on the committee to hammer out the wording and then voting for it when the actual vote was cast on January 9. He was also against the three amendments offered by the Unionists to water down the secession ordinance. One amendment would have adopted a wait-and-see attitude, with secession depending on the outcome of the several compromise attempts then going on in Washington, D.C. Another would have required the secession of several other slave states before Mississippi's secession went into effect. The third would have put secession to a vote by the people of the state. George voted against each one of these proposals and then voted for the ordinance, which passed. He signed the document on January 15 with most of the other delegates. Some would call it revolutionary, and others would call it treason, but it was nevertheless a large step in the pattern of opposition that was already developing in George.[10]

With secession accomplished, the convention settled down quickly and buried itself in mundane, detailed matters. One delegate, in fact, wrote of how busy they were in those first days of the convention: "I have been so much absorbed in the questions of the day that I have neglected my domestic affairs." Indeed, this act of secession now had to be supported with money, military means, and numerous other details contingent on establishing a new nation or sovereign state. Several major committees were established, and the president of the convention placed George on the Committee on Federal Jurisdiction and Property. The lawyer and court reporter George was an obvious choice for this committee. George worked on the issue of federal lands within the state, including forts, lighthouses, and arsenals, as well as circuit and district courts.[11]

George and the committee wrote an ordinance, which passed on January 16, stipulating that all U.S. land in the state be "hereby resumed and vested in the State of Mississippi." It also gave the legislature the "power to provide by law for the custody and preservation of the records and judicial proceedings of the Circuit and District Courts of the United States in this State; and to prescribe the manner in which suits and proceedings, civil and criminal, now pending in said courts, shall be tried and determined." In addition, the ordnance took "admiralty and maritime jurisdiction" for the state, and kept federal marshals in their same places and duties. A supplemental ordinance from the committee was passed on January 26 regarding "the sale of waste and unappropriated lands."[12]

But George did not limit his action to the purview of his committee. When he saw something that needed to be challenged or improved, he was not afraid to let his thoughts be known. Such was the case with the Committee on Postal, Financial, and Commercial Affairs, which dealt with the state's finances. In debating this committee's ordinance to fund the state, the convention passed a tax hike, but George was not satisfied. He offered an amendment that incorporated an increased tax on slaves. "That in order to make the State tax on slaves equal to the State tax on other personalty and on land," George wrote, "the above mentioned tax of fifty per centum on the present State tax, shall not apply to slaves: but instead thereof, an additional special tax of one dollar and twenty-five cents be imposed on each taxable slave, to be collected and disbursed as the other taxes herein provided for." According to one member of the convention, George argued that "they [slaves] had brought on the war and must pay for it." Consuming a lot of the convention's time, a good bit of political wrangling and maneuvering then took place. Ultimately an amendment to George's amendment that changed much of what George had wanted was barely passed, with George voting against it. He thus voted against his own amendment, now amended, and it lost by a vote of sixty-eight to seventeen. Delegate William R. Barksdale saw only trouble ahead on this issue, writing a friend, "If the people have not got patriotism enough to bear such a tax as this then they have not got enough to sustain this movement of secession." But George profited from the debate politically. Historian Stephen Cresswell has argued that George's proposed tax on the rich endeared him to the small farmers of Mississippi, which would constitute a major base of support for many years.[13]

George also became involved in another slavery-related issue. Members passed a resolution to outlaw the African slave trade, which George vehemently opposed. When it passed, George went so far as to lodge a protest against the resolution, arguing that the issue was not within the convention's duties. The journal of the convention laid out his reasoning:

> Mr. George asked and was granted permission to spread a Protest upon the journals, against the adoption, by this Convention, of the resolution offered by Mr. Holt this morning, in reference to the African Slave Trade, for various reasons having no reference to their individual views on the subject matter of said resolution. The Legislature had already declared a policy on this subject in exact conformity with the resolution adopted, and the action of this Convention was

unnecessary. The question was not made the subject of debate in the late canvass, and the resolution was an usurpation of the just powers of the Legislature, and a negation to that body of the right to exercise a plain constitutional function which had been delegated to them by the people.

George managed to get eleven other delegates to sign his protest, but it did nothing. George nevertheless felt so strongly that he "obtained leave to have the same spread upon the Journal of the Convention."[14]

George's protest and his slave tax proposal illustrated just how involved slavery was in the convention. George, of course, owned slaves, as did a number of other delegates. He and the other delegates obviously saw secession as a step toward preserving slavery and white supremacy. If there was any question of this, the "Declaration of the Immediate Causes Which Induce and Justify the Secession of the State of Mississippi from the Federal Union," which passed at the end of the convention, cleared up any doubt. The statement "declare[d] the prominent reasons which have induced our course": "Our position is thoroughly identified with the institution of slavery," the delegates stated, "the greatest material interest in the world. . . . [A] blow has long been aimed at the institution, and was at the point of reaching its consummation. There was no choice left us but submission to the mandates of abolition, or a dissolution of the Union, whose principles had been subverted to work out our ruin." The statement also read: "We must either submit to degradation, and to the loss of property worth four billions of money, or we must secede from the Union framed by our fathers, to secure this as well as every other species of property. For far less cause that this, our fathers separated from the Crown of England." Obviously, George and the other delegates had slavery foremost in their minds as they left the Union.[15]

Other issues were much less significant, such as when George moved that language inviting members of the High Court of Errors and Appeals be given a seat in the convention be changed to sitting members as well as anyone who had ever held a seat on the court. Because of George's connection with the court, he desired to take care of the judges with whom he had worked throughout the years. George also successfully offered a resolution appointing his friend Wiley Harris to help audit the convention expenses.[16]

With their work done, the delegates adjourned in late January, and George prepared for the future. If war came, of course, he would participate in it. But there were other political actions still needing his attention.

One of these was a reassembling of the secession convention in March, after the state's delegates to the Montgomery Confederate organizational meeting had returned.[17]

President Barry called the secession convention together again on March 25 to ratify the Confederate constitution. With several of the members already in the army, fewer delegates met for this session. The president appointed a special committee of five to go over the document and recommend approval or rejection, with George one of those five. The committee brought out an ordinance the next day, but the Unionists of the convention saw one more opportunity to weaken the secession movement. They offered numerous amendments and counter-amendments, mostly in an effort to place the new Confederate constitution before the people of the state for a vote. All the amendments were voted down, and the delegates ratified the ordinance accepting the Confederate constitution on March 29 by a 92 percent margin.[18]

Thereafter, and at times even in the midst of the heated debate over the constitution, the delegates took care of several other mundane matters. George offered several resolutions, mostly concerned with judicial procedure, most notably how to deal with pending federal court cases in the state and the attending paperwork. He also offered a resolution to "inquire into the expediency of requiring" all state, county, and local officers and members of the bar to take an oath of allegiance to the Confederacy. He also successfully made a motion to nominate Mississippi's delegation to the provisional Confederate Congress, a motion to urge haste in organizing the Confederate government, as well as a resolution "to define the power of the Legislature of this State in relation to the Ordinances and resolutions adopted by this Convention."[19]

With the delegates' work done, the president closed the convention on March 30, thanking the members for "the great work for which you were assembled" and declaring that "no man here need blush to the latest moment of his life." Certainly J. Z. George could see no reason to blush at this open opposition to the ruling authority.[20]

Big changes had come. Mississippi had declared itself a sovereign nation and then a member of the new Confederate States of America. Soon it would go to war to defend this act of secession, and George and his family would be affected. But one other major change took place when George returned home to Carrollton after the March meeting of the convention. Between the time he returned from Jackson and the time he left for war, he and Bettie made a land purchase that would affect the remainder of their lives. Today, the name James Z. George is synonymous with his plantation mansion, Cotesworth. Prior to 1861 George had lived at various locations, including in Georgia, Noxubee County, and around Vaiden before making his home and living as a lawyer in Carrollton. Successful planting, slave purchases, and land speculation had provided the Georges with a comfortable life. Now, with a war on the horizon, George decided it was time to purchase a large plantation. What thoughts went through his mind are not known; perhaps he wanted Bettie and the children to be well cared for in the event of his death. Perhaps he wondered if war might ruin his livelihood and decided to make his major investment in land before the war. Perhaps he wanted to move Bettie and the children out of town to a secluded place that hopefully would never see war. For whatever reason, in June 1861 George purchased the same house and land he had leased and then lost in 1853. It would remain his throughout his life, and is still owned by his descendents in the early twenty-first century.[21]

The original portions of Cotesworth had been built as far back as 1840 as a simple two-story structure with large columns and wide windows. A large central hall led into the various rooms on each floor, which were connected by a long staircase on one side of the hall. Through the years many additions had been added, including an original library wing connected by a breezeway in 1860 as well as a kitchen and cooks' quarters. Many slave cabins and outbuildings also came with the house. Cotesworth originally served as an inn, sitting as it did on the Grenada Road, which ran from Grenada to Carrollton. Only about two miles north of Carrollton, the house sat on a beautiful section of rolling hills and valleys along Beasley Creek, with the house sitting on the crest of a large, round hill. Perhaps George first noticed the beauty of the house and grounds when he served as overseer on the Grenada Road earlier in the 1850s.[22]

In June 1861 George paid $5,000 for the house, outbuildings, and 492 acres of land, which joined other landholdings he had already purchased. In all, the estate would eventually grow to around 900 acres. George named the house Cotesworth after his friend Cotesworth Pinckney Smith, who was the chief justice of the Mississippi High Court of Errors and Appeals.[23]

Thus George's life changed a great deal during the first half of 1861. He had helped form a new nation. He had purchased a large plantation and estate. Perhaps most important, he had a new calling—that of a soldier. He was not content to just talk his way into opposing the ruling authority. He intended to take action and show his opposition. He thus joined the newly forming Confederate States army.

CHAPTER 6

"The Duties of My Office"

Captain, 1861–1862

With Mississippi's secession, J. Z. George, like most other Carrollton men, prepared for war. In the stir of excitement he knew all too well from his Mexican War days, the well-off George threw his lot with the Confederacy. But there were differences this time around. Now he would be challenging the national authority, not fighting to expand it. And this time George's Civil War experience would not be mostly positive. There would also be much heartache and suffering.[1]

Having just returned from the second part of the secession convention's proceedings, George and a group of Carroll County men met together at Carrollton to decide their part in the conflict. Just seven days after the opening guns at Fort Sumter, they established a company, the Carroll Guards, and soon mustered into state service. The men elected as their captain Daniel R. Russell, who had been an officer in the company of Carroll County men that had fought in the Mexican War and had led the men at Monterrey when their captain was sick. Russell was a local attorney who had been the state's commissioner to Missouri during the secession crisis. The men made George their first lieutenant, second in command, no doubt a result of his growing stature as well as his prior military experience. George set about his duties with the gusto with which he entered every position he ever held. While awaiting orders, he wrote his superiors asking for "arms & tents." He also noted that the men needed buttons: "We need them now," George wrote. He also served as a mustering officer at nearby Vaiden while waiting for orders to move to one of the organizational areas in the state in May, mustering in the Carroll Rangers, a company that would eventually be a part of the First Mississippi Cavalry regiment.[2]

As the new Confederate government called on the states to raise regiments, Mississippi began to organize its independent companies, one of which was the Carroll Guards, into newly formed regiments of ten companies each. Lieutenant George and his company thus moved to Iuka, Mississippi, one of the four major troop organization centers in the state. There George and his men waited until "the requisite ten were in camp." By July 10 ten companies were present and a regiment took shape, the companies in the state service, including the Carroll Guards, being transferred to Confederate service. This regiment subsequently became the Twentieth Mississippi Infantry, and as the Carroll Guard's captain ranked third in seniority among the captains of the regiment, the company therefore became known as Company C. When the men elected regimental officers, Company C's own Captain Russell was elected colonel of the regiment, which he accepted. On July 15 the Carroll County men elected George as their captain.[3]

Throughout all this activity, George corresponded with his family and friends. He told Bettie how her letters were well received, and not just by him. One particular day one of her letters was handed to him while he was drilling the men. "I stopped immediately," he wrote, "telling the men that I had received a letter from my sweet-heart," causing a chuckle to run through the company. A family member told him: "all your family are well . . . we have had no sickness since you left." Another wrote George, "All are well and getting along finely. The children are all very anxious to come to see you." George was obviously missing his loved ones, writing Bettie in July, "Kiss the children all. I would be glad if you bring them all." But George was a realist, and cautioned Bettie that she had better not come see him right away. The regiment might move out any day, and he also admitted that he had to stay with his men and "you can not stay in camp." "But I want to see you so much," he added.[4]

Because of his absence from his legal career, George was worried about his finances. "My pay is $130 a month," he wrote Bettie in July, "but I fear our Government will not be able to pay me except in bonds or Treasury notes. Hence I shall be hard pressed for money." But he did get some good news about his crops that fall. "I examined your crops on yesterday," a friend wrote. "The corn is much better than I had expected." He also noted, "I learn your corn crop at Shongalo is very poor—Your cotton is good though."[5]

Another problem for Captain George and Company C, along with the entire regiment, was the absence of weapons. The brand new Confederacy had trouble issuing the units the necessary equipment. On August 7 the Confederacy offered the regiment to Major General Leonidas Polk, commander of Confederate Department Number Two, under the condition that he would arm it. That did not happen, so the War Department armed and sent the Twentieth Mississippi to Virginia.[6]

As soon as the regiment arrived in Virginia, George wrote his wife from Lynchburg at what he termed "Camp Davis." On September 12 the regiment was transferred to the Virginia command of Brigadier General John B. Floyd, then operating in the Kanawha Valley of Virginia (now West Virginia). The regiment traveled over the rough mountainous country that typified that area of western Virginia, arriving at Sewell Mountain on September 26.[7]

The rough terrain and the coming winter concerned George because his Deep South soldiers were not used to such weather. He called on Carroll countians for help. Prominent citizen C. M. Vaiden had earlier offered the company money, and George even had his wife working on the issue. She organized a group of women at his law office to sew clothes for soldiers, and they continued this effort throughout the war. In late August George wrote Bettie asking for his "winter vests" and blankets, and advised her to drum up support from the home folks. "I want you to do all you can to have the company well clothed this winter," he wrote, noting that with her being pregnant and due in October, she could not do much herself. "I know you can't do much work, but you can have it done," he wrote. "See your friends and have them to work." Later in the fall George wrote again, "I am glad to learn that your sex are doing so much for the poor soldiers in Carroll."[8]

George also commented on famous Choctaw chief Greenwood Leflore, a Unionist throughout the war. "I learned today that Col. Leflore had sent the Ladies Association at Carrollton $1,500 for the benefit of the soldiers," he wrote Bettie. "I infer from this that the old man has come right at last. I am glad to hear it, not so much on account of an importance I allot to his position, [but] as because it affords strong evidence of the intensity of the Southern feeling in Carroll. Nothing else could have driven that stubborn self willed old man to the support of the war."[9]

Meanwhile, George served under and battled some of the biggest names of the war. The Federal commander confronting him was William S. Rosecrans, destined to become one of the major Federal commanders in the conflict. Likewise, the Confederate commander, Robert E. Lee, would eventually become the most famous of all Confederate generals. George seemed destined for combat.[10]

"This morning we were surprised," Captain George wrote Bettie on October 6 from Camp Defiance, atop Sewell Mountain. But it was not a surprise attack; it was a surprise retreat. Rosecrans had come to the conclusion that attacking Lee would be counterproductive. Adding to the disappointment of no battle, rains continuously hampered the efforts of the troops and did not help the health of the army either. General Floyd reported that the eleven days he and his men were atop Sewell Mountain "cost us more men, sick and dead, than the battle of Manassas Plains." The lack of combat, coupled with the stormy weather, made for low morale, dejection, and illness in the Confederate camps. "The health of my company is still bad," George wrote in mid-October, "I don't know that it is improving much."[11]

As George and his troops miserably sat in camp in October, he thought of home. "The happiest moments I enjoy here," he wrote, "are those when are spent in reading your letters, and the next when I am writing to you." Foremost on his mind was the new baby Bettie was to have any day, Frank, who came on October 22. George's anxiety could be felt in his letters home; "I pray God that you may have a safe and comfortable time," he wrote, and hoped that the new baby would have the "virtue of its mother." George did not discount the other children either, and his eyes no doubt dampened when he received a letter from little Cothran saying, "How, do you do?"[12]

Although Lee left for South Carolina, Floyd continued maneuvering in the mountains with the "fine regiment from Mississippi, under Colonel Russell," as he described them. George explained the maneuvering to his wife in letters home. On November 4 he related that his letter had been interrupted on the previous Saturday because word came to get his company up. "We halted near a ferry over the Kanawha and at the foot of Cotton Mountain," he wrote. He also told of the hard time his men had as they put the two cannons assigned to them into position. "The men dragged, pulled and pushed the cannons," he reported.[13]

George also related an entertaining incident. He took a moment to rest, and as he lay down, word came from regimental headquarters that he had been "detailed as Field Officer of the Day." He was to report to General Floyd's headquarters for duty. This was, he said, "six miles distant." Fortunately, Colonel Russell provided him a horse so George did not have to make the long walk. Another such incident was not so easily rectified. Ordered to take a certain position, George wrote Bettie: "I had only 32 privates, the rest being sick or on duty which prevented them from going."[14]

Despite the rain, the mild fall weather proved less onerous on the troops from the Deep South than first feared. One member of the Twentieth Mississippi, in fact, wrote about happy times. "The 'boys' are all sitting around their log fires laughing, talking, playing the fiddle, and cooking," he reported with obvious enjoyment. By December, however, the mountain weather changed and began to take a toll. George himself reported feeling sick with a "slight pain in my bowels." No doubt he worried that sickness might send him home just as it had in Mexico in 1846. The sickness among the soldiers became so bad that the Confederacy sent an officer to help. Assistant Inspector-General George Deas reported that nearly one-third of Floyd's command was ill. He related that measles were widespread, but they were a well-disciplined and dependable brigade. Nevertheless, realizing the Mississippians were not acclimated to this weather, he recommended that the units from the Deep South should be "ordered into a milder climate." "The severe winters of Western Virginia will be fatal to those southern men," he reported.[15]

As winter set in, the suffering of the soldiers increased. George described "the disastrous retreat of Floyd's army," and the "mud frozen as hard as stones." He griped, "It is time . . . we were in winter quarters," and added, "What the men are to do I don't know." But George's spirits lifted when his half-brother Fayette Durham wrote in that bleak December that the "children are all well." He added one particular tidbit about daughter Mary. Her books, he wrote, were "the last thing she thought of at night and the first thing when she waked in the morning." The studious lawyer George must have liked hearing that.[16]

George remained busy throughout the entire campaign. He wrote Bettie that he only had "a little leisure" on Sunday afternoons, when he usually wrote her. Then he received a short leave early in December. George traveled home, where he saw his newly born son, Frank, for the first time. By early January the leave was over, but George had trouble finding his unit. During his absence, orders had come sending the Twentieth Mississippi to South Carolina, again to serve under Robert E. Lee, who had been sent there to shore up the coastal defenses. Then the orders quickly changed again, and the regiment detoured to Tennessee. General Albert Sidney Johnston in Kentucky was facing a formidable threat, and a major battle looked probable. George later wrote to Bettie that when he heard his men had been sent to Kentucky, he had letters from prominent friends written "introducing me to General Johnston." Because of the rush of events, however, George never saw the general and admitted to Bettie, "In all probability they will never do me any good." For once, George's political connections failed him.[17]

George soon returned to the army, trying to catch up with his regiment in Kentucky. Leaving Carrollton, he caught a train at Winona, passing through Grand Junction and Jackson, Tennessee. In Bowling Green, Kentucky, by January 18, he was having a hard time finding his unit. "I am sometimes told the 20th Mississippi Regiment is at one place and sometimes at another," he wrote in frustration. Making his situation worse, he had just had another of his "sick headaches," not to mention he was "cold and wet" from the hard rain. He managed to obtain a room at a tavern, but even that did not suit him. He told Bettie it was a "damp cold room," and had "the smell of a sick-room." He became depressed, and it almost got the best of him in Bowling Green. He could not find his command, he felt sick, and he had not had any meaningful conversation for the entire train trip northward. "I have been quite melancholy ever since I left home," he wrote Bettie, adding that "when I was not thinking of you and my children . . . my mind [was] ever upon the condition of my country." "But this will wear off soon," he added, "because the duties of my office will furnish food for the mind and it will not dwell upon my [absence from my] family."[18]

Perhaps part of George's depression was the condition of his troops upon returning, and indeed the Confederacy as a whole. "I have had gloomy forbodings," he wrote, "a long and exhaustive war—thousands upon thousands of my fellow soldiers dying from disease and on the battlefield." He also complained to Bettie about twelve-months' troops not reenlisting for the duration of the war. "I hope . . . they will see the great danger to the country arising from their desertion of her standard at the end of 12 months, and re-enlist promptly," he wrote. Once he reunited with his company, George was also not convinced that the men of his company were ready for a fight. As they headed through Kentucky ultimately toward Fort Donelson, he hurriedly wrote his wife, "It is expected that we will have an engagement there, but this is not certain of course." Then he added, as if in contemplation of the upcoming fight: "I fear to the health of this command," and continuing, "Poor fellows, they have a hard time of it and many—many will fall by disease." Yet there was an even larger issue than just health in George's mind, and indeed in other minds as well. He wrote Bettie, "We are still under General Floyd." He went on to admit that it was "unanimously agreed to petition to be transferred from Floyd."[19]

George arrived inside Fort Donelson with his company on February 13, just as the enemy arrived across the way. He and the men of the Twentieth Mississippi were placed in reserve directly behind the center of the Confederate line. Five of its 552 men present for duty died in the early skirmishing. The regiment continued to occupy the reserve position until midnight, when the Mississippians were told to occupy a stretch of trenches formerly held by the Seventh Texas. Major William N. Brown, now in command of the regiment because Colonel Russell was sidelined with an ankle injury, reported, "at that time a brisk fire was going on." George and his men promptly set to work strengthening the trenches they occupied. In the process, they had to remove water and snow that had accumulated since nightfall. Making matters worse, the wind shifted to out of the north, sending the temperature into the teens, freezing the falling rain. It was ironic that George and the Mississippians had been sent to a warmer climate and then were subjected to this freezing weather.[20]

After an unsuccessful Union naval attack, John B. Floyd, being the senior general present within the fort, decided to withdraw his army from Fort Donelson in a breakout attempt against the Federal right flank. George and the Twentieth Mississippi were attached to Colonel William E. Baldwin's Mississippi and Tennessee brigade for the operation. Major Brown received the order at 1:00 Friday afternoon, and the order "was executed in a very short time."[21]

The attack began soon thereafter. Baldwin's Brigade was in the advance of the attack, with George and the Twentieth Mississippi third in line within the brigade. As they trudged forward in the advance, "formed in column by platoon," a private in Company D went down. They marched on for perhaps 100 yards more when the order was received to countermarch and return to the trenches. Major Brown reported, "we did so in proper order." The reason given for the halt was that by the time the ironclads on the river were repulsed, there was not enough daylight left to finish what had been started.[22]

At 1:00 A.M. Saturday, February 15, the Twentieth Mississippi was once more ordered to join Baldwin's Brigade and take part in another breakout attempt early that morning. The attack was to commence at 4:00 A.M. George's company and the rest of Baldwin's Brigade promptly obeyed and were in position at the appointed time. Other units were late in arriving, however, and the attack did not get under way until 6:00 A.M.[23]

When it did begin, the men met the Federals only a third of a mile out of the trenches. As forward regiments deployed into line, George and the Twentieth Mississippi were left in column on the road. Soon, Gideon Pillow, who was in immediate command of the operation, came up and personally directed the Twentieth Mississippi to form in the woods, perpendicular to the road and behind a field on the left. This done, another order "from the same source" directed that the regiment wheel to the right, parallel with the road. The regiment wheeled into position, which put them in the field on the left of the road. "This movement," Major Brown reported, "subjected us to a cross-fire, and very much exposed us to the enemy on both sides." The major quickly reported his perilous position to Pillow, who immediately ordered the unit back to its original deployment. While this was transpiring, the left half of the regiment was exposed to a galling fire from the enemy in the woods to the front. When the order was given to retreat, those five companies on the left did not hear the command. George's Company C was the company just to the right of the center of the regiment and therefore was not in the hottest part of the fight. Fortunately, the five mangled companies presently received word and were soon with their comrades in their former position.[24]

"On several other occasions during the day we were ordered to advance and charge through the woods," Major Brown reported. At noon the regiment was ordered to join the command of Colonel Joseph Drake of the Fourth Mississippi, but the disjointed nature of the Confederate high command forced an end of the attack and a determination to escape. The high command decided not to take advantage of the escape route just opened by George and supporting units, so there was nothing to do but return to the trenches. The Mississippians could see other units returning to the works, but they held their ground for several more hours. With the regiments on the right having gone back to the trenches, an avenue was opened for a Union flank attack on the Twentieth Mississippi's right. With ammunition running low and a flank attack imminent, Colonel Drake ordered his men back to the fort.[25]

In the ordeal, the Twentieth Mississippi lost nineteen killed and sixty wounded for a total of seventy-nine casualties, George not among them. Many lives had been lost in the offensive, which went for naught. The Confederate high command had balked, and the Federals quickly shut the escape route. One wonders what George was thinking at the time. He and his Carroll Guards, along with thousands of other Confederates, were now trapped inside an untenable Fort Donelson. Their fate had been sealed by the incompetence of their leaders.[26]

CHAPTER 7

"My Far-Distant Prison Home"

Johnson's Island, 1862

It was a disastrous night for the Confederacy, as well as for J. Z. George. The commanding officers of Fort Donelson and its garrison spent that Saturday night, February 15, trying to decide what to do. With no hope of another breakout or of thwarting the Federal attack that was sure to come at daylight the next morning, they determined to surrender the fort. In a comedy of errors, Floyd refused to surrender himself, he being a wanted man in the United States for allegedly, as secretary of war, sending large shipments of guns and ammunition into the South immediately before the war. He passed the command to Pillow, who in turn refused to surrender; Pillow passed it to Simon B. Buckner, who finally opened communications with Ulysses S. Grant and received the "unconditional and immediate surrender" reply that became so famous.[1]

Not only did Floyd refuse to surrender the fort, but he also had no plans to surrender the troops that constituted his former brigade, to which George and the Twentieth Mississippi now reverted. Major Brown reported to Floyd at 1:00 that morning, at which time he received instruction to move his regiment to where the Virginians were, on the left of the line. Midway through the execution of the order, a command arrived from Buckner, now in command of the fort, notifying Brown to go to the steamboat landing. Major Brown checked with Floyd, who said that it was official. George and the regiment then proceeded to the landing. There they would escape with Floyd aboard two steamboats waiting on the river. At the landing, the regiments boarded according to rank, which put the Twentieth Mississippi last due to Brown's rank of major. Because they were last, Floyd ordered them to guard the landing from other units. Brown formed the regiment "in a semicircle around the landing." They "stood like a stone wall," he noted, protecting the Virginia regiments and awaiting their turn to board the steamboats.[2]

What happened next was shocking. With the dawn of February 16 fast approaching and Buckner fretting about his duty as a soldier to surrender everything in the fort at dawn, he sent word that if the boats were not gone by daylight, he would destroy them. All the Virginia regiments had already either ferried across the river or boarded the boats, so Floyd ordered the captains to shove off. This left the Mississippians trapped; according to Shelby Foote, they stood "howling ruefully on the bank." The irony was not lost on most of the Mississippians. One member of the regiment remembered they "whipped [the] federals and was currendered." Later in the war another soldier still harbored resentment toward the man who had left them to be captured. "Floyd has at last gone up," W. A. Rorer wrote his cousin upon hearing of the Virginian's death in 1863. "All of our old politicians are failures as generals," he added.[3]

A few members of the regiment, about twenty-five, got away by their own devises, but Buckner surrendered everything else inside the fort, including the Twentieth Mississippi and J. Z. George, at dawn. George surrendered himself and sixty-five other members of his company. After stacking arms, a total of 454 men of the Twentieth Mississippi surrendered. Family members decades later reported that George refused to surrender his arms and threw them into the Cumberland River. While this cannot be documented, it certainly seems plausible for the often-rebellious George.[4]

Despite this surrender, the Twentieth Mississippi received much praise for its work in the two major campaigns in which it had participated. In his report of Fort Donelson, Colonel Baldwin stated, "the whole regiment was among the foremost in every advance." Major Brown also praised the regiment, stating that "without sleep for four nights . . . and . . . encountering a severe snow storm, without tents or cooking utensils, every order was obeyed with the greatest alacrity, every man seeming to feel that much depended on himself." The men had "done credit to themselves and their State for the arduous service they have performed," he said. Nevertheless, the Mississippians were now prisoners of war.[5]

George first went to Camp Chase, a prison camp near Columbus, Ohio, arriving there on March 1. On April 10, however, he was sent to Johnson's Island, at Sandusky, Ohio. Johnson's Island had been built specifically as a prison, with work beginning in November 1861 and just getting completed in February 1862—in time for George and the Fort Donelson prisoners. Located just off of a spit of land in southern Lake Erie, the island itself was small, but it could accommodate several thousand inmates. Its location provided several important resources and was, in fact, the reason it was chosen as the site for a prison. Nearby Sandusky offered rail connections to the outside world, while the island itself offered little hope for any Confederate prisoners trying to escape.[6]

Accommodations were not all that bad early in the war, but the barracks soon became overcrowded as more prisoners came throughout the summer of 1862. Johnson's Island was originally intended to be a prison for officers, but soldiers of all ranks were sent there at first. Thus men from George's company and regiment were able to support one another. The reclusive and often melancholy George especially needed the support of his men.[7]

George's habitat was a walled prison, encircled by a plank stockade fourteen feet high. Inside the stockade were the quarters, some thirteen different two-story barracks, each made of wood frames. Each building was around 3,000 square feet in size on each floor, the prison designers thinking that would house 250 men each. Each barrack was known as a "block" for administrative purposes. Most of the barracks remained unsealed, with large gaps in the walls exposing the prisoners to the elements, most notably the frigid winter wind. Fortunately, George did not arrive at Johnson's Island until after the worst of the winter had ended. A few of the blocks were sealed and divided into individual rooms, although most were unsealed and contained two large rooms where the prisoners slept in groups on three tiers of bunks along the walls. Precisely where George was quartered is unknown.[8]

The rooms on all the blocks were heated with wood stoves during the winters, hardly alleviating the harsh cold. But George spent most of his time in prison during the summer of 1862, when the cold was not a major issue. The cleanliness of the blocks was a concern, however. All the cooking and washing were done in the same rooms, and the buildings were poorly ventilated. The collection of grease, soap, and smoke had a negative effect on the prisoners.[9]

George's major source of fresh water came from the bay itself, augmented by several wells nearby. Eventually, pipes would carry water from the bay to the blocks, but of course these pipes froze during the winter, when the bay did. As the island contained only a shallow layer of topsoil on top of hard rock, the prisoners had trouble keeping open latrines. The shallow sinks filled quickly, necessitating digging new ones frequently.[10]

The prisoners were able to receive goods from home or from acquaintances, and were allowed to buy additional food and goods from sutlers. George's ration during his stay in 1862 was fairly good; the size of the food allotment would not decrease until later in the war when news of the suffering of Union prisoners in Confederate prison camps encouraged the Union government to reciprocate.[11]

At times the prisoners performed duties at the camp, such as chopping wood, carrying water, or digging latrines. It is unknown if George took part in this work, but his attitude could be surmised to be similar to other officers who saw themselves as commissioned personages above the work of privates, or rather masters above the work of slaves. As the prisoners went about their business, though, they had to abide by the regulations. Several prisoners were shot, for example, when they came too close to the dead line, which limited how close they could get to the stockade wall.[12]

George later wrote that he was deeply depressed upon his arrival. Soon his spirits began to rise as word of possible exchange spread. "For sometime back we have all been much cheered up," he wrote Bettie in July, "with the hope of a speedy exchange." "We are often disappointed . . . on this subject," he wrote, "but we still hope that at no very distant day we shall once more be permitted to press the soil of our native South." George was counting on such an exchange, telling his wife, "whether in that event I shall have an opportunity of visiting my home and its dear inmates is doubtful. I shall not come if duty forbids." He assured her, "but I will certainly come if it be consistent with my duty." He concluded his letter, "I am in good spirits and hopeful."[13]

George and his command made the best of the accommodations at Johnson's Island. He had all his men with him, and later in the war he wrote how good they had been for him in those dark days. "All my command was in prison with me," he wrote. Not having to endure the long northern winter and cold winds of Lake Erie immediately upon arrival also helped. "My health still continues good," he wrote Bettie that summer, "though I am much reduced in weight—have lost at least thirty pounds." He related how "we have the necessaries of life and through the kindness of some friends we have found here we have occasionally some of its comforts." Friends from Chicago, as well as Bettie's brother, also sent items for his relief.[14]

One of George's most favored occupations in prison was reading, which fit the lawyer well. He apparently did not partake in the games such as baseball that the prisoners played between the barracks in the common area. He had many choices of books, including some he owned personally, they having been sent to him from outside. "I manage to pass my time pleasantly, at least without positive misery," he wrote Bettie from prison. "My old law publishers have sent me some books which I have read very diligently," he wrote, noting that he had his choice of several legal texts, including Blackstone. He also had volume three of Thomas Babington Macaulay's *Critical and Historical Essays Contributed to the Edinburgh Review* (1850). George signed his name on the front cover, and it was also stamped upon inspection by "John I. Manor, Captain 123 OVI, Superintendent Prisoner Roll and Prison Correspondence, Johnson's Island."[15]

George undertook a more activist approach to law as well—that of teaching its rudiments to the young soldiers. Much as Cothran had taken him under his wing and taught him the law profession, George likewise returned the favor for several prisoners who had nothing else to do in their spare time. One of George's sons later told how his father taught law classes to prisoners, "a few of which later became successful practitioners in Mississippi and other states." One of his students was James M. Pearson of Alabama, who after the war studied further in George's office in Carrollton.[16]

George's chief concern while in prison was the lack of mail. "I am still without a single letter from you," he wrote Bettie in July. "I know you have written frequently but fortune has been against me." He rattled off several prisoners who had received much mail, but then listed an equally lengthy list of men, including himself, who "have [not] been as favored." Letters from other family members no doubt lifted his spirits, including one from his mother, who wrote in July 1862 telling him "all of the family join in sending much love to you." In addition, George received other goods, such as money from J. T. Young of Bettie's family.[17]

Unfortunately, George received some crushing news as well. In his mother's letter, she wrote a tragic postscript: "PS—Your boy Frank died last spring since you was a prisoner." Little Frank had been born in October 1861 while George was in Virginia. Fortunately, he had been able to return home on leave in December 1861 and January 1862, so he saw the five-month-old before he died on March 30, 1862. Bettie had him interred next to his brother James Jr. and his grandmother, her mother, in the family plot in Evergreen Cemetery just outside of Carrollton.[18]

George's mother's letter was not the first news of Frank's death. He wrote Bettie in July that he had heard of it "sometime ago" in someone else's letter from home. The broken-hearted captain tried his best to comfort his wife over the "death of our little boy." He admitted, "the sad news made me melancholy indeed in this my far-distant prison home, but more on your account than on my own." He continued, "But I did not doubt that the merciful Providence whose hand had thus afflicted us would give you strength and fortitude to bear the heavy blow with courage and a calm resignation to his will." No doubt more sensitive to being away from his children, he ended his letter with "kiss all the children for me and remember me to all our household."[19]

The heartbroken George remained in prison several more months, despite the rumors of release, but his spirits were eventually lifted with news of pending exchange for Union prisoners held in the South. On September 1 George was sent to Vicksburg to await the swap. He was officially exchanged on November 8. In all, he had spent six and a half months in prison at two different camps. Obviously, this was not the glorious part he envisioned playing in the war, but now he had a fresh chance to participate again.[20]

CHAPTER 8

"I Report to Gov. Pettus"

State Brigadier General, 1862–1863

"I hereby resign my office of Captain of Company C, 20th Mississippi Regt. to take effect this day," J. Z. George wrote President Jefferson Davis on October 13, 1862, "when I report to Gov. Pettus for duty in accordance with a telegram from you to him." The newly exchanged captain thus resigned his position, but he would soon take on even larger responsibilities. The governor of Mississippi, John J. Pettus, had appointed him a brigadier general of state troops, and he was already busy in that capacity.[1]

Such an appointment was not uncommon during the war, especially in the state troops and militia, commanded by the governor, which were very different from the regular Confederate army. Yet there was the bureaucratic paperwork that needed to be seen to, and the lawyer George knew as much. When released from the Federal prison camp and exchanged, he was still captain of Company C. Of course the regiment was re-formed, but he was not there. In the company return for August 1 to October 31, in fact, he was reported "absent on detached service by order of War Department." To be officially transferred, George had to write out his letter of resignation. He would never serve with his Carroll countians again.[2]

There was some disagreement as to what George's duties would be between the time he resigned and when he went into state service after official exchange. His resignation actually took effect on October 23, but in correspondence between Davis and Pettus, the president would only accept George's resignation when he entered Mississippi's state troops. The lawyer George thus wrote a lengthy explanation of the Davis-Pettus correspondence for the record and entered state service.[3]

George's first activities were reorganizing portions of the state's militia and state troops. Throughout October and early November, while waiting for official exchange, George was in frequent correspondence with Governor Pettus working through issues of furlough, conscription, and absences from the state service, the last usually caused by it being harvest season and many of the men needing to be home gathering crops. Pettus's instructions were to furlough all "who are necessary for the safety or convenience of their neighborhoods." Obviously, George would not have much of a command if he sent all his troops home, so he retained some. He utilized them to respond to calls from sectors such as the Yazoo River valley and the Tallahatchie River bottoms, where Federal incursions were occurring. In mid-December, for example, George had to send troops to help block the Yazoo River from Union naval expeditions, one of which resulted in the Federal loss of the gunboat U.S.S. *Cairo* by an underwater mine. George was told to send troops to block "the Yazoo River by felling trees."[4]

After completing preliminary organizational activities, George next visited the commands under his care. Accustomed to being several states away, he wrote Bettie from northern Mississippi, "It does seem after my long imprisonment in Yankee land that just to be sixty or seventy miles from home with mail communication is really to be at home. But, still I don't see you or the children and hence I want to hear from you occasionally."[5]

George first traveled to Batesville and other areas of northwest Mississippi. What he found there was not encouraging. Only a few men (actually around thirty at Batesville) were in camp, and the rest "pay no attention to the summons." He related to the governor that the "militia officers are afraid to assume any responsibility—it is almost impossible to get an order carried out." "There is everywhere pervading all classes, especially the slave owners, a great repugnance to entering into the service of the State, or the Confederate States. Every protest is seized upon to secure an exemption. Diseases have suddenly developed to a most alarming rate extent, outside appearances are nothing, so termed stout looking, active men are afflicted with some deadly malady," George joked. And this was not just the case in the militia. The people themselves were revolting against conscription because of a "distrust in the military management of the area," and George actually thought the people were beginning "to doubt the final issue of the struggle and are beginning in their own minds to accept subjugation as inevitable." "The practical lesson I learn from all this," George wrote to Pettus, "is that the enrolled militia called out suddenly to meet the enemy will do but inefficient service."[6]

But George did not have long to get his troops in line. By mid-November 1862 Ulysses S. Grant's Vicksburg campaign was beginning. Brigadier General George, formally exchanged on November 8, was busy for the next few months as the enemy made several attempts to get to the river city. George would not be part of the major campaign, however. He spent the majority of his time on the fringes, mostly in northwestern Mississippi. In fact, he wrote Pettus in early November, "I know nothing of the plans of our Generals." As might be expected, the regular Confederate army was used to block and stop Grant's moves, with the state troops serving a peripheral and less important duty. Such was the case when cavalry commander Earl Van Dorn assigned George to command the post at Oxford, Mississippi, on November 10. "General George, with the State troops under his command at and near Abbeville, will take post at Oxford, Miss., to guard the public property at that place," his orders read. Wanting little interference with the regular Confederate commands, Van Dorn stipulated that "General George will assume command of that post, but will give no orders to post quartermaster and commissary except so far as to supply his own command." Obviously, Van Dorn did not want state troops interfering with Confederate command authority.[7]

George planned to remain at Oxford, even renting a "comfortable house with three rooms" for himself and his staff. He invited Bettie to come for a visit. "You will live with us," he told her, "one room shall be for you." George cautioned her not to bring the children, though, and not much baggage, although he did tell her to "bring enough . . . to be respectable." Bettie never visited because Grant's central Mississippi campaign soon threatened Oxford. George apparently had to be satisfied with just letters, of which he received quite a few. He told Bettie to keep writing, as the letters were "so comforting, affectionate . . . so hopeful and cheerful amidst the gloom which is now almost universal."[8]

As John C. Pemberton and the Confederate army retreated from Holly Springs to Abbeville, in front of Grant and his army, General George and his state troops guarded the Oxford area. When Grant moved through Oxford toward Grenada, George evacuated southward. Grenada was spared due to Van Dorn's cavalry raid on Grant's base at Holly Springs in December, forcing the Union army to fall back into Tennessee. George and his troops did not return to Oxford, but remained in Grenada, where they spent the winter. George was the senior officer of the motley brigade stationed there.[9]

As Christmas came and went in camp, George wrote Pettus that his job of organizing the militia was not going well. "I am sorry to report that the State Troops are not what they ought to be," he wrote. "It will be found next to impossible to make the State Troops efficient under the present organization." Desertions were frequent, he reported, and he did not even have a surgeon who could care for the sick. As a result, ill soldiers had to be sent home, further reducing the command. He was also getting little cooperation from his superiors. George complained to the governor, "I have written three times to General Tupper," but still could get no reply. "Will you be kind enough to have an answer sent me?"[10]

George let off a little of his steam by writing to Bettie. "A happy Christmas to you and all the family," George wrote her on December 25. "I wish I could be at home with you but it is impossible. Possibly before another Christmas I may be at home," he wrote. His spirits were somewhat improved by the presence in camp of his slave Aleck, but even he "wants to go home to see you all," George wrote.[11]

George had little time for such further musings. He continued to organize his troops, dealing with the many furloughs that the state soldiers requested. At other times units under his command made contact with the enemy. Major Green L. Blythe in late January, for instance, sent George "ten prisoners and three Jay Hawkers." But the biggest headache was a near revolt on the part of his soldiers concerning the Confederate draft. Many soldiers wanted to know if their state service exempted them from Confederate service, and George did not know. He sought an explanation from Pettus, telling him that there was "considerable commotion in the Militia Camp." When told that their prior service would not count, George sought the chance to allow his men to choose which companies and regiments they would join.[12]

More trouble was brewing, however, and George reported to Pettus that "demoralization of the militia [was] complete." The men "will desert any time" if not furloughed before being sent into Confederate service, he reported. "I am mortified and disgusted at the present state of affairs in the militia," George wrote. "I have done all I can to prevent it.... I feel almost certain that my self respect will compel me to abandon all connection with an organization which produces such fruits, but I'll struggle a little while longer."[13]

With such bare nerves among officers and men, confrontation was bound to erupt. An issue arising from surgeons' discharges during the winter soon led to an outright rebellion on the part of some of George's command near Grenada. As George had no "medical director," he relied on a "board" of regimental surgeons, who sent men home for almost any reason. "I have no confidence in them," George told Pettus, "they are not responsible to me." George petitioned Pettus for a brigade surgeon he could trust, thus making enemies of the surgeons and the men in the ranks. In addition, George had revamped the furlough system, limiting the furloughs in a "ten percent system." Thus in late January and February a group of officers under George sent a petition to Governor Pettus requesting he be relieved of command because he did not care for his troops. They cited frustrations such as having no say in whom their commander was and that "we know nothing of Gen. George's military capacity as he has never drilled this brigade." The officers asked Governor Pettus to return their old commander, Richard H. Winter. The perpetrators openly admitted to George they had "harshly sent a petition to his Excellency Governor Pettus impeaching your character as an officer." Just as quickly as the situation flared up, however, it was over. George faced the criticism head on and explained himself to his officers. One of the petitioners wrote Pettus thereafter that George had "made an explanation of the matters," which was, he said, "generally satisfactory." It helped George's case that another group of officers under his command likewise sent a petition to Pettus supporting George. "Having heard that a petition having been gotten up against our able and worthy General George impeaching his character as an officer and being unworthy to fill the position that he does," the officers told the governor, "we look upon him as an able officer, one that looks to the welfare of his command." The officers went on to say that a "hasty injustice has been done to him" and "respectfully submit[ed] that he be retained as our leader." George's explanation clearly satisfied his disgruntled officers, and they soon sent another petition to him saying they "take pleasure now in recalling those sentiments and express ourselves fully satisfied with your statement and we feel that no one more worthy than yourself could hold that position." Another original petitioner "request[ed] that no action be taken <u>based</u> on the allegations."[14]

Following this internal squabble, there occurred a much larger and potentially more troubling episode that saw the independent George confront a Confederate brigadier general and wind up under arrest. While at Grenada in early March 1863, George was technically under the command of Lloyd Tilghman. The two had some acquaintance, even going back to the Fort Henry and Fort Donelson episode in which they both became prisoners. But when both were exchanged and returned to duty in central Mississippi, they had several disagreements. Tilghman ordered George to take orders from one of his subordinates, a colonel, with the idea that a Confederate colonel outranked a state brigadier general. This, of course, upset the prickly George. "I could not see what right he had to command me his superior in rank," George wrote. Then Tilghman told George to follow orders from his quartermaster, saying staff officers had the same authority as generals. George wrote to Governor Pettus: "by the same logic he can easily arrive at the conclusion that he is invested with all the powers of the President of the Confederate States or even of the Almighty himself." Once again, George did not take any drastic action, although when Tilghman "arbitrarily and illegally ejected my QM [quartermaster] from an office which he had rented for his own use," George had just about reached the breaking point.[15]

Adding to his problems, George, no doubt, was still wobbling from the accusations that he did not see to his men's welfare. Thus when he received an order during the late hours of March 1 to send 100 men for guard duty on a steamboat, he told Tilghman that most of his troops were "old men and unfitted for such duty." He reminded the general that he had two regular Confederate regiments at Grenada as well. He also argued that he had too few men to cover all the fatigue, guard, and wood-gathering duties assigned him. George waited for a reply, but he only got a staff officer from Tilghman asking if he had sent the men. George replied he had not and that he had a letter pending to Tilghman. When a staff officer "suggested the propriety of my going to see General T[ilghman]," George rode to the general's headquarters.[16]

After the two politely discussed another issue, George brought up the order. Tilghman immediately changed his attitude and "in a short and domineering tone refused to listen to me," George insisted. He pressed the matter. "I claimed the right to be heard in defense of the full rights of my command," George told Governor Pettus, but Tilghman "again . . . refused to hear me." To this George replied, "If you will not hear me, I shall be compelled to refuse the detail." Tilghman immediately ordered George under arrest for disobeying an order.[17]

This sudden act awakened the lawyer in George. He began to comb the army regulations, and wrote a lengthy letter to Governor Pettus saying that he felt compelled to "lay before you a correct summary of the Proceedings and transactions which have ended in my being deprived of my command and placed under arrest as an alleged criminal against the laws of my Country." He reminded the governor, "my past life furnishes a guaranty that I would not fail to discharge any duty however painful or unpleasant. Whatever sacrifices the condition of my Country calls upon her sons to make I will cheerfully throw upon her alter." But he drew a line at obeying illegal orders. "I have committed no offense," he wrote. "It is as much my duty to refuse Obedience to an illegal order as to obey a legal one."[18]

Then George made two basic arguments. One was that the order had been "illegal and improper" due to its violation of several paragraphs of the army regulations manual, most notably that of sending officers to participate in fatigue duty. George insisted that he had shown "beyond a shadow of a doubt" that the order was illegal, but he did not stop there. He also maintained that the order was "oppressive and injurious to my command." Then George argued that Tilghman had "persistently and constantly ignored my rank and attempted to deprive me of my just powers as an Officer." He cited several examples, such as the colonel and staff officers who were supposed to command George.[19]

George reminded Governor Pettus that he had served honorably under Earl Van Dorn, John Pemberton, and William Loring, and had never been treated with anything but "courtesies and respect." He asked "to be released from arrest at once and restored to my command where my service is much needed." As fate would have it, the courier by whom he sent his explanation was sidetracked and did not go directly to Jackson, prompting George to write Pettus again several days later requesting the governor hold off any decision until he heard George's side of the story.[20]

Governor Pettus sent Charles D. Fontaine, one of George's fellow secession convention delegates, to investigate, and this officer reported to him on March 9: "I am left without a doubt as to the legality . . . of his [George's] conduct," and recommended the "speedy release of Genl. George from his illegal arrest." George was quickly restored to his command, and the matter ended. Making the tense situation less hostile was the fact that Tilghman was soon ordered to Yazoo City with his brigade, leaving George in command at Grenada. But George had only 488 men and reported that this number would likely fall in the coming days. "Thirty-three desertions in the last forty-eight hours," he reported to Pemberton. Nevertheless, the Confederate high command turned from attacking one another to stopping the Federal thrusts that multiplied as the weather became better in the spring.[21]

One of the Federals' attempts to get to Vicksburg involved George's Grenada area. The Federals tried to get through to the Yazoo River by the Yazoo Pass. In February 1863 William W. Loring ordered George to harass the enemy in the Yazoo Pass region, particularly along the Coldwater and Tallahatchie rivers. George sent Major Green Blythe, in command of the partisan rangers in that area, to do the job. Blythe simply had too few men and was ineffective against the Federal transports. But his scouts were very helpful in keeping the Confederate high command knowledgeable about the enemy venture.[22]

Because of the failure to stop the Federals at Yazoo Pass, Union troops, by March 26, were at Fort Pemberton on the Yazoo River near Greenwood. George received several more urgent pleas for help. Pemberton ordered him to send some cavalry to the mouth of the Coldwater River to intercept any supply or courier boats, and when the first attempt to take Fort Pemberton at Greenwood was turned back, George was asked to harass the Union retreat as much as possible. But then a second wave of Federals was soon back testing the fort in early April. This time Pemberton personally ordered George and his troops to serve under Loring's orders at Fort Pemberton. George and his state troops were together at Winona and Vaiden at the time, near his hometown of Carrollton, and he immediately sent forward 100 men with 285 additional soldiers ready to go when transportation arrived. General George eventually arrived on the scene himself; he wrote home on April 10 from Greenwood, indicating the crisis was over. "The enemy have been gone from our immediate front for several days," he wrote, but he joked that "they disappointed me in leaving without having first made greater efforts." All joking aside, he admitted, "where they will turn up next I can't tell." Nevertheless, he returned with his command to Grenada to watch and wait.[23]

Although he expressed some excitement amid the Yazoo Pass operation, George was still chafing under the lack of action at Grenada. Writing his wife in April, he confided that when the Federals finally left for good, "I shall go to Jackson with the hope that I may get more active service. I do not know that I shall succeed, but I hope I will. I intend to see more of the war than I am likely to see at Grenada in command of the militia."[24]

The Federals had indeed quit on their Yazoo Pass operations but had not given up on capturing Vicksburg. Events soon shifted to the general proximity of the city, leaving George and the state troops in northern Mississippi to deal with the Federals near Memphis guarding supply depots and transportation routes. Thus General George and his men remained inactive at Grenada in April, when Governor Pettus told him to take a few months to recruit and organize new companies of cavalry and to eventually report to Brigadier General James R. Chalmers at Panola. George became commander of the state's "District No. 5," although his immediate superior was a regular Confederate general.[25]

In this new position, George was involved in actions peripheral to the capture of Vicksburg. For instance, he was ordered to mobilize and scout the area east of Grenada in mid-April as a major Federal raid moved through the state. As Benjamin Grierson's raid moved southward toward

Newton and then on toward Baton Rouge, Louisiana, George responded to frantic calls for assistance and intelligence about the enemy column's whereabouts. Other Federal actions were also reported in the vicinity, keeping George and the Confederate high command chasing shadows.[26]

Once Grierson's column moved to the south, events quieted later in April and into May. George returned to his conscripting, impressing, and organization of the state troops in his district. He found the going difficult. There was a lack of interest among conscripts and furloughed soldiers who refused to return to the ranks, and the government in Jackson ignored him because of the crisis in that area. When Grant crossed the Mississippi River south of Vicksburg and then headed northward, he eventually reached Jackson, which fell on May 14. As a result, Pettus was busy overseeing the evacuation of the capital and the removal of the archives, treasury, and executive departments. George seemed to have little or no knowledge of the events around Jackson in the early days of May. He repeatedly sent telegram after telegram asking for mundane instructions concerning the legality of conscription and impressments. He desired to know if impressments were to be temporary or permanent, if he should mount his troops, what were terms of impressments, and state versus Confederate authority regarding the men. He received no answers from a state government in crisis south of his position at Grenada. But George kept trying. "You did not answer my dispatch," he wrote Pettus on May 4. "Please answer my dispatch of yesterday also mine of several days ago." There was no answer.[27]

More telling, the independent George had begun to assert his command authority in a way that probably irritated his Confederate superiors. He was a brigadier general, but that rank was in the state service, and there was tension between Confederate and state forces. George's questioning of orders as well as his dexterity for offering advice probably did not help the situation. Messages containing phrases such as "Had I not better send my cavalry?" and "Why may not the whole regiment at that place be sent?" no doubt rankled the professional military men. In addition, he had a habit of sending messages full of questions, and ending the messages with the one word, "Answer."[28]

As for Governor Pettus, George told him how to run his state even during the crisis of early May 1863. "A regiment ought to be sent here [Grenada]," George wrote in early May. On May 10, as the Federal Army of the Tennessee bore down on the state capital, George wrote Pettus, "There seems to be no pressing necessity for me to remain here. Please relieve me so that I can report to Genl. Chalmers and organize and equip the cavalry." Pettus had larger issues to worry about, and George was left at Grenada organizing state troops. Later in the month George seemed to have accepted his fate, concentrating once again on organization. But he let Pettus know of his troubles, which included lacking saddles, bridles, and men for the horses.[29]

Finally, with this lack of action, no response from Pettus, and untrustworthy troops, George had had enough. He asked Pettus in late May either to disband the militia, which would allow him to move to another command, or to relieve him of the command at Grenada so that he could get into the action in north Mississippi. Pettus curtly refused, citing Joseph E. Johnston's specific requests that there be troops at Grenada. George, it seemed, was destined to sit out the war in Grenada, fidgeting with almost useless state troops and seeing no enemy but those within his own command.[30]

George was never a beloved commander of the state troops, and as late as July 1863 was telling his wife, "Just now I am the subject of more abuse and slander than any man in the State." His superiors joined in the criticism. When George questioned several orders, fellow secession convention delegate Chalmers wrote through a staff officer, "it is the duty of an officer to use every exertion to carry out any orders that may be given him—and if he fails in spite of them, he can then render his excuses with better grace than before the effort was made." Probably, though, George's unhappiness came primarily from dwindling morale. He wrote Bettie at the end of May, "Lincoln will enforce his conscript law and that will give him soldiers enough to carry on the war forever." Later, he wrote, "I confess to a great deal of depression myself," and warned her to try to pack up and save his library if possible from any invading Federals. George nevertheless philosophically endured his trials, saying, "Better men than I have suffered greater things."[31]

George's tenure as a brigadier general in the state service clearly had not been what he had hoped. He wanted an active command, but he had spent most of his time in organizing, equipping, coddling, begging, and fighting with his own soldiers and commanders. His personality quirks came to the forefront, and George had several altercations with superiors and subordinates. Historian Richard McMurry has written that one of the marks of a great commander is the ability to get along with both superiors and subordinates. Unfortunately, George's personality was such that he continually stayed at odds with both. If his personality was well fitted for the courtroom, it was a hindrance on the battlefield.[32]

CHAPTER 9

"With Gallantry Discarding Caution"

Confederate Colonel, 1863

During the summer of 1863, a welcome change came for J. Z. George. Federal activity in northwestern Mississippi in support of the Vicksburg campaign required the Confederate commanders in the area to concentrate their forces. Thus James R. Chalmers, commander of the Fifth Military District, ordered George northward to Panola to help repel Federal expeditions south into central Mississippi from Federal bases at Memphis and La Grange, Tennessee. George immediately began preparations to move, glad to be leaving the doldrums of Grenada. "I have bought another horse," he wrote Bettie, likely knowing that he needed a better mount for the more arduous operations he realized were coming. He also asked Bettie to send his trunk to him in Panola and send the key by letter.[1]

George arrived at Panola by May 30, as did his trunk. "I have now more clothes than I can well take care of," he told Bettie. He also had more serious duties. Chalmers was in the process of reorganizing his troops into three brigades, one of which he gave to George with orders to hold the Tallahatchie River line. George's new brigade consisted of the Second Mississippi Partisans, Dunn's Mississippi Battalion Partisan Rangers, and McGuirk's Mississippi Battalion Partisan Rangers, all in state service. "I have a pretty fair brigade," George wrote Bettie in June, and vowed to support his commander, Chalmers, no matter what happened. Unfortunately, the Confederates were terribly outnumbered and outgunned in north Mississippi.[2]

George was overjoyed to be leaving Grenada. "I am happy at the prospect of leaving this town," he wrote Bettie at the end of May. "I have been here about 6 months and not exceeding a half dozen courtesies have been extended to me during the whole time. I hope the Grenadians are better to other people than to myself," he wrote. Other minor issues also tugged at him. He had lost his "old knife," and worried about losing his slave Aleck. "Aleck is well," he wrote from Panola in June, but admitted that "if he intends to escape to the Yankees he will have plenty of opportunities of doing so." In fact, one of George's other slaves had already escaped across the lines.³

Also on George's mind during this transition was the pending birth of another baby. Elizabeth Watt George, his ninth child, was born on June 24, 1863. George wrote Bettie, "I do not fancy the name you wish to give our little daughter. . . . One has been named for me and I think now that one ought to be named for you. So, let the little stranger be named for her mother." She was; Elizabeth George quickly gained the nickname Lizzie.⁴

But the Union threat to north Mississippi was George's chief concern for the moment. The Federals, as expected, made a major raid to Panola between June 16 and 25, 1863, in support of their Vicksburg campaign farther south. At the time, Chalmers was absent on a raid of his own, and General George was in command. The Federal units moved southward, evidently intent on breaking the railroad bridge over the Yocona River. With only about 800 men in his entire command, George could do little to stop the raid, which consisted of about 2,000 enemy troops led by Colonel John K. Mizner. George retreated in front of the invaders, staying between them and the important railroad town of Grenada. When the enemy finally left, George led his men back northward, nipping at the Federals' heels.⁵

Although George issued a congratulatory order to his troops stating "his high satisfaction with the gallantry and energy displayed," this first independent command had not gone well for him. He had showed obvious inexperience, often asking subordinates what to do. He filled his report with such phrases as "in accordance with Colonel McCulloch's suggestion," and "on consultation with my colonels." He indicated that he had immediately changed the direction of his march on the suggestion of a colonel. He even admitted that he had generally followed Colonel McCullough's suggestions, "owing to his greater experience in the cavalry service." More important, George was unable to save the railroad bridge or a cache of supplies at Panola. Union Colonel Mizner reported that George "evacuated during the night, somewhat hastily, . . . leaving his sick, a quantity of guns, ammunition, and camp and garrison equipage, also two caissons and battery wagons and battery forge." The setback was not lost on the people of the region, George complaining that "I have heard that a good deal of unfriendly criticism upon the retreat has been indulged in by that class who have seen proper to take no other part in this war than to remain at home and to embarrass the operations of the army by abuse of those who are intrusted with command."[6]

George went further in complaining about the lack of numbers he had at his disposal during the raid, even suggesting that if no more soldiers could be sent, the Confederate units in the region should be divided into guerrilla companies. Later in July George went further and sent his commander unsolicited suggestions. He admitted that he sent the message "with the greatest diffidence, and with no view of dictating a policy to the military authorities of the Confederate States." He "offered [it] solely," he said, "as the contribution of a heart earnestly solicitous for the welfare of the State and the protection of its citizens." George argued that, with the loss of Vicksburg, the Confederacy could not keep large numbers of troops in northern Mississippi. Instead, he recommended "that the State forces in the section referred to be employed in the future as guerillas, or in detached companies." He stated that they could thus "furnish some protection to the country and annoy and injure the enemy to a considerable extent." He also said that they could live off the land and evaporate instead of retreating when large numbers of the enemy were sent against them. Chalmers forwarded George's message to the departmental commander, admitting "there is much truth in what is said by General George, and it is deserving of serious attention." But Chalmers also contradictingly wrote that he did not have a high regard for guerrillas. "My own experience here has been that these guerilla companies cost the Government much more than they are worth, and that it has been a cover for many men desirous of avoiding all duty." He derisively added, "Their ranks are very thin until a muster for pay is ordered, and then they are quite full." Nothing ever came of the unsolicited advice from the state militia officer.[7]

Some of George's complaining probably stemmed from the discouragement he felt concerning the Confederacy's future. He had earlier written that he felt "anxious" about Vicksburg. On July 4 he wrote Bettie, "I am somewhat depressed at the condition of our national affairs and especially am I so at the prospect of Mississippi and Tennessee." On the day the city fell he ironically wrote, "I can't see how Vicksburg is to be retained." His discouragement extended to his own area of operations as well: "In this district the prospect is not more promising." He told Bettie they were outnumbered three to one, "if not more." He also ominously told her, "You had better move to the plantation."[8]

With the fall of Vicksburg in July 1863, matters changed precipitously in northern Mississippi. Widespread demoralization convinced George to send home most of the state troops under his command. When the Federals were back on the move to Jackson in mid-July, Chalmers took his best troops southward to offer any aid he could to help stop that advance. He thus left George and his command at Panola to counter any Federal advances from the Memphis area. Chalmers left explicit instructions for George about how he was to retreat in the event a major raid pushed him back. By late July, however, even George's small command was needed farther south, and Chalmers sent him to Vaiden "to watch the movements of the enemy in that quarter and prevent the advance of marauding parties." George was also ordered to burn any cotton he found during the march to and upon his arrival at Vaiden. Once again, George questioned Chalmers as to the wisdom of such as move. A terse response told George to move immediately, and he did, although another scathing letter followed, stating, "it is impossible for any officer to exercise the proper control over his men who admits that he cannot command them before he has attempted to do so." Despite the ruckus, within days the Federal threat to the south minimized while another one in the north developed. Chalmers sent George's men back to Panola with the other brigades.[9]

George himself did not return to Panola, but subsequently moved his headquarters back to Grenada of all places, where he spent the rest of his service in the state troops organizing and reorganizing regiments and dealing with the mundane paperwork of district command. Good news arrived in August, however: George was relieved of command of his brigade and told to collect men who would be sent to the Confederate army. He was authorized to enlist all those who were not already in service as well as wounded men who were not presently with their commands. Best of all, he was ordered to organize a regiment or battalion. If too few men could be found, he was to send them to organizations already in the field.[10]

On August 31 George was officially ordered to "proceed at once" in collecting the companies to form a new cavalry regiment. Mississippi governor Pettus had sought the permission of Jefferson Davis, who approved despite some interference from local commanders. George fumed, "I concluded to quit at once," he told Bettie, but he ultimately received the clearance needed to begin his recruitment. He also received the support of his former commander James R. Chalmers, whose aide told George that the general hoped "that you will have no difficulty in raising your regiment and will be most pleased to have you in his command." George quickly organized the regiment out of unattached companies in the area, with its first designation being the Nineteenth Mississippi Cavalry Battalion. When the full complement of companies was reached, the unit became the Fifth Mississippi Cavalry Regiment.[11]

By early October the regiment remained unorganized, and therefore it was not assigned a part in Chalmers's raid to Collierville, Tennessee. In fact, Chalmers wrote, "I left the new regiment, commanded by Colonel George, which was not fully organized, to picket the river." George spread his men out along the Tallahatchie River near Abbeville, and as the raid drew to an end and Chalmers retreated in front of the enemy, he requested George to gather ammunition for his retreating command. Then Colonel R. V. Richardson, one of Chalmers's brigade commanders, ordered George and his men to the town of Wyatt, five miles west of Abbeville, on the Tallahatchie River. George arrived there with sixty of his men, the number that he could supply with ammunition. Nothing came of the resulting standoff, and George and his men were soon deployed to hold a ford less than a mile upriver. George's troops drove the Federal pickets away and held the ford the remainder of the day, until the Confederate forces retired. After returning to Wyatt once more and finding the enemy had retired, George took his men to Water Valley to finish the regiment's organization. Casualties were very light in the skirmishing, with only one officer wounded. George himself admitted, "the affair at Wyatt was a small one, our action being defensive, the enemy not pressing much."[12]

On October 18, with the regiment finally organized, George was assigned to Colonel W. F. Slemons's Brigade of Chalmers's Division. The regiment was reported as having 350 men. Elections were held on the 30th, and George, not surprisingly, was elected colonel. He was mustered into Confederate service on November 1.[13]

With Grant's activities around Chattanooga requiring William T. Sherman's troops at that place, Chalmers once more planned to attack Collierville, Tennessee, in order to disrupt travel on the Memphis and Charleston Railroad. Originally intending to demonstrate against Collierville while other troops broke the railroad to the east, Chalmers changed his plans and headed directly toward the weakly defended town. His scouts reported to Chalmers that only one Federal regiment of cavalry held the town.[14]

Slemons's Brigade received their marching orders at midnight on November 2, and soon crossed the Coldwater River and moved toward Collierville. "After a good deal of slight skirmishing," George wrote Bettie, in which several prisoners were taken, the brigade arrived within half a mile of the town. There the brigade was put into line of battle. George's regiment constituted the right of the brigade while the Third Mississippi State Cavalry made up the left. A portion of another regiment, the Second Arkansas, was detailed as flankers. To their left, Colonel Robert McCulloch's Brigade formed and continued the line. The line advanced and "halted under a hill," but by this time George realized that more than cavalry were confronting them. Federal artillery had opened up on the advancing troops. The men could not see the town or the position of the batteries, which they could only guess at "from the sound of the cannon," George noted.[15]

George's orders were to charge the battery. He led his men, he wrote his wife, "first to hunt for the battery and then to take it." The attack made its way up the hill. "The boys followed in good order and with a shout arriving at the crest of the hill," he wrote. At the top of the hill, he noticed "a very strong fort on my right," and the battery on his left. Both were located at the edge of Collierville, on the opposite side of the railroad. George stated that both opened on him as his men, "in good order," topped the hill. He quickly realized that the possibility of taking the fort was slim, so he directed his men to concentrate on the other battery.[16]

The terrain was "uneven and intersected with gullies," and George himself soon became a casualty of this terrain. Within 100 yards of the Union line, his horse "fell in a gully and very near dismounted me," George told Bettie. He managed to get his horse back on track, but, although still ahead of the regiment, Captain William N. Scales, a Carroll countian commanding George's Company D, and others had passed. Quickly rising to a "short gallop," George caught up to these officers before they reached the railroad.[17]

George and his troops were within sixty yards of the railroad when the Federals, armed with "Colt revolving rifles" George later learned, rose and poured a devastating fire into the gray ranks from rifle pits, "the existence of which I was totally ignorant," Colonel Slemons later admitted. George wrote Bettie, "the battery was not advanced beyond the enemy fortifications as I think Col. Slemons supposed and the result was that the charge could not be successful." George and the officers leading the attack continued on, but the regiment did not follow them. George raced to the Union lines "with gallantry discarding caution," according to his brigade commander, and crossed the railroad. A Federal officer later remembered only "a few men reached the guns; among them General George and two officers." The officers suddenly found themselves within Federal lines. George saw a Federal within twenty feet of him "take deliberate aim at me and fire." "Strange to say, I was not hit," he told Bettie. "Not even my clothes were touched," but his horse, which had already had a bad day, was "badly wounded and fell." George also fell and in doing so hurt his right hand. Later, he also found a bruise on his left arm, which he deduced had come from a shell fragment or a spent ball. But that was not the worst of it. Having miraculously waded into the incoming fire without being killed, George knew it was useless to try to escape. Thus he became a prisoner of war for the second time in less than two years.[18]

George's superiors commended him for his bravery and courage. Colonel Slemons reported that he had "a reputation too well established for gallantry to be benefited by any comment from me." Perhaps George's superiors had to wonder at his thinking in moving so far ahead of his troops, however. Chalmers reported, "Colonel George led the charge made by Slemons' brigade, and rode into the town followed by Captain Scales and Lieutenant Lamkin, of his regiment, and a few of his men. The main body of his regiment did not follow him, and, as we were mistaken about the force at Collierville, it is, perhaps, best that they did not."[19]

In two letters to Bettie over the next two days, George defended his regiment and his own actions in the skirmish. "They are not to blame," George wrote of his men. "I do not believe any Regt. would have done better. I know from the enemy that after they faltered they fought bravely." He did tell his wife, "If the Regt. had advanced as I expected we would have taken the battery I think, but we could not have held it as we would have been subject to an enfilading fire from the Fort which was not more than 150 yards to the right of it." George felt the most need to defend his own actions. "I put myself at the head of the line and ordered them to follow," he wrote. "I was in the advance as I ought to have been." Later, he continued, "I have been unfortunate but it is no fault of mine. I charged as ordered and I feel conscious that I did my whole duty bravely and well. No friend of mine need be ashamed or mortified at my conduct." Yet George was clearly worried about how his actions would be perceived. "If the charge was a reckless or foolish one . . . I am not responsible for it. I obeyed orders as it was my plain duty to do," he wrote. Even after he was in captivity, George asked Bettie to send him a copy of Confederate papers telling of the fight at Collierville. "I have seen the Yankee accounts . . . and I am anxious to see our side of it." He wanted to know how he was treated in the press.[20]

With the attack on Collierville a failure, Chalmers returned south to fight another day, but the war was over for George. In a letter to his wife written two days after the fighting, he opened with a devastating line:

"The fortunes of war have again placed me in the hands of the enemy." He quickly went to work trying to obtain a parole, but bad news again reached the George home in a letter dated November 7. George wrote, "I shall not get a parole." He was heading to an enemy prison camp again.[21]

Ironically, George had written Bettie last Christmas: "Possibly before another Christmas I may be at home." Little did he know then that by that next Christmas he would be a prisoner in enemy hands again.[22]

CHAPTER 10

"My Prison Home"

Johnson's Island, Again, 1863–1865

J. Z. George's capture made news within the Federal high command. The area commander, Stephen A. Hurlbut, notified his superior, Ulysses S. Grant, of the capture. The Federals also noted George's bravery. In describing the action of the Second Iowa Cavalry, Federal commander Edward Hatch reported they were attacked by "a regiment mounted, led in person by General George." He also noted, "A few men reached the guns; among them General George and two officers."[1]

George was first held by the provost marshal in Memphis. He reported that he was handled fairly, telling Bettie, "I have been treated with the utmost courtesy by the officers and men belonging to the enemy. I have not been robbed at all." In fact, he wrote that he gave a private $100 to recover "for me my overcoat and shawl." "He afterward returned the money to me," George said. He also noted that the Federal officers had "very much complimented" him on his charge, which he took as the reason he was treated so well. In all likelihood, his rank as colonel probably had more to do with his treatment than any gallantry in the charge on Collierville.[2]

George's mind quickly turned to trying to understand what had just happened to him. "I argued my escape as providential," he wrote his devout wife, "and I shall not spurn or neglect the teachings of Him who . . . has shielded . . . [me] from Death and harm." He assured Bettie, "I have your last letter with me. I have read and pondered over its contents and shall endeavor to regulate my conduct according to the monitions of my Christian wife." But he had to admit that "I shirk somewhat from the rigors of a northern winter in a northern prison." He told Bettie to "tell Judge Cothran and Gov. Pettus and Judge Harris to use their influence to have me speedily exchanged. I have been in prison so much since the war began that I think I ought to have some favors given me." If he received a parole, he wrote, he would go to Richmond "to effect an exchange." "I long once more to be in the field. My regt. is a good one and I want to command it and make it useful to my country."[3]

George was also worried about his family in case of a long absence. "Do not give way to melancholy," he wrote his wife. "I shall return in due season to honorable service to my country." In the meantime, he instructed, "Teach the children . . . encourage them to read." He told her to tell his sons "to be good boys." George also gave instructions about his belongings, including moving his various law and literary libraries to Cotesworth and keeping his slave Aleck with them; "he is one of the best boys I ever knew." "You had better move to the plantation," he wrote Bettie, and told her to do whatever she thought best about the slaves he held in Georgia.[4]

Through it all, George's spirits remained remarkably high. "I am not depressed now as I was when captured as Donelson," he wrote Bettie. He had her last letter to him and told her, "I shall often read it in my prison home and endeavor to profit by its contents." Also helping his feelings while he was in Memphis was his friend T. S. Ayers, whom George described as "a brother in distress." He similarly tried to aid others, including Captain Scales, who had been wounded in the charge. "Though I am treated with courtesy by the officers of the prison," George wrote Bettie, "yet the guard is strict and vigilant and we have no opportunity of going into the city even under guard."[5]

By November 7 George had received the disheartening news that he would not be paroled; he was going to a prison camp. "I learned that I go north this evening," he wrote, "to what particular place I am not informed." "Use every effort in your power to have me exchanged soon," he added. "Put my friends to work. I do not care for the rigors of a Northern prison." He had "a stout heart and a calm resignation," he said, "[but] I naturally desire to be returned soon for service in the field." Soon George learned he was going back to Johnson's Island of all places, where he knew "all chances of escape are absolutely closed out and I am to await the slow and uncertain process of exchange." He reminded Bettie to write only one-page letters and to "remember that all your letters as well as mine must undergo examination." Returning to his old prison did have some advantages, however. He "shirk[ed] instinctively at the idea of encountering the piercing cold of the Northern Lakes," but he had made friends near Johnson's Island and "shall resume my acquaintances with my Chicago friends and with Mrs. Mary Scott." He also planned to "while away my leisure hours by reading and writing and make myself as comfortable as possible."[6]

Ironically, as he was traveling north on November 11, the Mississippi state legislature acted on his reporter position. Since his reelection in 1859, George had been busy with secession, military service, and prison, and had not spent much time in his reporter duties. He had not completed any of his required work during the war. But the high court had not been active anyway. Nevertheless, the legislature elected a new recorder. The combined House and Senate elected A. Y. Harper as the new recorder with sixty-nine votes to George's forty. It is unknown whether the legislators knew George was a prisoner, and it is equally unknown if George knew he had been replaced.[7]

Even later the bureaucratic wheels continued to turn. George was officially made a Confederate colonel, "appointed under the constitution by the president," on February 5, 1864, with the commission dating back to December 7, 1863. In fact, as late as August 1864 George was listed as the colonel of the Fifth Mississippi Cavalry. But by that time George was out of the war for good. Although he was never transferred, he was one of several officers recommended by Federal commanders to be sent to enlisted men's prisons to distribute goods and command the Confederate inmates.[8]

George soon began to settle into his familiar surroundings at Johnson's Island. He wrote Bettie in January, "I am not so well situated as I was during my former imprisonment. My room is more crowded and besides most of my room-mates now, [were] entire strangers to me before my arrival here." This situation had a striking effect on the semihermit George: "I do not and cannot read and write so much as formerly thence am more restless and uncomfortable. If I could get a letter from you occasionally it would help me a great deal." By February, he admitted, "I have made several acquaintances among my fellow prisoners," and there were men from Carrollton in the prison, too.[9]

Although he wrote every week (prisoners could only write two letters per week), and although he never knew until much later that she received very few of these, he wrote, "I have been imprisoned 3 months and am still without a letter from you or any of the children." "I write to you or one of the children every Sunday," he said, and told Bettie to "confine yourself to family and neighborhood matters, avoiding all allusion to political subjects and public affairs." Bettie and the children were actually writing, but their letters were not getting through. "I still live in the hope that after a while I shall get a large bundle of the truant messages who have been understandably delayed in their journey hither," he wrote. He finally decided that her letters contained inappropriate topics for prisoners: "I fear your letters do not pass muster and are condemned as contraband. Be particular to write nothing but personal and domestic matters."[10]

Finally, on March 2 George received his first letter from his wife. "This is the only letter I have received from Dixie since my imprisonment," he wrote in the return mail. "I had almost begun to despair of ever receiving one fearing my ill luck in that respect would always attend me." He insisted that he was cheerful as Bettie admonished him to be in her letter. "I am generally so. I seldom despond," he wrote, although he admitted, "Imprisonment now is more irksome to me than formerly but I am patient." With a "letter from home occasionally I could stand almost anything," he added. He also requested to know who were the officers in his regiment as well as casualties in his old company and regiment.[11]

Over the next few weeks George received notes from several of his children—Mary, Kate, Alfred, and Emma. The enjoyment of a proud father was evident as he told Bettie, "Little Mary's letter is very well written and affords me gratifying evidence of her improvement in her studies." Soon even more letters from the children as well as some from Bettie arrived, one including a picture of her. The letters and the picture "gave me great pleasure," George wrote her. Letters from Judge Cothran and other Carrollton residents lifted his spirits as well.[12]

As time passed George settled into life at Johnson's Island even more. In March 1864 he wrote Bettie, "I have a great many friends and have become more social than on my first arrival. I do not read and write so much and do mix now with my fellow sufferers." Yet he wrote that this second imprisonment "has been more irksome to me—then all my command was in prison with me; now most of it is in the field and I have been especially anxious to rejoin them." His personal condition was good enough, though, and he assured Bettie that he "bathe[d] myself every morning."[13]

George provided his wife a detailed account of daily life. "Major [Jo] Gee and myself mess together and we get along first rate.... Gee is a pretty fair cook and we manage to fix up our rations so as to make them palatable. There are six in our room but we manage to keep it tolerably clean, that is for men: you would not so regard it." Later, he wrote, "As the cold weather approaches I become more still and quiet, keep my cover very closely and read a good deal. If I had all my room-mates of similar tastes and habits it would cause my imprisonment not to be altogether a blank in my existence. But as it is I can do but little. I read rather to pass the time which hangs heavily on my hands than to attain any certain and specific aim." Later, the bored colonel reported, "My roommates and myself have commenced a garden for summer vegetables so if we stay here we shall have a supply. The working of it supplies me with some employment and amusement."[14]

George suffered through the harsh winters of the Great Lakes, just as he feared he would. He wrote Bettie in January 1864, "I am now very well—but have been sick a good deal. . . . We have had colder weather here than I have ever felt." In late February he wrote, "We have had some extremely cold weather though I learn the weather has been much more moderate than usual." But as the temperatures warmed in the spring and summer, he began to feel much better. "I am tolerably well," he wrote in March, and "have suffered less from cold than I anticipated. I do not however regain my flesh. I am fitted neither in body or mind for long imprisonment." By April he wrote that he was "regaining my lost flesh. My appetite is good."[15]

The summer of 1864 was not uniformly happy for George. Letters from Bettie indicated some type of trouble with her neighbors, prompting George to write, "I am somewhat annoyed at what you write in relation to your neighbors." He also became sick in June, and by the middle of the month he was down to 160 pounds from his normal 175 pounds, and described himself as "frequently 'ailing' but never seriously sick." Later in June he reported to Bettie about "an occasional headache," and his weight being down to 150 pounds. He described the problem as "the combined effect of a mustard poultice and a slight attack of pleurisy." He rated his feeling as "very week and languid." The sickness caused him to despair: "my mind is necessarily turned with the melancholy attendant on long imprisonment and no news and debilitated condition of the body." Fortunately, several of the prisoners were surgeons. Captain J. F. Sessions was particularly attentive, and George wrote a thankful letter to him upon news of the surgeon's exchange in October 1864.[16]

By the fall George was regaining his strength, although he "dread[ed] the coming winter," his second on Johnson's Island. He did have a slight problem later in the fall when he reported "owing to the very infirm condition of our rations my bowels are irregular and I sometimes suffer from gout." His bowels continued to plague him in the winter, perhaps part of it the result of the stress he felt. He felt "doomed to a hapless imprisonment for years."[17]

Fortunately for George and the other prisoners, the winter of 1864/1865 was a mild one. "The cold is not nearly so severe as it was last winter," he wrote, "though it is hard enough surely." There was also a revival of the hope of exchange. George frequently mentioned this hope, but it was wishful thinking. But it seemed to help, and he even seemed in a content mood in January 1865 when he wrote Bettie, "I have now a plenty of clothing and bedding and as many books as I want to read. Altogether I pass my time more pleasantly and more useful than one would imagine." He was most concerned about not getting mail, though, saying he was "much disappointed and annoyed," and sharply told his wife, "I do think that a very little care and foresight would secure more punctuality and speed."[18]

During his imprisonment, George continually forwarded rumors of impending exchange to Bettie, which kept his morale up and perhaps kept him from dropping into depression. Throughout the long imprisonment, George and the other prisoners were on a continual upheaval of hope and despair. Eventually, he realized that exchange was not coming. "I chafe under this disappointment considerably," he wrote Bettie in June 1864. In early 1865 he even told Bettie not to travel to Richmond to lobby for his release. The deaths of friends in prison certainly did not help him either. George related that Captain Scales had died at Camp Chase in April 1864, and his wife's brother died in the fall of that year.[19]

George was particularly angered when others were able to get out of prison after only a short time in custody. He tried to laugh at two such prisoners, telling Bettie of "two young gentlemen captured while attending a dance party." "That is a good way to be captured," he wrote, "it is less dangerous than capture on the battlefield and it appears also to possess an advantage in the way of exchange. I infer from this that the Confederacy has all the soldiers she needs and that her wants are in the direction of fiddlers and dancers. I hope however they are not wanted to play the part of Nero when Rome was burning."[20]

On a happier note, George received goods from a variety of people. Bettie's brother forwarded him "a box of good things." He also had friends in Chicago, whom he described as "tho poor have managed occasionally to contribute materially to my comfort." He also had a cousin in Kentucky with whom he corresponded and who sent him several items. He received a ham, sugar, canned fruit, flour, meal, oranges, eggs, butter, biscuits, coffee, and tea. He especially requested honey and tobacco, but it is unknown if he ever got any of those articles. Bettie and the girls sent packages, but he never reported receiving them. In January 1865 George was upset to discover "my box of tobacco has been at Fortress Monroe since Oct. 13. Something or other keeps it from coming forward."[21]

At times George also received money, but by the summer of 1864 he reported that he was nearly penniless, a fact that must have rankled the well-to-do colonel. He asked Bettie to have a bale of cotton sent through the lines to add to his account. Fortunately, his publisher, T. and J. W. Johnson and Company of Philadelphia, Pennsylvania, advanced him funds.[22]

Even in his deprived condition, George still aided the less fortunate. In one letter he instructed Bettie to care for a destitute widow and her children. "He was a man for whom I have no admiration and but little respect," he told her, "but my prejudices whether well or ill . . . are buried in his grave." He also shared some of the money received from his publisher in Philadelphia with prisoners less fortunate than he.[23]

George's major worry while on Johnson's Island was his family. He realized he had no way to help. "I am a poor judge of what should be done," he wrote. He also chafed at the lack of news from home, especially after a Federal raid went near George's home in February 1864. "Did it go to Carrollton and who were the sufferers," he wrote. "How much damage done?" The status of his immediate family took precedence, however. "I do not even know where you are," he wrote Bettie, "whether at Vaiden or Cotesworth." Fortunately, Bettie had her brother-in-law William Cothran to look after her, and George approved. "Say to Judge Cothran I would like to hear from him," he wrote. "You and he do just as you please about my affairs." Still, he could not help but offer some advice, and routinely encouraged Bettie to make the children read and behave. He wanted her to "watch over their morals and principles." He also advised her to "enlarge the dwelling at the plantation" and see to his library, something he was most proud of and constantly reminded her to protect. Concerning the farming operations, he told her, "Mr. Fullerton," apparently his overseer, would "assist you in all farming operations." He told her to "plant a little sorghum," and gave instructions for his boys to tend their sheep. Later in the year George was much relieved at the prospect of a good crop. The obviously attached father always had sweet admonitions to "kiss all the children for me," and, being a good son, asked Bettie to notify his mother living at Kosciusko that he was well.[24]

As George remained in prison, and as the South's fortunes began to waver, he became increasingly pessimistic about the Confederacy. He told Bettie to make the children study hard as no one knew what would happen in the future: "it is not impossible that they will never have other opportunities or facilities for education." He admonished them to "learn fast." He also began to wonder about his future. "If I should survive," he wrote to Bettie, "I may not even have the liberty of choice" regarding property.

He became so upset during the summer that he began to doubt his own survival and talked of losing "both my life and fortune."²⁵

As the year 1864 waned, along with the Confederacy's chances, George began to view the future as a conflict between the races. Speaking of returning to the United States, he wrote Bettie, "We will remain in it as inferior men—mere hewers of wood and drawers of water for our Northern masters. And what a set of masters we will have? Dutch, Puritans, negroes." He instructed Bettie to teach the children: "Whatever may be my fate teach them that the holiest of earthly causes is the independence of this country." Perhaps he had race relations in mind when he counseled Bettie to stay at Cotesworth instead of in town. "Would not the negroes be better satisfied if you were on the place?" He later counseled her to take all the slaves to Cotesworth and to plant grasses. "When all else is gone these will furnish you beef and milk."²⁶

George also fretted, as month after month passed, over wasted time:

> The idea of having so much time in prison without benefit to my country or anyone else is annoying. I am dissatisfied and discontented about that. I feel that I have not done what was expected of me in the war. Misfortune in war is the same as mismanagement. Nobody troubles himself to the distinction. I have been in but three fights and was made prisoner in two of them. The only decent position I had during the war I was unable to hold but a few weeks and then I was captured. I had set great store upon my new regiment and had no doubt that with it I should do honorable and useful service. How sadly have I been disappointed.²⁷

By May 1865 George and the other prisoners could see that the end of the war was near. Their enthusiasm for going home was tempered by the realization that the nation they had suffered for had lost. Nevertheless, like most other officers, George applied for amnesty, but it took several weeks for the documents to be issued. He reported that out of around 2,800 imprisoned officers, less than 100 "still regard it as their duty not to apply." "I know of only one Mississippian who has not applied and he is a strange boy," George wrote home.²⁸

When the amnesty papers were finally issued, George took the oath and was released on June 9, 1865, on promise of allegiance to the United States of America. His oath of allegiance information listed him as thirty-eight years of age, fair skinned, with brown hair and blue eyes. He was five feet nine and a half inches tall. His weight was not listed, but he had lost weight in prison.[29]

George had been a prisoner this second time for nineteen months. If his prison experience after Fort Donelson, six months and fifteen days, is added on, he spent a total of two years, one month, and twenty-one days in Federal prison camps. Captured twice, he endured the frigid winters and the less than blissful conditions of Federal prison camps, all in a losing cause. His challenge of authority had nearly cost him his life.

Yet the war was over, and the fight between the races, which George had predicted, was about to begin. This time, he would not be on the sidelines as he had been for most of the Civil War.

CHAPTER 11

"One of the Ablest Lawyers in the State"

Reconstruction, 1865–1873

Bettie George had forewarning that her husband, who had spent the last nineteen months as a prisoner of war, was coming home that June 1865. She determined to make his homecoming special. "My mother knew he was coming," remembered one of their daughters, "and made herself a new dress for the occasion." "She had an old black silk, which had been worn and turned until there was no more use to be gotten from it, so she washed it to get it thoroughly clean and raveled it and used it for the filling with a cotton warp and spun the cloth for her dress. She found an old purple velvet bonnet of ante-bellum days and made the collar and cuffs and covered the buttons with that. And she felt fine indeed when she put it on," her daughter remembered. She "never had a dress of which she was so proud," Bettie later remembered, and she wore it on the special day when her warrior husband finally returned home.[1]

But not all else was so good when George returned to Carrollton. Much as Abraham Lincoln had begun to plan for Reconstruction even during the war, George had begun planning for his own family's reconstruction as he sat in the windy prison barracks at Johnson's Island. As he realized that the war was over, he began to include an increasing number of instructions in letters home after May 1865. For example, George expressed his thoughts about how the South should respond to the defeat. "My own opinion," George wrote Bettie, "is well settled that hopeless, objectless war is not only unwise but inhuman and sinful. I have struggled for the independence of the Confederate States, but am unwilling to carry on the war for revenge or through passion." This was George's unwavering stance for the remainder of his life. He would always respect his heritage of war and never apologize for the South's actions, but he would nevertheless let the past slip away and move forward. He never continued the war either through action or rhetoric, although he would come close in the chaotic Reconstruction years.²

Racial matters were something entirely different, however, and George was not as compromising or reconciliatory when it came to the status and rights of former slaves. George became very upset when Bettie wrote to him in prison that some of their former slaves were "unkind." And although his attitude toward blacks would develop over the course of the next few decades, in 1865 he realized he needed them as much as they needed him. He told Bettie to try and persuade their former slaves to remain at Cotesworth to help work the crops. "Make some arrangement with our negroes," he wrote, so that they will remain to "cultivate and gather the crop now planted." Later, he instructed, "Make some arrangements with them by which they will be compensated, as fair as practicable, without incurring a positive loss to us for the labor." "When I get home," he continued, "if they desire to remain with me I will make if I can arrangements to keep them. If they wish to go out for themselves, all well." He added, "If we are able to keep any house servants, which I doubt, I will keep them." One of the most trustworthy of George's former slaves, known simply as Jake, did remain and would become a longtime family friend.³

George's concern for profit illustrated his greater concern for loss of affluence. "Our family affairs must be immediately put upon the footing of poverty except as to the education of the children," he wrote Bettie while still in prison. "I think my assets are sufficient to pay all I owe on my own account and yet save a home and the books and sufficient household furniture," he wrote. But he added his greatest concern: "I fear that I am surety on two debts. . . . If I should be compelled to pay them we will have nothing left." He instructed Bettie to ask Judge Cothran to investigate his financial standing.⁴

He also realized that he owed Cothran a great deal for all Cothran had done for him. The affluent Cothran had never concerned himself with repayment, but George knew of Cothran's own financial problems coming out of the war. Cothran had actually lived with Bettie and the children at times during the war, seeing after them while George was away. "On a settlement between Judge C[othran] and myself I would be indebted to him several thousand dollars," he told Bettie. "This debt I never expected to pay for I never thought the Judge would need it or want me to settle, but if he has lost all his property it seems but right if he desires it that a settlement should be made as near right as possible and that he should be paid." George continued, "Considering his age and his liberality towards me and my family and his reduction from wealth to poverty I regard it my duty to pay him above all others."⁵

Knowing he was in debt, George instructed Bettie to start selling land. He knew it would be tight, but wrote, "I do not doubt but with energy and good health I shall be able in a year or two to support you all including my mother and unmarried sisters comfortably." He planned to return to his law practice in Carrollton, but also left open the possibility of moving to Memphis or New Orleans. With much of his slave labor gone, he was not interested in "farm[ing] or plant[ing] another year."⁶

From prison, George asked Bettie to tell his law partner, Colonel Robert W. Williamson, who had served as a captain in the Eleventh and Twenty-ninth Mississippi as well as colonel of the Twenty-fourth Mississippi during the war and had been wounded at Stones River and Resaca, to "open the office and go ahead till I come." He also asked Bettie to be patient until he got back on a firm footing. "The loss of wealth will be no great hardship," he wrote her, "when we get used to it. We will be as happy as ever if we are contented. I shall almost be able now and I do not doubt I can make a comfortable provision for all who are dependent on me."⁷

Upon returning to Mississippi, George began to make that provision, although he found the going difficult at first and sought to recoup any money he could from any area. As soon as he returned to Carrollton, he began his law practice again in partnership with Colonel Williamson. Arriving before George did, Williamson began the operation of the office, which George joined when he arrived in June. Slowly, he began to emerge from debt.⁸

George's effort to get back on his feet in the late 1860s was made within the context of a situation changing around him. Despite some early non-Democratic appointments by President Andrew Johnson, such as Unionist William Sharkey as governor immediately after the war, and occupation by mostly black army units, George returned to a Mississippi solidly in the hands of former Confederates by the end of 1865. Former Confederate general Benjamin Humphreys was elected governor, in fact, as Mississippi settled into Presidential Reconstruction life not altogether different than before the war. Black Codes intended to keep former slaves from voting were instituted. Eventually, however, Republicans on the national level took over Reconstruction policies and implemented a vastly different manner of reconstructing the South, ushering in what historians have termed Radical Reconstruction. The military occupation legislation of 1867 broke the South into districts, and Federal troops registered blacks in

Mississippi to vote. With those new numbers at the polls, combined with efforts to disenfranchise former Confederates, Democrats were removed from state offices during this period and replaced with Republicans. Eventually, Mississippi would see a Union general as governor and blacks serving as lieutenant governor, in the state legislature, and as U.S. senators. A new state constitution implemented mostly by Republicans came about in 1868, institutionalizing many of these changes. George and countless other Democrats faced what they perceived as a major bias against them, resulting in higher taxes and other laws tilted against white Democrats. They believed they had no political say and could only fight back with intimidation and violence, which came to be embodied in the Ku Klux Klan (KKK). There is no evidence George was a member, but he was certainly supportive of their terrorizing blacks enough to keep them out of the political process.[9]

Within that context, George began to recover from his losses during the war. Yet by the mid-1870s he was still not as wealthy as he had been before the war. In fact, George wrote fellow Democrat L. Q. C. Lamar, "I have but little time to think of anything but the eternal never ending work necessary to subsist my family." He tried cases not only in Carrollton and Vaiden but also in neighboring areas such as Choctaw, Sunflower, Tallahatchie, and Yalobusha counties, as well as in the U.S. district court in Oxford. George also returned to Jackson often to try cases before the High Court of Errors and Appeals, his first case after the war being decided in the January term in 1866. He and Williamson argued a case together in 1867, and George covered many cases by himself or with other lawyers from different firms in the ensuing years. Between the end of the war and the end of Reconstruction in Mississippi in 1875, George was involved in eighty-four cases before the court, along with three cases before the U.S. district court in Oxford and two cases before the regional U.S. Court of Appeals. One of the Oxford cases was pro bono representation George and former Confederate general Edward C. Walthall provided for several KKK members who had been intimidating local blacks. The rebellious George was beginning to challenge the new authority in Mississippi.[10]

One contemporary Mississippian described George's legal acumen. "He was not a specialist. He frequented courts of law, of equity, of admiralty, and of bankruptcy alike, and he was at home in all of them." He "loved the strife and combat of the courtroom," he stated, and "rained down upon the opponents with all the swiftness and vigor that his strong arm could command." And George was tenacious: "Motions for new trials, appeals, and applications for rehearing were everyday occurrences in his practice, and through them he often recovered the ground he had lost."[11]

Just as before the war, George's work took him away from home. He begrudged his time away from Bettie and the children as he had before the war and in the prison camps. "I am very tired of Jackson," he wrote Bettie while trying cases before the high court in 1867. But it was necessary in order to begin to recover the losses of the recent years. The court's calendar was also frustrating. In January 1867, for instance, he was stuck in Jackson not knowing when his case would come up. "I have a mind to go home and come back next week," he wrote, but added, "I am afraid to leave." He contemplated going to New Orleans for a couple of days to see about cotton business, but admitted that "I really have but little business there and it seems hardly worth while to go." Determining to wait out the court, the reclusive George was happier when he finally got a room alone. "I am now in a room to myself," he wrote Bettie, "Genl. [Reuben] Davis and Col. [James] Phelan having left this morning."[12]

George certainly missed his children, but he and Bettie kept adding to the family. Although Fannie and the other girls were nearing their late teens, George and Bettie continued to produce children. After a somewhat remarkable stretch in which all six of their first children lived to adulthood, two of the last three had died in infancy. Nevertheless, George and Bettie produced two more sons in the 1860s: Pinckney Smith George, named after Cotesworth Pinckney Smith, on March 11, 1866, and Joseph Warren George, named for George's father, on August 23, 1869.[13]

As the years passed, no longer were he and Bettie parents to small children alone. Their children were growing up fast, marrying, and giving the Georges grandchildren. In fact, all four of George's older daughters married during the Reconstruction era: Fannie married George's secession convention colleague William R. Barksdale in 1867; Emma married one of George's later law partners, J. B. H. Hemingway, in 1872; Mary married William H. Leavell, who would be a future U.S. ambassador to Guatemala in 1874; and Kate married Francis Minter Aldridge, son of George's friend and fellow secession convention delegate Francis Marion Aldridge, in 1875. Alfred also married during that volatile time, in 1876.[14]

One thing George did not miss at this stage of his life was Bettie's religious zeal. She had always been a devout Baptist, and had urged George to attend church with her, but he rarely did. When he returned home, she redoubled her efforts to have him baptized. She asked the local

Baptist church pastor, Henry Pittman, to confront George on every occasion he could. Newspapers later reported a story surrounding his conversion and baptism that perhaps said more about the gruff George than it did his actual conversion. The story went that in 1867 Pittman proselytized George at every opportunity. One winter day as George was riding back to Cotesworth from Carrollton, reading his mail, the preacher "burst out of the woods" and began pressing the lawyer again. George was near a creek, probably Big Sand Creek at the foot of the hill on which Carrollton sits, and told Pittman, "I'm tired of bein' harried around the kentry like I was a cotton tail rabbit an' you a pack o' nigger dogs. Baptize me right here." The creek, George described, was "saddle-pocket deep," but the two waded in, and Pittman baptized George then and there. George emerged from the creek and mounted up. Looking down at the "shivering evangelist," he barked, "you go home and stay home. I'm through with this . . . foolishness."[15]

George's pastor in later years told a somewhat different account of his baptism. He remembered that George had become a Christian during the war, probably after Collierville when George wrote Bettie, "I argued my escape as providential and I shall not spurn or neglect the teachings of Him who . . . has shielded . . . [me] from Death and harm." When he returned home, he asked Pittman to baptize him, insisting on a certificate of baptism so he could join a church later. The Reverend Pittman demurred, saying that George needed to join a church immediately. George argued that the churches were in a "disorganized state" at the time, and reminded the minister that the Ethiopian eunuch in the Bible had requested baptism and the evangelist Philip had done so. "His case was so forcibly presented," a later pastor wrote, "that the man of God finally consented and baptized him." The pastor also noted that the "cares of public life" so sidetracked George that it was decades before he actually joined any church.[16]

These two descriptions of George's conversion present many of the same details, such as the era of his baptism, the minister involved, the certificate of baptism, the fact that he did not join a church immediately, and George's argumentative and independent manner. The major difference in the stories comes from the presentation of George's personality. One shows a brusque and noninterested man and the other an interested convert who sought out baptism. Perhaps with so much common detail, the two stories are not mutually exclusive, but support one another as different portions of the same event. Perhaps, too, the differences in George's personality resulted from the teller of the story rather than the differences in the event itself.[17]

George's religion may have had something to do with his charity. Numerous sources described him as extremely compassionate despite his outwardly gruff personality and his tight money situation. After the war, a newspaper reported, he asked a local colonel from Winona to help him dispense money to families of killed and wounded Confederate soldiers. George gave the colonel $500 every year without the needy families ever knowing the source. The writer ended, "This is but one noble deed among hundreds that will never be known."[18]

George also had other issues on his mind, such as forming a veterans' organization of his old Mexican War regiment. In addition, George was a budding researcher and writer, and turned out several newspaper articles dealing with such legal questions as vendors' and agricultural liens, landlords and tenants, and the sale of lands. He also worked on his unfulfilled responsibilities as court reporter. Having served as recorder of the High Court of Errors and Appeals from 1855 to 1863, it was his responsibility to publish all proceedings of the high court through 1863. Obviously, George had had little time during the war to do so, although the high court was not nearly as busy during the war as normal. Right before the war began, George had published his last volume, covering the cases up through the April term in 1860. He thus began work on collecting the material needed for his tenth volume, which covered the rest of the 1860 cases as well as the various terms held in 1861 and 1863. George eventually published this final volume in 1867.[19]

The writer-lawyer also produced another compilation volume of legal cases during this period: *A Digest of the Reports of the Decisions of the Supreme Court and of the High Court of Errors and Appeals of the State of Mississippi, From the Organization of the State, to the Present Time*. This nongovernment-sanctioned book appeared in August 1872, although George had hoped to publish it in the summer of 1870. Other writers were working on similar projects, and George fretted at how slowly the work was going, "as I feel it necessary to read every case." Nevertheless, he finished the volume, and the others dropped their projects when his massive tome appeared. George published the volume on his own, although he did use as publisher his friends in Philadelphia at the T. and J. W. Johnson and Company, who had published all his volumes of reports. The volume was just what it said it was, a ready reference of all high court cases in the state's history up to 1870, arranged by topic. Thus any lawyer could quickly determine the most important cases on any subject just by looking up that particular topic in the *Digest*. A reviewer in a Jackson newspaper wrote it was "a most valuable contribution to the legal learning of the State."[20]

George described his effort as a "labor of love," explaining that it took five years to produce amid other "professional pursuits." He hoped it would "be found accurate and faithful, convenient and useful; that it will greatly lessen the labors and facilitate the investigations of my professional brethren in Mississippi, and will supply to the bar of other States, who have no access to our Reports, a safe guide in respect to the jurisprudence peculiar to this State, as well as furnish them many useful illustrations of the principles of the Common Law and Equity, as they prevail in England and in the States of the American Union."[21]

George dedicated this volume to his friend Francis Marion Aldridge, a Yalobusha County attorney who, like George, was a member of the secession convention; George's daughter Kate would years later marry Aldridge's son. Aldridge had been killed at Shiloh while fighting in the Fifteenth Mississippi Infantry. George wrote glowingly about those who had sacrificed for "the cause," saying, "All those who, like Aldridge, whether they fell or survived, gave their best efforts to their country, are enshrined in my recollection; but I here select his name, not because it is the highest or the brightest amongst them all, but because it was to me the best beloved."[22]

Another of George's major concerns and activities during early Reconstruction was his land. In addition to his law profession, George also recouped some of his lost wealth by dabbling in land speculation. Between 1867 and 1870 he bought fourteen pieces of property, much of it around Cotesworth, but also some around Carrollton and Vaiden. Much of this land was bought cheaply at auction, probably the result of landowners who could not afford their taxes. Between 1871 and 1875 he bought four more tracts but sold eleven in Carroll County, no doubt making a large amount of money in the sale of land cheaply obtained.[23]

The biggest land investment he made was in neighboring Sunflower County, today's Leflore County. George bought several hundred acres of land in 1868 for $2,100, and then added an even larger tract, some 1,137 acres, in 1874 for another $2,700. Over the years he added additional acreage. One of the two major tracts had been known as "Shanty" before his purchase, and he named the other Shongalo after the area around Vaiden where he had come of age. With the addition of a third tract later, George named the entire plantation Runnymede, after the place where the Magna Carta had been signed in England. He also owned other lands in Leflore County.[24]

Runnymede soon began to make George a lot of money in cotton. He of course utilized sharecropping freedmen as much as possible to work his various tracts, but he also employed white men, some of whom lived with him. In particular, George hired two immigrants to work his land at Cotesworth: James Ryne from Ireland and Charles Gildy from Canada. His older children aided him in other areas such as his law work, and the younger ones attended school.[25]

George's land efforts caused some confrontation with Republican state officials. Like many former Confederates, he thought the new Republican Reconstruction state government was extremely tilted against him. In fact, George had a hard time during the period keeping some of his land, not so much because he was destitute, but because his taxes were extremely high compared to before the war. He lost some land to the state Liquidating Levee Board, which was set up after the war to retire unpaid bonds taken before the war to build levees in the Delta. This board was allowed to collect taxes on land and cotton, and these higher taxes, in addition to state taxes, forced many landowners to default, with the levee board taking possession of the land. Working through the county court system, the board took some of George's land in 1870 for defaulting on the high taxes.[26]

George fought back in court, where he appeared frequently as a defendant or plaintiff on issues ranging from child custody to debt. In 1871 he sued for his land, citing several obscure provisions in the state law. He won the case on the county level, but the levee board appealed to the Mississippi Supreme Court, where George won again, as he did in a motion to reargue the case. In these supreme court cases, George's friend Wiley P. Harris represented him. Not only did George get his land back, but he also showed a crack in the land board's Reconstruction armor that led to numerous similar cases in the future.[27]

Despite all his activities, George remained a lawyer by trade, and he was making his name in the state. One Mississippian testified to Congress in the 1870s that George "stands at the head of the profession; one of the ablest lawyers in the State." Nevertheless, George took the ultimate step in his law career in the early 1870s. When he parted with Williamson in 1871 because Williamson moved to Winona, George needed a new colleague. On July 1, 1872, George took a new partner: Wiley P. Harris of Jackson. After finishing his digest of court proceedings for publication, George and Bettie and the children moved from Cotesworth, and his practice based in Carrollton, to Jackson. This surprising move expanded his law practice and allowed him to argue cases before the high court without the long stretches of time away from home. Perhaps most important was the partnership with one of Mississippi's best-known statesmen. Harris had long been a major force in Mississippi politics as well as law, and was often referred to as "the recognized and unchallenged leader of the bar in Mississippi." He had been a leader in the secession convention in which George served, with one member of the convention remembering that Harris's "voice was regarded as the voice of an oracle." Harris also played a prominent role in the Montgomery convention that established the Confederate States of America. George and Harris had worked together on numerous cases before partnering together and in all argued some fifty-six cases together before the high court. Mississippi congressman Thomas C. Catchings described Harris's partnership with the well-known and increasingly regarded lawyer George: "It is my deliberate judgment that the law firm of Harris & George was as able as any that ever existed in any age or any country. My acquaintance with both of its members was intimate, my observation of their methods and struggles was almost constant, and I unhesitatingly affirm that in my opinion they had both reached the very summit of professional excellence and power." A more recent historian has termed the partnership "one of the brilliant chapters in the legal annals of the state."[28]

George thus left his beloved Carroll County as well as his home at Cotesworth. The people of Carrollton threw a huge going away party for the Georges on New Year's night in 1873 at the local Odd Fellows College. "His friends met him and his family and 'good-byes' were exchanged," one newspaper reported in describing the "social assembly." One wonders what the reclusive George thought of such high society.[29]

By 1873 George had come out of the fog of war. He had been hit hard financially as well as personally, but was able to keep his land and even obtain more. His law practice offered him the chance to make even more money, and with his move to Jackson, he became one of the state's most prominent lawyers, partnered with another of the state's most important citizens.

The move to Jackson also led George into the political arena, putting him solidly amid the growing tension between state Democratic and national Republican officials over Reconstruction policy. Although there is no record of whether political issues helped spur his move, it nevertheless ushered him into the political arena, and George would not miss the opportunity; he would stay in the public eye the rest of his life.

James Zachariah George was one of Mississippi's most important statesmen of the nineteenth century. He was a lawyer, soldier, chief justice of the Mississippi Supreme Court, and Mississippi's longest-serving U.S. senator to that time. Courtesy of Katherine Williams.

Elizabeth Brooks Young George, called Bettie, was J. Z. George's constant companion throughout life. George became homesick and almost depressed when away from her, and he died only two weeks after her death. Courtesy of Katherine Williams.

Judge William Cothran was perhaps J. Z. George's biggest influence in life. Father figure and mentor in the law, Cothran took George in and made him a partner in his law office as well as introduced him to his future wife, Bettie, who was Cothran's sister-in-law. Cothran also cared for Bettie and the children while George was away at war. Courtesy of Carrollton #36 F&AM.

George named his plantation home Cotesworth after his friend Cotesworth Pinckney Smith. First leasing the plantation in the 1850s, he would own the house and grounds from 1861 until his death. This view shows how the house looked during George's lifetime. Courtesy of Katherine Williams.

Mississippi Reconstruction governor Adelbert Ames was George's chief opponent in the volatile election of 1875. The two had a famous meeting in the governor's mansion in which both compromised in order to try to keep the peace. Brady-Handy Collection, Prints & Photographs Division, Library of Congress, LC-DIG-cwpbh-00604.

L. Q. C. Lamar was a major contemporary of George's. Both were members of the 1861 secession convention, and both then worked to take back Mississippi from Republican control during Reconstruction. Both were rewarded with U.S. Senate seats, where they were colleagues until Lamar became secretary of the interior and finally a U.S. Supreme Court justice. Brady-Handy Collection, Prints & Photographs Division, Library of Congress, LC-DIG-cwpbh-03965.

Edward C. Walthall was a Confederate general who later became George's colleague in the U.S. Senate. Courtesy of U.S. Senate Historical Office.

Hernando D. Money was a friend of George's from Carrollton, Mississippi. Money served in the U.S. House of Representatives while George was a senator, and Money took George's seat in the Senate upon his death in 1897. Brady-Handy Collection, Prints & Photographs Division, Library of Congress, LC-DIG-cwpbh-03686.

J. Z. George spent many hours in the U.S. Senate chamber. This view shows the chamber about the time of his death. Detroit Publishing Company Photograph Collection, Prints & Photographs Division, Library of Congress, LC-D4-14216.

By the mid-1890s George was having major health problems. His age can be seen in this photograph of him at Cotesworth in 1896. Courtesy of Katherine Williams.

One of George's closet friends was "old Jake," a former slave who stayed on to work for George after the Civil War. George included him in many family events and confided to Jake his deep sorrow upon Bettie's passing. Jake was the chief mourner at his old friend's funeral two weeks later. Courtesy of Katherine Williams.

J. Z. George and much of his family, including his wife, two infant sons, and numerous other children, are buried in the family plot in Evergreen Cemetery just outside Carrollton, Mississippi. Also buried in the foreground is George's mentor, William Cothran. Photo by George Smith.

The state of Mississippi placed a statue of J. Z. George in the National Statuary Hall Collection in the U.S. Capitol in 1931. He was regarded then as one of the two greatest statesmen Mississippi had produced. The other was Jefferson Davis. *Acceptance and Unveiling of the Statues of Jefferson Davis and James Z. George* (Washington, D.C.: Government Printing Office, 1932).

Cotesworth still stands just north of Carrollton and is still owned by the George family, although there is a movement under way to place the house under the care of a nonprofit group that intends to turn it into a cultural heritage center. Photo by George Smith.

George was especially proud of his library, which he built on Cotesworth's lawn in 1887. The unique hexagonal building still contains much of his book collection, including many *Congressional Record* volumes stamped with his name. Photo by George Smith.

George practiced law in Carrollton and the surrounding area, keeping an office on the court square in Carrollton, just across from the courthouse, where it still stands today. Photo by George Smith.

CHAPTER 12

"Surrounded with Difficulties Unprecedented"

Politics, 1873–1875

When J. Z. George and his family moved to Jackson, they came in contact with a variety of political issues. Mississippi Democrats, most all of them old Confederates and white leaders, had begun to rebel again, this time politically. Democrats throughout the South began to try to take back their states from Republican rule, which they saw as racially, sectionally, and economically alien. It was bad enough for these Democrats to see Unionists from the war era such as William Sharkey and James L. Alcorn as governors of the state, but a new state constitution authorized in 1868 by what Democrats termed the "Black and Tan Convention," made up mostly of blacks, "carpetbaggers" from the North, and white Republican Mississippi "scalawags," created a situation in which a Northern general from Massachusetts, Adelbert Ames, became governor. Many blacks served in state government offices, in the legislature, and in the U.S. Congress as senators and representatives. Mississippi Democrats thus began to wage a campaign of harassment and intimidation to take back, or "redeem," their state. Becoming more politically minded through the years, the often rebellious George was right in the middle of the growing controversy. His move to Jackson put him at the center of the operations.[1]

George's participation in the Democratic Party went back to the 1850s. During the 1868 and 1872 presidential elections, he had served on the State Conservative Democratic Executive Committee. At that time, George had taken a major step forward in leadership. In 1868 the committee was deadlocked arguing whether to even nominate a slate of candidates in Mississippi, some wanting to boycott the election entirely. George wrote an open letter to a committee member, Fulton Anderson, which appeared in several of the state's leading papers. George argued, after "much anxious reflection," that the party should field candidates and fight, even though it might be a losing battle. "We are now surrounded with difficulties unprecedented in our history," George wrote, adding that "I regard the result as doubtful, and I am satisfied that success can be attained only by the most prudent measures." But, he argued, any little help Mississippi could offer might tip the national balance the Democrats' way: "We ought therefore to conduct the canvass in such manner as will most help our friends at the North." To George, it was a battle worth fighting, because the stakes were so high: "If the Radicals elect the President, then we are doomed to Reconstruction under African rule—if the Democrats succeed, we shall be restored to our just constitutional rights." Despite George's effort, Ulysses S. Grant won the first of two Reconstruction-era terms as president. Joining with what he perceived as the lesser of two evils in 1872, George canvassed the state in support of New York Republican Horace Greeley in his bid against a second Grant term. Reconstruction politics made strange bedfellows.[2]

At the heart of George's feelings was his concern about his dealings with the now freed slaves. He found it difficult to work within the legal parameters of the new Reconstruction governments of the state and the nation, especially after Presidential Reconstruction gave way to Radical Reconstruction, which included Union military occupation, disenfranchisement for former Confederates, and Republican state government. George's dealings with his former slaves were waged within that context, and he had to tread carefully amid the new system. He had little hope for the process, writing, "I have but little confidence in the apprentices [former slaves] doing us any good," and stating that even his best workers were not reliable; "as soon as we turn loose the balance they will go too," he wrote Bettie. Yet he had to have workers on his land or it would be worthless.[3]

Before moving to Jackson, George dealt with freedmen as best he could because his law practice often took him away from Carrollton. Mississippi laws required non-job-holding blacks and those under eighteen to be legally assigned or apprenticed to employers. He left Bettie in charge, often giving her directions from afar. "[I am] sorry to hear that the freedmen are doing so badly," he wrote her, but he also wanted to retain their labor. "The fact is they are all illegally apprenticed and I cannot lease them without taking out a new indenture," he wrote her. He told Bettie to "send Davy and Sidney into town and have them surrendered to the court and let the court do what it pleases with them," and "you had better have May and Short sent in and re-apprenticed to me." The records in the local courthouse bear out the legal work. One document related that

George apprenticed "certain Freedmen or Free Negroes or Mulattoes formally belonging to him." Each former slave bore the last name George, and George was referred to as the "legal master of the above." For all the court work, William Cothran aided George and provided the monetary bond for the document. Obviously, working freedmen within the context of the Reconstruction-era regulations was not easy.[4]

George also had misgivings about the ability and fairness of the Republican state government. He told Bettie that "the lawyers here [Jackson] complain of a dearth of business. I fear after this year there will be but little to do in our profession in Mississippi." His own experience with a request for a listing of Mississippi Confederate officials for a biographical publication, not the only request for war reminiscences he received, indicated his negative feeling toward current political rulers. George informed his requestor that this information was in the state archives in Jackson and that he would have to talk to "the Rev. James Lynch (colored) who is Secretary of State." George added, "I doubt whether he can get up a correct list, but the Gov. (J. L. Alcorn) could have it done, and would probably do so if requested by you, and especially if he believed that his name would appear in the *Biographical Dictionary*." George went on to say, "I would cheerfully undertake, on my next visit to Jackson, to examine the archives for you, but my examination would not be favored by the authorities who would probably suspect a rebellious and treasonable design in any effort of mine to exhume the records of the past."[5]

George and the majority of the state's Democratic leaders opted eventually to overthrow the Republican government, but some Democrats wanted to accept life under Republican rule in the best interest of peace and tranquility. One such leader was former governor and George's friend, Albert Gallatin Brown. George had admired the governor since the early 1850s, when Brown had helped George become the state senate's engrossing clerk. George had also requested his aid in getting out of prison during the war, when Brown served as a Confederate senator. When Brown opted to work with the Republicans, however, he lost a lot of white support in the state. George wrote Bettie during one of his trips to Jackson that he still planned on visiting Brown "and spend[ing] a day or two with him." George wrote, "I understand he is low-spirited and I feel it almost a duty to show him that I respect him still."[6]

George's move to Jackson and his partnership with Wiley Harris thus put him front and center in the politics of the state. But other than being elected to the secession convention, he had never held political office and generally shunned the spotlight, which brought the need for social intercourse and small talk with which the shy George was not gifted. He much preferred to work behind the scenes. Yet George had definite views about how things should be run, and he opposed the state's current crop of leaders. As time passed, George grew increasingly hostile. Mississippi politics by the mid-1870s was almost dominated by Republicans, both white and black. The state's governor was a northern Civil War general from Massachusetts. The lieutenant governor was a black man, as were other lower officers such as superintendent of education and Speaker of the House of Representatives. Republicans of both colors dominated the state legislature, and they elected two black U.S. senators, Hiram Revels and Blanche K. Bruce. Throughout Reconstruction, almost all appointments to positions from judges to clerks were Republicans. George was extremely dissatisfied with this situation, remarking that "the aspect in which the Republican Party has hitherto shown itself in Mississippi, it is true, has not been such as to commend itself to the whites, or any intelligent friend of good government." He later labeled the Republican government one of "ignorance and vice," and said "they were omnipresent for evil—powerless for good."[7]

Given the growing volatile situation, George was extremely careful in what he said and did, and to whom he spoke, during Reconstruction. He carried on an extensive correspondence only with those he trusted and whom he knew were no threat to him. For example, in writing L. Q. C. Lamar in 1874, George stated that he "would like to write you a long letter about public affairs." But he warned, "I do not think it opportune to talk about [it] now publicly." He nevertheless described the problems faced by many white Mississippians, of the "inexorable demands of the legislature," and labeled the current government as the "most corrupt government which ever existed in a capital city."[8]

Slowly Democrats began to make headway against the Republicans, mainly through intimidation and violence. One of George's prominent colleagues described it outright as "the struggle of the white men to throw off Republican and alien rule and re-establish white supremacy in the State." George, in fact, wrote that "there is a giant reaction going on in the Northern mind against negro government in the South" and that "the Northern people are beginning to see the end of all this misrule." By 1875, in fact, there seemed to be a good chance that Democrats could win a stellar victory and take back, or redeem as it was called, the state government and place it in Democratic hands. Confederate soldiers were once again allowed to vote, but because the state's population contained a black majority in the state, there was still a gap of some 30,000 black votes to overcome. Intimidation was the tool of choice to close the gap.[9]

The state Democratic Party, not really functioning since 1872, opted to put great emphasis on the state's 1875 legislative election because the Republicans had given the Democrats a perfect opportunity to strike. In 1873 Republicans in Mississippi split along the old "carpetbagger" and "scalawag" lines as supporters of Adelbert Ames and James L. Alcorn parted ways over the gubernatorial election. White conservative Republicans in the state, who had supported Alcorn, increasingly flocked to the Democratic side to oppose the more liberal Republican faction led by Northern and black politicians. One partisan observer noted that "the better class of white Republicans abandoned the Ames Administration." The Republican split went so far as to allow the Democrats to win several of the U.S. House of Representative seats in the state in 1874, helping push the House itself Democratic for the first time since 1860. With the Republicans split, and emboldened by the 1874 advances, Democrats saw their chance. If they could woo enough moderate white and black Republicans to the Democratic side and scare away enough of the remainder, perhaps the Democrats could again retake the state government. The main goal was to seize control of the legislature, which would assure that Democratic senators would be sent to Washington as well as allow the possibility of thwarting Governor Ames by impeachment, if necessary.[10]

George was a leader in reorganizing the state Democratic Party in a January 1875 convention of "taxpayers" held at Jackson, serving on the committee on resolutions that turned out several recommended actions that reconstituted the party. George addressed a meeting of the formation committee in May, and by August the various committees had worked up enough support to hold a convention in the House chamber of the capitol on August 3, 1875, with George a participant. Former governor Charles Clark presided over the convention, and there were other luminary delegates, such as John M. Stone, Wiley P. Harris, Josiah A. P. Campbell, Winfield S. Featherston, Robert Lowry, Edward C. Walthall, and Ethelbert Barksdale. George addressed the convention, advising moderation: "We must ... discharge our duties as American citizens, insisting on an equality of benefits, as we are willing; to bear our share of the common burdens of the government. Our statesmanship must embrace the whole country, seeking to advance the common interests, the common happiness, and the general welfare of the American people." The speech evidently so impressed the delegates that they surprisingly elected George as their party chairman. Despite living in Jackson, the forty-eight-year-old George had come to the convention as a mere representative of Carroll County; he left as head of the party.[11]

The newly elected chairman set up shop in the Neal Building in Jackson and prepared for the coming campaign. It was a huge task for George; he had to lay aside all other work, including his legal profession, as he entered a job that quickly consumed all his time, effort, and energy. As Harris was a loyal Democrat who sought redemption as well, there was no rift between the partners. Harris agreed to take over much of the firm's load; George thus tried few cases during that year.[12]

George weighed every decision heavily. "I remember how carefully every possible phase of the situation was discussed," remembered one of George's lieutenants, "and how fully every possible outcome of that course was considered." There was already a lot of intimidating violence from white Democrats in the state against Republican officeholders and voters. But George realized that the vote gap could not be made up strictly through intimidating enough blacks into not voting, and he worried about the response from the state and federal governments and the possibility of U.S. troops governing the state again. Governor Ames had in fact called on President Grant for troops, but the president declined several times. Making George's position even more ticklish as the year passed, Ames then organized and armed black militia companies throughout the state, drawing a predictable harsh response from whites. George had to find some way to win the fall election and remove the threat of black troops patrolling the state without provoking Ames and Grant into taking over through military rule. He had his work cut out for him, and issued a statement upon entering office calling on all Mississippians to do their duty: "In this contest Mississippi expects each of her sons to do his duty; brace up old age to one more effort, nerve manhood to put forth all its strength, and invite youth to its noblest enthusiasm."[13]

George had several chief colleagues and lieutenants who worked hard with him in the campaign. Foremost was L. Q. C. Lamar, a Democrat in Congress at the time. One observer noted that when Lamar returned to Congress, he "met a reception so cold as almost to chill the ardor of his great soul," but he was very much reconciliatory toward the Republicans, arguing for reunion. His most noted effort was in eulogizing Charles Sumner, the staunchly abolitionist Northern senator who had been beaten by a Southern congressman on the floor of the U.S. Senate before the war. In fact, George congratulated Lamar on his "splendid appeal for an oblivion of the past" while admitting that he himself had "not outlived the prejudices of the past." While George took care of state matters in Mississippi, Lamar sheltered the state's reputation on the national level in Washington. Another major player was newspaperman Ethelbert Barksdale, who could sway public opinion through his large Jackson newspaper. In addition, George's executive committee also contained such luminaries as former Confederate general Edward C. Walthall and former Confederate congressman Josiah A. P. Campbell.[14]

George and Barksdale became the two major leaders on the ground, however. Though allies against a common enemy, they were certainly not kindred souls. In fact, they headed different wings of the newly reestablished Democratic Party. Barksdale was more unreconstructed than George and advocated a return to old Confederate ways, or what was called the color line. "George represents and controls the old Whig elements there," a Republican in Mississippi wrote, "and is very liberally inclined—Barksdale the opposite." The Republican, former Union general Mortimer D. Leggett, continued, "these two men operate together—yet they have no love for each other and there is no affinity between them." Still, a common enemy made allies of George and Barksdale.[15]

George thus somewhat surprisingly moved to the head of the party in the state in 1875. And he was a good choice. Calm enough to counsel some restraint but firm enough to push for victory, George was exactly what the Democrats needed.

CHAPTER 13

"The Glorious and Decisive Victory"

Redemption, 1875

J. Z. George was stepping into bedlam when he agreed to run the Democratic Party during the 1875 election. And he had few choices available to him. As the election drew nearer, tension increased until a veritable race war erupted in the late summer and early fall. Antiblack riots were common throughout the state, with clashes occurring as early as 1874 at Vicksburg over the removal of the black county sheriff, Peter Crosby. Riots by blacks in Hinds and Yazoo counties only swelled the tension. Mississippi was in crisis.[1]

After several clashes, Governor Ames again called for federal troops to keep the peace, and George acted. He quickly wired U.S. Attorney General Edwards Pierrepont, telling him the Democratic side of the story:

> There are no disturbances in this State now, and no obstructions to the execution of the laws. There has been an unexpected conflict at a political meeting, and some subsequent disturbances, but everything is quiet now. The governor's call for United States troops does not even pretend there is any insurrection against the State government, as required by the revision of *United States Statutes* of 1875, p. 1034. Peace prevails throughout the State, and the employment of United States troops would but increase the distrust of the people in the good faith of the present State government.

In another telegram, George insisted: "The people of Mississippi claim the right of American citizens to be heard before they are condemned. I reassert that perfect peace prevails throughout the State, and there is no danger of disturbance unless initiated by the State authorities, which I hope they will not do." Many have insisted George outright lied about the tranquility in Mississippi; if he did not lie, he certainly stretched the truth in declaring "perfect peace."[2]

President Grant refused to send any troops, prompting the governor to rely on the state militia, many of whom were black. That was equally unacceptable to George, who confided to an aide, "I think they mean mischief." George was caught between two difficult positions with no good choices. He could not let the black troops control the state for fear that white oppression would do more harm than good, most notably in calling the state to the attention of national leaders who might then actually send federal troops. On the other hand, the more Ames talked of black troops, the more white Republicans sided with the Democrats, which was what George wanted. It was a fine line for George to walk.[3]

The number of riots and the violence only grew as the election neared. There were numerous occasions when whites attacked blacks in the state, trying to intimidate them from voting. On the other hand, George and the committee also tried to lure other blacks to the Democratic side, offering them chances for education and advancement. "If there be any one thing which the Democrats and Conservatives of this State are more determined to carry out than another, it is to provide the means of educating every child in the State, of whatever race or color," George wrote in an open letter. There were also occasions in which blacks attacked whites, such as the famous Clinton Riot that took place on September 4. George and the Democrats, of course, used that riot as a major weapon to draw even more white Republicans to their side in what was becoming a referendum on race in the state. The fear of black troops patrolling the state only added to the growing white fear after the Clinton Riot, prompting George to call on white Mississippians to enlist in the militia to circumvent the black troops. The result was an unparalleled unity among white Mississippians to overthrow what they described as black Republican rule. Still, George had to corral the white hatred and violence in order to keep federal troops out of the state. One writer has described the situation well: "The Democratic leadership cracked the whip to avoid open conflict and the resultant influx of Federal troops. With difficulty, it brought a roused populace to heel."[4]

George and his executive committee constantly worked the telegraph, keeping tabs on the state's whites and instructing them on what to do. One member of the Hinds County Democratic Party remembered, "Our county committee was in constant communication with him [George]. He advised us of the very delicate ground upon which we stood and urged us to do nothing which would give Ames a legal pretext to call for troops."

A Yazoo County member told basically the same story: George "kept us fully posted each day on movements of Governor Ames and his black and tan mélange at Jackson, Mississippi." George also sent speakers to various parts of the state, as his limited funds would allow, and these speakers infuriated the crowds with inflamed racial speeches. George also issued several pamphlets, with titles such as *The Legislation of 1865 Concerning Freedmen: A Letter, Decrease of the Wealth of Mississippi under Radical Misrule*, and *The Clinton Riot: A True Statement, Showing Who Originated It*. The last pamphlet, containing eyewitness statements called for by George (always favorable to the Democrats, of course), illustrated his and the executive committee's view. Such wordage as "a premeditated massacre of the whites" filled the pamphlets. George also reprinted newspaper articles, such as *Issues of the Canvass—Compiled From the Clarion, and Presented to the Democratic-Conservative Canvassers*. The theme of all the publications was "Radical misrule and corruption." George lectured the populace, "We have a fair chance to relieve ourselves now. If we let the opportunity pass, another may never come."[5]

George left no record of his thoughts about intimidation and violence, but it may be assumed that he was cooperative if not supportive of such actions as long as they did not grow to a level that would bring federal troops to the state. Of course, individual county leaders had more of a say than George did in Jackson, and many of them openly advocated intimidation of blacks and stuffing ballot boxes or switching Democratic for Republican tickets for illiterate blacks. George was in overall charge of the campaign, however, and should shoulder much of the responsibility. He even oversaw the loaning of artillery pieces for celebratory activities and salutes, probably knowing full well they would be used to try to intimidate Republicans. Democrats shot a cannon so close to the governor's mansion that it shattered the windows, for example.[6]

Some Democrats later reported on George's influence on coercion. "Gen. J. Z. George early sounded the note of warning against the use of such methods [stuffing ballot boxes]," an Oktibbeha County Democrat reported. "He early saw the creeping miasma of moral obliquity and advised the Southern white man to turn aside from such methods; to get guns and if necessary stand at the polls and use open violence rather than fraud." On at least one occasion George's name itself was used as intimidation. Democrats in Lafayette County formed the "James Z. George Club," which sent speakers to every Republican function. At one meeting members of the George Club slipped behind the Republican speaker and lifted a

Democratic banner over his head. The Republican speaker stated, "I stand under the great Union flag," to which the Democrats responded, "No, you are not, you are under the banner which you swore a month ago to support." A member of the Democratic Party in Lafayette County remembered, "This Club won many Negroes over to the Democratic ticket, since they were afraid of its members and generally did as they directed." A newspaper similarly reported that George himself, in speaking around the state and particularly at Duck Hill in late October, "made a glorious speech in his usual happy style, satisfying the colored people that they had been deluded."[7]

By mid-October, however, several key areas were reaching emergency status, and Ames was again calling out the black militia. In Yazoo County, for example, the deposed Republican sheriff was about to be reinstated by black troops, and whites were planning an attack in response. In addition, several counties were sending delegates to a specially called white convention in Jackson set for October 15. George had to do something or the state was about to erupt, and the only conceivable response from Washington would be to send federal troops.[8]

Such was the setting for the famous meeting between George and Governor Ames on October 15. The idea emerged that Ames was in such a quandary that any offer for him to, in the words of one of George's lieutenants, "recede from his position, with some dignity," would be accepted quickly. George thus decided to meet with Ames. Apparently George did not come up with the idea, but he thought it was a good one and implemented it quickly. Ames, who was fast running out of options, heartily agreed. George set the meeting with Ames for ten o'clock in the morning on October 15 at the governor's mansion.[9]

George not only had to deal with the governor and get what he wanted, but he also had to quiet the frenzied mass of whites who were calling for blood. The newspaper-called convention of counties was meeting that very morning in Jackson, and George decided he had better finish the meeting with Ames before the convention acted. He changed the time to meet with Ames from ten to nine o'clock. That would give George time to get a deal with Ames and then hurry to the convention to pacify the whites.[10]

The two men met for two hours in the parlor of the governor's mansion. One of George's lieutenants who attended the meeting with him recalled, "General George ... [did] most of the talking." George explained the Democratic point of view to the governor, emphasizing how the black militia was creating such anger among whites. "Governor Ames, I will pledge you myself that I would desire peace, order, and a fair election, and everything of that sort in this country, and I believe every other good, solid, white citizen in the State feels that same way; and I will pledge you, sir, that they will act that way," George waged. Ames readily agreed to stop the militia from aiding the Yazoo sheriff, and also decided to stop shipment of guns to other black militia units in DeSoto County. George asked Ames to disband the black militia, but the governor would not agree to that. But Ames made a counteroffer: to disarm the black militia and send the companies to their homes. "This General George accepted at once," recalled an observer. In return, George promised to hold Mississippi whites, as best he could, in peace during the election.[11]

Immediately after brokering the deal with Ames, George went to Angelo's Hall to address the gathered convention. The participants were in no mood for compromise, whipped up as they were by the recent riots and violence. George spoke to the convention, although one observer noted, "at the outset of the meeting the tone was excited and rather stormy." Another observed, "at one time it was thought that General George would lose control of the situation, but finally, when the full significance of the compact with Governor Ames was understood, the action of the committee was accepted as satisfactory." One of George's lieutenants, former attorney general T. J. Wharton, was not convinced. He commented, "it was hard to tell whether they had captured the governor or the governor had captured them."[12]

George left no record of his thoughts on the deal, whether, as many historians suspect, he intended the compromise as a bold lie to gain time or if he really meant to try to hold the Democrats at bay. Certainly he had to realize he could not control every hotheaded Democrat in the state, and he more than likely knew he would not be able to fully abide by the deal. On the other hand, George's actions following the meeting demonstrated he attempted in large part to hold the Democrats at bay, not so much because he cared for the blacks being terrorized, but because he feared such open violence would draw the attention of the federal government, which might send in troops.[13]

Despite the deal, tensions began to rise again as the election neared. Democrats began to use their underhanded and brutal tactics once more, despite George's promise. As for George himself, he tried to work with Ames and met and corresponded with him numerous times over the next few weeks. For example, he met with Ames at the governor's office in the statehouse to try to get control of the weapons turned in by the black militia. George wanted to appoint guards for them, but Ames kept them under the control of the U.S. military stationed in Jackson. At other times Ames specifically consulted George regarding appointments, saying "that if they had any objection to any man whom he purposed to appoint, he wanted them . . . to state the objection."[14]

George also took matters into his own hands to keep violence down. On one occasion a Justice Department official sent to Mississippi to observe the election, George K. Chase, confronted George with the case of a black man named Walker who was agitating the white people. George described him as "a bad nigger anyhow," and he feared Walker would be killed. George told Chase, "If you will get him to go up to my plantation I will hire him till after the election to cut wood. There are a lot of niggers controlled by him. He is a bad nigger, and will get killed yet." George's prophesy proved true once Walker refused to go. On another occasion, after trouble in Amite County, George responded "that the people there were acting like a set of fools, and would greatly endanger the cause of the State if they did not keep quiet."[15]

A thorough reading of George's private telegrams during the election, never intended for public consumption but later subpoenaed by Congress, reveals he personally worked hard to abide by his promise to Ames. The telegrams contain numerous clauses such as "a difficulty should be avoided by all means"; "keep quiet, observe order, and all will be well"; "Will you authorize us to pledge that peace shall be preserved; that there shall be a peaceable election; and that the Republicans shall not be molested in voting for such ticket as they may choose?"; "see that a peaceful election is held"; "Preserve the peace, and have a fair election"; "Don't let us have any trouble of that sort on our hands"; and "Be sure that you watch the box every minute, and allow no cheating." George also warned his county officials, "Faith must be kept on the peace agreement." His mentality carried over to some of his followers, one of whom wrote him, "We intend to carry the election by votes, not by force."[16]

There were instances when George suffered the ire of white Democrats in order to keep the peace or to try to keep his promise. On one such occasion, two companies of black militia were targeted for attack as they carried arms into a portion of the state. Special Agent Chase investigated the plot to, he said, "destroy the nigger militia-men," finding out that George had ordered the white Democrats not to attack. Chase reported, "General George said that he was found fault with for having done as he did; but he thought it was the best way to quiet it down and gave no fight."

On another occasion, Democrats planned to kill the state chairman of the Republican Party when he traveled to Madison to vote. Chase uncovered the plan and drove to George's house "in the upper end of town," where he told him of the planned effort. George immediately wired officials in Madison to stop the killing, saying: "If Warner [the state chairman] goes to Madison, see by all means that he is not hurt. We are nearly through now, and are sure to win. Don't let us have any trouble of that sort on our hands." The killing was thwarted, and the chairman later expressed his thanks to George for "sav[ing] his life."[17]

Still, George could not control every Democrat in the state, and violence began to increase as the days passed after the meeting. And it mattered little in the opposition's eyes whether George was involved or not; he got the blame anyway. But George was not totally blameless. When violence and outrage were reported to Special Agent Chase, he would inquire of George about his views on the matter. "He would have by the next mail or by telegraph at once," Chase remembered, "from two to ten statements that no such thing occurred, or that it was a personal fight with no political significance. I was met every time in that way." Chase reported that George "would get me a lot of statements that nothing of the kind had occurred, and that it was all peace and quietness." If George was not a participant in the actions or even sanctioned them, he certainly was trying to cover for his men to keep tensions lower. Chase noted each time the victims were black, and he quickly decided, as he testified to a congressional panel, "that there was no chance for a fair election without the aid of United States troops." Chase reported that some Democrats admitted that they "intended to carry the election peaceably if they could, forcibly if they must." Other Mississippians were not so diplomatic. A Madison County Republican reported that he and the governor "had some warm words on the subject [Ames's deal with George]. I was satisfied that General George could not control the people of the State; that he could not carry it out, as subsequent events proved that he could not." One Mississippi Republican from Aberdeen, John E. Meek, was more blunt: "J. Z. George & Co. hoodwinked the President of [the] U. S. about peace in Miss, election; Gnl. George knew better."[18]

George and his lieutenants denied any wrongdoing, of course, even responding to a published report of a Republican convention that looked into the abuses. A Democratic paper called this convention "the last card of the defeated and desperate office-seekers." George, along with Ethelbert Barksdale, Wiley Harris, and others, wrote an open letter to Governor

Ames immediately before the election stating that all the charges were "so general in their character" that they would not carry any weight. "If the state of general terrorism and intimidation exists as charged," George wrote, "it is certain there must also exist specific acts of violence and disorder." The Democrats then returned to their theme of a "desire . . . for a peaceable and fair election."[19]

Reactions to George's efforts have run the gamut, with the foremost authority on Mississippi Reconstruction going so far as to say George's actions and rhetoric contained "a large dose of hypocrisy." But perhaps the best assessment of George during the campaign came from George Chase, the federal agent sent to Mississippi by the Grant administration to watch events. Although he complained George was not successful in holding his Democrats fully to the pledge with Ames, he nevertheless stated in testimony before Congress, "I wish to add, in justice to General George, that on all occasions he proved himself a gentleman of honor; personally I have a high respect for him."[20]

The net result, whether legal or not, was a complete Democratic victory in the election of 1875. As George stayed in constant contact with various county officials on election day, the realization emerged that the Democrats had won a huge victory. George telegraphed the *Memphis Appeal* late in the day: "the State has been redeemed by a large majority." He also telegraphed officials in his home county, Carroll, "Tell our colored friends at Vaiden if they want to get in the Democratic wagon now is the time."[21]

The victory was indeed complete; the state legislature went heavily Democratic. The executive soon came under Democratic control as well when the new Democratic legislature began impeachment proceedings against Governor Ames. The governor obviously had never been liked by Democrats, and was often publicly humiliated, such as when they would stick "their fingers up to their noses to him, and hallooing to him to go back to Massachusetts, where he belonged." Ames resigned and returned north. But even in that victory George had to walk a fine line—he could not get rid of Ames before removing the black lieutenant governor, or else a black man would become governor. Alexander K. Davis was thus removed from office by impeachment before Ames resigned, and the next ranking officer, the president pro tem of the state senate, Democrat John M. Stone, became governor.[22]

George's campaign, although tarnished with controversy and underhanded tactics, nevertheless was successful. It was on George's watch that the state went Democratic again. He issued a congratulatory order: "The

Democratic conservative executive committee congratulates you upon the glorious and decisive victory which you have achieved in the election which has just taken place." He went on to say, "Upon the result of that election depended the destinies of the State for many years to come," and urged his fellow victors to "be moderate in the hour of triumph and magnanimous to the defeated. . . . The committee urge this moderation as due to the character of the people of Mississippi and as a fit tribute to the Giver of all Good who hath enjoyed them." He also wrote a letter after the election in which he warned: "I want merely to state that anything like disorder or riot or lawlessness or intimidation of Republican officials will be of material injury to our cause. We have carried the State by an immense majority, and we must so act as to show we are worthy of power. Do implore our hot-headed friends to be patient and resort to the law for redress. Allow, if you please, the expelled to return to their duties. If they are guilty of wrong, proceed according to law."[23]

Not surprisingly, the U.S. Senate held lengthy hearings on the election, with George's actions at the center of the testimony. The three Republicans on the committee agreed that the Democrats had acted illegally and that the election should be nullified, while the two Democrats supported George and their fellow Democrats. In a minority opinion, the two Democratic senators wrote:

> Perhaps the best proof that can be offered of the real intent and spirit with which the Democratic and conservative canvass was organized and conducted will be found in the telegraphic correspondence between Mr. George, the chairman of the executive committee, and his party associates throughout the State, who communicated with him during the canvass. This correspondence, although not referred to by any witness nor in any way supposed to be connected with the subjects to be inquired of by the committee, was, by the order of the committee, and against the formal and recorded protest of the undersigned, made public for the purpose of sustaining the charges of lawlessness and outrage against the Democratic party of Mississippi. Mr. George had not been made a witness; none of the parties who were his correspondents had been made witnesses; but the whole correspondence was seized and produced in bulk before the committee. . . . Let it be borne in mind that these communications were all supposed by the writers to be confidential, and that their contents would never be made public. It will be difficult for any mind, however prejudiced, to

construe any portion of this telegraphic correspondence so as to favor the suspicion that lawlessness of any kind was looked to as an element for the success of the Democratic party in that canvass. From first to last there is nothing but what is creditable to Mr. George and his Democratic correspondents as honorable, peaceful, and law-abiding citizens. We do not believe it will be possible to torture any of these dispatches into any other meaning.[24]

George was certainly a happy and relieved man that November after the election. Not only was his state's politics back in Democratic hands, but his personal life had several exciting events as well. Kate's marriage in late November no doubt added to his glee, with Alfred's coming the next February. But while the 1875 state election was the most important because control of the all-powerful state legislature was at stake, the 1876 national election weighed nearly as heavily on George's mind. In addition to the congressional election, that year saw the chance for national Democrats to take back the White House in an election between Republican Rutherford B. Hayes and Democrat Samuel Tilden. Despite the weddings of his children, George took little time off and worked feverishly to build on the success he had achieved in 1875, hoping that putting Mississippi in the Democratic column would help a national Democrat win the presidency. In fact, George spread his successful formula to other states as they picked up what became termed as the "Mississippi Plan," which has been described by one recent historian as "intimidation just strong enough to keep blacks from the polls but subtle enough to avert any real protest from the North."[25]

To be sure, the signs looked good for a Democratic victory in Mississippi in 1876, judging from what had occurred in 1875. As the time for the election neared, however, George wrote a colleague: "I feel very hopeful—even confident—but still when there is such a big majority of blacks—so well drilled &c, I can't but feel anxiety." To help the cause, George used such luminaries as L. Q. C. Lamar, who had served in the U.S. House of Representatives before being elected by the new Democratic state legislature to the U.S. Senate in 1876. George informed Lamar of an executive committee meeting in September, telling him, "The object is to have a full report from all parts of the State and to [develop] final plans for the Campaign." He continued, "I would, and I am sure the . . . Committee would, be pleased to have you come down and confer with us." Later in October George asked Lamar to help even more. "I think it very likely we shall carry the State by a large majority without trouble," he wrote, "but there is a chance . . . for a different result." He asked Lamar to tour the eastern portion of the state, making speeches in Corinth, Aberdeen, Columbus, Macon, and Enterprise. "I fear our friends at all these places need working up," George wrote.[26]

George also published more leaflets in order to whip up more public support, pamphlets such as *Address of the State Executive Committee* and *Radical Extravagance Contrasted with Democratic Economy*. But George did not need to fear, because Mississippi went solidly for Samuel Tilden in the election in November, with the Democrat carrying the state with 68 percent of the vote. Illustrating the completeness of the work done in 1875, Mississippi's vote was not in dispute as were the votes of other Southern states such as Florida, Louisiana, and South Carolina. Although the Democrats lost the election to Hayes in the Compromise of 1877, George had Mississippi firmly in Democratic hands, and it would remain so for the next century.[27]

The Reconstruction battles, of course, betrayed George's fundamentally negative view of African Americans. He believed blacks were human, as opposed to some lines of thought in those days, but inferior to whites and should not be allowed to govern. Numerous examples of his ideas are extant, even beyond his slave ownership, secession convention actions, and Civil War endeavors. In Reconstruction days, he commented that Mississippi was suffering from the "black cloud" of Republican refugees incoming from already "redeemed" states such as Georgia and Alabama. In dealing with Ames, George stated that "the best security that Governor Ames or anybody could have for peace and order in this Country . . . was the moral sentiment of the best classes of white people here."[28]

But George also courted black voters and offered them offices in return for support. There is much evidence that some blacks sided with the Democrats and against white Republicans in Mississippi elections in return for a portion of the offices. George realized that the two races would have to live together and sought the best possible solution that afforded everyone peace while still retaining white domination. George thus supported education for black children, which noted historian C. Vann Woodward has labeled the "fusion principle."[29]

George continued to head the Democratic executive committee through 1876, and was a topic of conversation even with presidents. One Republican in Mississippi counseled President Hayes in 1877, "I believe it would be comparatively easy to secure, through George, almost the whole of the old Whigs of Miss. to support, heartily, your administration. I respectfully suggest that you consult him if occasion occurs." By that time, though, George was not in a dealing mood as the full government of the state was coming under Democratic rule, and violence and intimidation were fading because the need was no longer there for such tactics. Only one major incident of note occurred during his last year as chairman, that being the so-called Kemper County Tragedy in which Democrats killed a Republican judge. George and the Republican chairman, John R. Lynch, traded charges in the papers and pamphlets, but by that time George and the Democrats already firmly controlled the state. The Republicans were powerless to do anything but complain.[30]

George's status in Mississippi certainly rose with his political victories; he was hailed as a hero among the white population of Mississippi for returning an age of white supremacy to the state. The *New York Times* reported, "He found his office a sinecure, and left it an institution." A contemporary, John Sharp Williams, called him "almost dictator as chairman of the executive committee of his party in the revolutionary campaign of 1875." But George's victory in Mississippi had larger repercussions. He not only led in "redeeming" Mississippi from Republican rule and black equality, but he also set the foundation for other Southern states to do likewise. In what became known as the "Mississippi Plan," other former Confederate states used the same basic formula George had used in Mississippi in 1875 (not enough force to bring down the wrath of the federal government but enough to dissuade enough blacks from voting to win the election) to nullify Reconstruction in their states and to establish complete white supremacy. George was becoming a force not only in Mississippi, but throughout the South as well.[31]

CHAPTER 14

"Eliminating the Last Vestige of Republican Domination"

Rewards, 1876–1881

After the state's politics were securely in Democratic hands, J. Z. George returned to his law profession. Once more he worked with Wiley P. Harris on cases around Jackson on the county level as well as numerous more cases before Mississippi's high court. He also argued cases on the federal district and circuit levels. In fact, by the mid-1870s the firm of George and Harris was the leader of the Mississippi bar.[1]

Unfortunately, a nasty incident soon took place in which George lost his partner and friend. George had never been known as particularly neat or well dressed, and Harris unfortunately made a joke that George took the wrong way. "During an hour of conviviality," one newspaper reported, Harris jokingly called George an "educated hog." The prickly George heard about the statement and immediately went to Harris and demanded an apology. Not satisfied, he dissolved the partnership. George took his son-in-law, J. B. H. Hemingway of Jackson, as his new partner and went off on his own. A newspaper reported, "Among his thoughtless speeches, Judge Harris never uttered one which he more deeply regretted."[2]

George had more important issues to consider than practicing law in Jackson, however. He was still involved in politics and accepted new and more important duties, largely in response to and as a reward for his successful work in the Democratic revolution. He once commented on his views of friendship: "I am gratified . . . to know that I have pleased my friends: and to the 'rest of mankind' I care little what they think of what I do or say." Now that version of friendship rewarded George for his work. The *New York Times*, in fact, described George's emergence onto the national scene as his being "rewarded for infamous work." With colleagues such as L. Q. C. Lamar and Ethelbert Barksdale, George had run the political machine that brought the state government back into Democratic hands, and now that Democratic government intended on repaying these leaders with prized appointments. The first prize, a Senate seat, went to Lamar in 1876, which put him on the path toward becoming a cabinet member and U.S. Supreme Court justice.[3]

George also landed several positions, small ones at first. The new Democratic governor, John M. Stone, appointed George to the board of trustees for both the state university at Oxford, known as the University of Mississippi, and the new Agricultural and Mechanical College at Starkville, now known as Mississippi State University. George's appointment to the state university board came on February 14, 1878, while his appointment to the agricultural school was on May 8, 1879. As with all state positions, George had to have state senate confirmation to take office.[4]

George met only once with the University of Mississippi board, that meeting occurring on June 24–28, 1878. He was appointed to the committee on buildings and made several recommendations concerning the university facilities. But due to fiscal shortages, George and the committee were not able to do much. He could not get renovations to the law school classrooms or obtain an organ for the chapel. Neither was funded. George made several other recommendations that were passed, though, such as paying a professor a small amount for extra work, granting an honorary degree, and honoring former governor Charles Clark upon his death.[5]

George resigned his state university board position on May 7, 1879, when he took his seat on the Agricultural and Mechanical College board of trustees. George alerted Governor Stone that his time on the state university board had been "pleasant," but that he could "do better service for the State in the position which you have tendered me." George probably thought he was much better suited to the agricultural college than an academic state university. Thus his major work in higher education from then on concerned itself mainly with the budding university at Starkville.[6]

George was not a founding father of the board, but Governor Stone placed him in the first vacancy to occur. Still he was instrumental in the founding of the university, serving on a three-man committee, along with Stephen D. Lee, that observed a similar college in Michigan to get ideas for building the Mississippi agricultural college. He also spoke at the laying of the university's cornerstone in September 1879. He asked that the university "unite what has heretofore in Mississippi, at least, been separated—high mental culture and manual labor." He touted such schooling in agriculture, fences, manures, cattle, and a host of other items, praising the art of manual labor. "We propose to make here no dreamers, nor splendid and dazzling intellectual prodigies, with neither the capacity nor the will to do the world's work," George said, "nor on the other hand, do we propose to make machines of men, mere automations to be worked and moved by the will and intellect of others."[7]

George carried out his board duties with gusto and served on the board for the remainder of his life. He served on various committees of the board, such as that overseeing the university's farm. He attended the meetings every year in June right up until his health no longer allowed him to do so. George was a firm supporter of the Agricultural and Mechanical College.[8]

His strong support of the college caused George to later become involved in an argument with one of the University of Mississippi's major professors, all over the prestige and endowment of the two schools. While on the board of the agricultural and mechanical school, George took the state university to task over fiscal matters, most notably comparative funding. At issue was a legislative appropriation that rewarded the state university compensation for "seminary funds" that had been lost during the Panic of 1837, long before either of the institutions was established. George argued that the Agricultural and Mechanical College should get a portion of such monies since the original funds were not specified for any particular institution. Edward Mayes, who served as chairman of the faculty at Ole Miss, responded to George's criticism with a detailed rebuttal, stating, "I maintain that . . . [George's] argument is fallacious and misleading and his conclusions wholly mistaken and untenable." George responded, as did Mayes again, and the entire dispute was carried out in pamphlets and the press, although nothing was ever decided, and the dispute soon died out. George did not hold a grudge against the university, though, and later helped obtain for it a large tract of more than 23,000 acres of land.[9]

George was considered for other more important positions as well, with Senator Lamar leading the effort. Since George had played such a role in throwing off Republican rule in Mississippi, the next available major government post would go to him. Thus, when it looked possible that Samuel Tilden might win the presidency in 1876, Mississippians began promoting George for a nomination to the U.S. Supreme Court. "Numerous bar meetings were held all over the State," Lamar remembered, producing memorials "directed to the contingency" of Tilden's victory. When Hayes won, Senator Lamar still approached the Republican president with the idea of appointing George, knowing that Hayes was looking for ways to gratify the South. Lamar wrote that the state memorials "were many, widely diffused, and powerful." He told the president:

George is a man of vast legal acquirements; is a profound jurist and publicist; stands at the head of his profession in this state, and I believe has few equals in this country. I have known few men so admirably fitted to that exalted position, and but feel assured that he would add honor to it, although so honorable already. In addition, he is a man of unassailable moral integrity, and of great personal influence throughout the state. I do not believe that anything could be done which would be more grateful to our people than his advancement to the bench; and I gladly and earnestly recommend it.

Lamar also added a postscript to entice Hayes even more: "P.S.—Genl. George has always been a Democrat, but is an open and outspoken supporter of your [Reconstruction] policy." Hayes, of course, chose not to appoint a Democrat and former Confederate to the Supreme Court so early after the war and Reconstruction, but George's name was obviously rising.[10]

Other positions were soon offered to George. Despite the legislature becoming Democratic in 1875 and the election of a Democratic governor the next year, it took a few years for all of the Reconstruction-era officials to be fully removed. Offices that had longer terms such as court judges and senators remained in Republican hands for a few more years. In terms of Mississippi's revolution, it took several years for all the Republican officers to be replaced, and George was front and center in replacing two of the last Republicans in the state.

Although George did not get the 1876 Senate seat or the U.S. Supreme Court appointment, a seat was reserved for the fifty-two-year-old George on the Mississippi Supreme Court. A *Vicksburg Herald* article, which was picked up by other papers such as the *New York Times*, applauded the move, complimenting George on "his modest simplicity, his profundity, his earnest patriotism, and his massive brain."[11]

Although a Confederate supporter during the war, the presiding chief justice of the court, Horatio F. Simrall, had been appointed by Reconstruction governor James L. Alcorn in 1870. His term ended in May 1879, necessitating a new appointment. Democratic governor John M. Stone thus appointed George, in the words of the state supreme court's historian, "eliminating the last vestige of Republican domination of the Supreme Court." The appointment carried a nine-year term.[12]

George's appointment and Senate confirmation occurred in February 1878, although he did not take office until May 1879, when Simrall's term ended. On May 10 George took the oath of office, which stated, "I, James Z.

George, do solemnly swear that I will faithfully support and true allegiance bear [to] the Constitution of the United States, and the State of Mississippi, and obey the laws thereof; that I am not disqualified from holding office by the Constitution of the United States or the State of Mississippi; that I will faithfully discharge the duties of the office upon which I am about to enter, so help me God."[13]

One of George's fellow justices on the three-man court was old friend Josiah A. P. Campbell, who had been active in state and Confederate politics, having served as Speaker of the Mississippi House before the war and as a Confederate congressman and colonel during the war. Stone had appointed him in 1876, and Campbell became a fixture on the court for nearly two decades. The other member was Confederate veteran H. H. Chalmers, brother of George's old wartime commander James R. Chalmers. Like Campbell, H. H. Chalmers had come to the court in 1876 with an appointment from Governor Stone. Thus, with George's appointment, three Democratic-appointed Confederate veterans oversaw the highest court in Mississippi. The "redemption" of the state, at least in legal affairs, was complete.[14]

The reconstituted court met together for the first time on May 10, but quickly made an unconventional decision two days later by electing the newest member as chief justice. Chalmers and Campbell decided George should be given the honor of presiding over the court. Such a move was almost unheard of; Edward C. Walthall called it a "rare distinction." The May 12 entry into the court's minutes read: "James Z. George, having been chosen to be Chief Justice or Presiding Judge of this Court, it is ordered that this fact be entered of record and that the said James Z. George is hereby made Chief Justice or Presiding Judge of this Court."[15]

The duties of the chief justice were not entirely different from those of the associate justices, except that he had the duty of presiding over the court when in session as well as taking care of its administration. Little is known of George's presiding style, as transcripts of hearings and arguments are nonexistent. The minutes of the court reflect only a synopsis of each case as well as any administrative actions. As chief justice, it was George's duty to approve the daily records of the court as compiled by the clerk.[16]

Over the course of George's tenure on the court, he, Campbell, and Chalmers heard a total of 254 appeals from all parts of the state. The three judges split the cases equally among themselves in order to write the court's opinion on each case. Thus George wrote a total of eighty-seven different opinions. He was so thorough in writing these opinions, one contemporary noted, that "the only criticism I ever heard of them is that they are too long." In addition, George had a heavy correspondence with judges, litigators, and clients during this period.[17]

During his tenure as chief justice, George and Bettie, and most of their children, lived on State Street in downtown Jackson. Some thirteen people lived in the George household, ranging from the chief justice and Bettie to their grown children who had already married and borne George grandchildren. George's son Cothran also lived in the George household even though he was twenty-one and was working as a clerk in the state treasury department. Also part of the household were four black or mulatto servants, two of them with the last name of George. They had been George's slaves before the war and remained with him afterward, even taking the family name as theirs. His children's education was very important, and those still young enough to do so attended school in Jackson—Lizzie, for example, at the Fair Lawn Institute.[18]

Being chief justice of the state's highest court was not the end of George's reward for his 1875 efforts, however. In January 1880 the rumblings of a new U.S. Senate election were occurring. One of the last Mississippi Reconstruction Republicans leaving office was African American senator Blanche K. Bruce. Obviously, Bruce would not be reelected by a Democratic legislature, so the party turned its attention to a host of qualified candidates, including Edward C. Walthall, Ethelbert Barksdale, and Otho Singleton.[19]

In 1880 L. Q. C. Lamar effectively headed the Democratic Party in the state, having been elected to the U.S. Senate in 1876. His two main subordinates were George and Walthall, and George was already on the state supreme court. Lamar desired a similarly high post of honor for his other supporter, Walthall. The Senate seat vacated by Bruce gave Lamar the ideal opportunity, and Walthall became the front-runner for the Senate seat.[20]

But other prominent Democrats challenged Lamar's hold on power. With no common enemy to unite the party after Reconstruction, the Democrats split into two factions, the conservative, or Bourbon, wing, and the liberal wing. Lamar, George, and Walthall led the liberal wing, which proposed a peaceful reunion with the North and integration into its industrial economy. The Bourbons, on the other hand, sought to retain an isolated Mississippi, based on the memory of the Old South, the Confederacy, and the Lost Cause. The major common ground of both was white supremacy, which has led many historians to place George and other liberals in the Bourbon camp when they were more liberal than Bourbon. Ethelbert

Barksdale, George's ally during the 1875 canvas, led the conservative wing of the Democratic Party and promoted his own candidacy. A sitting congressman, Otho Singleton of Canton, also ran for the seat.[21]

These Democratic splits led to a dispute over the 1880 Senate seat, and the Democratic legislature meeting in Jackson in January 1880 deadlocked. Barksdale won more votes, but not enough to be elected. Walthall stubbornly held his support firm, and other lesser candidates took some support away from the two front-runners. Despite numerous ballots, neither side could attain the required majority.[22]

Finally, Walthall withdrew and had his supporters nominate George. Barksdale, apparently convinced he could not defeat the chief justice, also threw his support to George. With both Walthall's and Barksdale's support, George became the front-runner, but his election was still not ensured. When a joint session of the House and Senate met on January 21, George's old friend Winfield Scott Featherston nominated him, but he actually received fewer votes than Barksdale and about the same as Singleton, both of whom were still receiving votes. By the time the two houses met again the next day, the process had been worked out, and George, again nominated by Featherston, received a large majority of both houses. In fact, both Barksdale and Singleton had dropped out by then, leaving only Greenbacker A. M. West in the running, although a few members still voted for Walthall and three voted for the sitting African American senator, Blanche K. Bruce. In a swift turn of events that he had not completely expected, George was bound for the busy streets of Washington, D.C. His Senate term would run from March 4, 1881, to March 3, 1887.[23]

George's election caused various reactions. Barksdale loathed the result, and George reciprocated by loaning money, as did Walthall and Lamar, to Barksdale's chief newspaper rival to continue the fight against him. Some supported the election, with Walthall accepting the outcome with outward graciousness, mainly because he and George viewed most issues in the same way. George, of course, thanked Walthall for his support. But the niceties went only so far among the liberal wing of the Democratic Party in Mississippi. Years later Walthall admitted that he and George had endured some "occasional disturbances of a friendship." One Mississippian who was particularly unhappy was L. Q. C. Lamar. The state's senior senator had nothing against George personally, but he had openly asked that Walthall be elected. Thus George's election was a slap in the face, illustrating his weakening control over the Democratic Party in the state. "The election of George," Lamar wrote, "does not gratify me as it ought."

A newspaperman described Lamar's check as a "signal punishment," and Lamar agreed, saying, "It is one which grows sharper and more bitter every day. It is my one great disappointment in life, & the only one of a political nature that I could not have borne with composure." One newspaper went so far as to editorialize, "The Lamar crowd hate[s] George worse than the devil hates holy water." C. Vann Woodward would write in understatement that the maverick George "was never on intimate terms with his two colleagues [Lamar and Walthall]."[24]

Because George would not take his Senate seat until early 1881, he decided to remain in his current position until that time. But he did not deem it wise or necessary to remain in the chief justice's position. He thus resigned as presiding justice, reverting back to an associate justice. H. H. Chalmers became chief justice on the basis of a new 1880 code of regulations, which stipulated that the chief justice would be the member who had the shortest term remaining. George remained on the court until February 19, 1881, when he resigned in order to make his way to Washington to be present when the new Congress convened in March. Replacing George on the high court was Timothy E. Cooper.[25]

The difference between the bustling avenues of Washington, D.C., and the quaint towns of Mississippi symbolized the change that was about to take place for J. Z. George. Washington was completely different from Jackson, Mississippi's capital of only around 5,200 souls, and even more different from tiny Carrollton, George's hometown. Similarly, as George made his way into the busy lifestyle of the nation's capital city, he entered the realm of national politics, of which he was woefully unknowledgeable. He had been a major factor in Mississippi politics and had even garnered some regional clout, but the nation's capital was a very different arena. It did not help that George had recently made war on that very capital or that his social skills were still lacking.[26]

George nevertheless left his familiar surroundings of Carrollton and Jackson, including Cotesworth and his supreme court, although he continued to maintain his law partnership with son-in-law J. B. H. Hemingway in Jackson. Perhaps the most substantial loss, even if only brief, would be the separation from his beloved wife, Bettie. George had never done well when away from her, sliding into melancholy and perhaps depression when separated for long periods. But like some other senators' families, neither she nor their children would accompany the new senator to Washington because George knew that his duties would not allow sufficient time for his family; living arrangements were likewise uncertain in Washington.[27]

But the hardships incurred in such a dramatic turn of events would pale in comparison to the chance George saw to help his constituents, state, and nation. His assertive manner again emerged, and George threw himself completely into his new line of work as the junior senator from Mississippi.

CHAPTER 15

"I Have to Go to the Capitol Now to Do Some Work"

First Senate Term, 1881–1886

Most congressional sessions in the nineteenth century began in December. Such a schedule would have placed the beginning of the Forty-seventh Congress on December 5, 1881. But George became a senator some nine months early due to a special session of Congress called to facilitate a new administration and approve its new appointments. George consequently moved to Washington in February 1881, and was present when the special session opened on March 4.[1]

George suddenly found himself thrust into national politics, and he discovered it was very different from Mississippi affairs. In Washington, George rubbed elbows with famous senators and representatives as well as the president and cabinet officers. He soon became familiar with the Senate chamber, which would become his home away from home, and the processes of the body. At his desk, George sat on the right of the chamber when looking from the rostrum. He held no rank as a newly elected senator, and thus had to accept a seat on the back row. He was flanked by Democratic senators Johnson N. Camden of West Virginia and James G. Fair of Nevada. Two seats down to George's right sat L. Q. C. Lamar, George's colleague from Mississippi.[2]

The first order of business was the swearing-in ceremony. George was called in the second group, and at the front of the chamber he raised his right hand and with the others took the oath of office from Vice President Chester A. Arthur. George then had to take another oath: one for former Confederate officers. Nevertheless, George was now a member of the U.S. Senate. He also witnessed the inauguration of President James A. Garfield on the east portico of the capitol.[3]

Washington society apparently did not know what to make of this new man from Mississippi. "Mr. George is not a man who would be picked out by a stranger in the gallery or in the street as a Senator handy with the organic law," one newspaper reported. "He is a shock-headed, rusty-bearded Southerner, who wears a slouch hat that looks as though it had been jammed by every awning post and umbrella between the Treasury and the capitol; and he is not fastidious, though presentable." Another described him: "Senator George, of Mississippi, is one of the most bow-legged men in Congress, and, by the way, there are a great many of them," says the *New York Tribune*. It is one of the traditions of the country where he comes from that his trousers are cut with a circular saw. The result is that these garments are usually conspicuous for a baggy appearance where they are widest." A Mississippi newspaper summed him up by saying, "he is rough to look at but he is thoroughly equipped to meet any Senator on the other side."[4]

The Senate soon began its work, and George received his committee assignments. As a junior senator with little status or recognition, the majority of his appointments were second rate; he served on none of the major committees such as Judiciary or Military Affairs. Instead, George was placed on three committees: Agriculture and Forestry, Claims, and Education and Labor. Agriculture and Forestry was, of course, an important committee due to the nation's economic dependence on farmers. This appointment was appropriate as George was a planter and knew what farmers needed. Moreover the vast majority of his constituents were farmers. George probably liked the Claims Committee least, because he was always placing petitions before the Senate on behalf of citizens, which took much of his time. As for Education and Labor, time would tell if George was a friend of public education, but his position on various university boards in Mississippi made this appointment logical, too.[5]

George said little during most of the special session, as well as during a second special session called by Chester A. Arthur on the event of President Garfield's death in September. The second session ran from October 10 to October 30, 1881. George offered no bills or amendments during these sessions, but did demonstrate his independence on one issue. In the last days of the second session, there was a heated debate over compelling senators to attend a vote on a disputed presidential appointment. Several senators, including George, lodged a protest, but George was not satisfied and added his own explanation regarding the unconstitutionality of the procedure: "I concur with the protest with the understanding that . . . ," he wrote.[6]

George spoke only once during these two sessions, but he did so with force and conviction. He demonstrated his aggressive and blunt personality, literally picking a fight on the Senate floor. On April 1, 1881, Republican senator Henry L. Dawes of Massachusetts made a passing reference to Mississippi. He alluded to the fact that a Massachusetts man who lived in Mississippi had tried to help several freedmen, and he had been killed and his house burned in retaliation. This event allegedly occurred during Reconstruction. The ill Senator Lamar began defending Mississippi, but he grew weak in the exchange, and George took up where his ailing colleague left off. He demanded specifics. He wanted to know who, where, and when this event took place. Dawes dodged the questions, but George tightened his hold, arguing "the circumstances which have been recited by the Senator are untrue."[7]

As leader of the fight for "redemption" in Mississippi, George knew almost all that had and had not occurred in the state during those turbulent times. "Now, Mr. President, I know a little more about that than the Senator does," he remarked. Then he began attacking Dawes's story piece by piece. George belittled the accusation of murder, stating, "I believe murder occurs everywhere in every state possibly in the Union." George gave personal testimony that he himself had built several schools for black children, chiding the senator from Massachusetts: "and I have never been murdered for it." Dawes responded, admitting that it had not been a house but a cotton gin that had been burned. George insisted that the Massachusetts man had never been murdered and that most likely the man had never even been to Mississippi. "I do not [even] believe he had a gin house," George cajoled, causing a roll of laughter to spread across the floor and galleries. Despite the humor, George continued the pattern of denying any wrongdoing that Chase had found so frustrating in 1875.[8]

As the exchange continued, others joined in the fight. Republican senators Samuel McMillan of Minnesota, George Hoar of Massachusetts, and Angus Cameron of Wisconsin all took aim at George. With his lawyerly ability, he countered the assaults with questions to which his counterparts refused to yield. Conversely, perhaps because of his inexperience, he yielded to every question from every assailant, thus accepting attacks from all directions. George remained adamant, but failed to persuade his opponents. Dawes scolded that "the Senator [George] shuts his eyes and fills his ears with cotton."[9]

George kept quiet for the remainder of the special sessions, even traveling home between the two. When the regular session of the Forty-seventh Congress began, however, he began the normal functions of a senator. He performed his committee assignments and spoke on several occasions on the floor. But none of his service boosted his career during his first two congresses. He remained the junior senator at his desk in the back of the chamber. He quietly but steadily did his work, slowly transforming himself into a veteran senator.[10]

George's fortunes changed in the Forty-ninth Congress, which began in December 1885. Mississippi's senior senator, L. Q. C. Lamar, resigned his seat to take the office of secretary of the interior. George thus became Mississippi's senior senator. His replacement was Lamar's friend Edward C. Walthall, George's old ally if not close friend. On January 25, 1886, George presented Walthall's credentials to the Senate, then escorted his fellow Mississippian to the desk for his oath.[11]

Not only did George become senior senator during this Congress, but he also attained a more powerful senatorial position. On April 16, 1886, George was appointed to serve on the Judiciary Committee, a post he had desired since his arrival in Washington. His lawyer training and service as a judge in Mississippi suited him well for the position, but it took him five long years to gain the seniority required for the post.[12]

George's advancement in standing was symbolized by his physical advancement in the Senate chamber. By the Forty-eighth Congress, George had moved from his back-row seat to the second row. He still sat on the right of the chamber, but this time he was seventh from the aisle, which put him in the center of the right half of the chamber. In this new position, George was flanked by Democrats Wilkinson Call of Florida and James B. Beck of Kentucky. North Carolina Civil War governor Zebulon Vance sat directly behind him.[13]

As he became a greater force in the Senate, George's personal life conversely suffered in Washington. He lost several dear members of his family during this period. His stepfather, Seaborn Durham, had died in 1877, but George was probably sadder over the loss of William Cothran, who passed away in November 1880 while George was a member of the supreme court. Cothran had always been a father figure to George. Most notably, his mother died within a few months of his joining the Senate, on October 29, 1881. George was in Washington at the special session of the Senate when his mother passed away. Fortunately, the session ended the same day, and he quickly returned home. Probably worst of all for the reclusive and already saddened George, his wife and children did not accompany him to Washington, and he found life difficult during his first two Congresses. George lived at various places in Washington, including hotels such as the St. James, St. Nicholas, and New York; his address changed each session.

Such a life in boardinghouses and hotels without company played on the family man's mind. He enjoyed the times when the Senate was not in session, when he returned to Mississippi and his family.[14]

During the Forty-eighth Congress, Bettie and the children joined George in Washington. But Bettie returned home often, sending the senator into more gloom. Trips to other parts of the country also took her away from him, such as when she traveled to Boston with her daughter and son-in-law. "Of course you can stay as long as you wish," he wrote her, but added, "I want you to know I am awfully tired of being alone."[15]

Fortunately, George's children kept him busy, somewhat filling the void. Fannie's first husband, William R. Barksdale, died in the mid-1870s, and she married Thomas J. George—no relation—in 1882. At least several of his children also stayed in Washington at different times to keep him company, especially Pinckney and Elizabeth, known as Pink and Lizzie. Lizzie served as the senator's private secretary some of the time. George was a busy but doting father, telling Bettie what all he had bought them despite limited funds. He even contemplated buying one of them a pony and buggy, asking Bettie, "What do you say?" Apparently he and Pink spent much of their time together. George wrote Bettie: "We get along fairly well but there is no house keeping without a woman so we want you back and bad." At times even his older children came to visit in Washington. In 1884, for example, when Cothran came, George wrote that he had "been a great Company and Comfort to me." Joseph also came for a while, wanting to attend the Mardi Gras festivities, presumably in Washington. George wrote his wife, "I have not the money but I have to send him." Even his children's presence did not make up for Bettie's absence, however. He sent letters with such pitiful phrases as "I want you to know I am awfully tired of being alone," and "I am anxious for this summer to come as I am very tired and want to be home with you." He assured her that he and the children were all right, though, telling her "Lizzie and I go to church every Sunday."[16]

Meanwhile, the sometimes ill-natured George was gaining a reputation in the Senate for being brusque and short, and his children were not immune from his irritability either. Certainly Bettie had endured his moodiness throughout their marriage, but George seemed to be mellowing as he grew older. "You are mistaken in your supposition about your father being disagreeable," Bettie wrote to Lizzie. "I have not seen him for years so pleasant as he is now." She went on to say, "Your father bears adversity better than prosperity" and that "he is in a good humor all the time."[17]

One issue with his children continually bothered the senator, however: his financial condition. It was certainly more stable than it had been during those trying days immediately after the war and even as late as 1870 when he lost part of his land. Agricultural prices were down, and George's legal career was almost nonexistent now that he was in the Senate. That salary, while good, was not spectacular, and he had difficulty making ends meet. Yet he continually sent his children money, especially Lizzie, who stayed on and off in Washington and Mississippi. "This <u>must</u> do you till you get here," he wrote Lizzie in 1883 while sending her money. "I hope to make a little money this year by farming, but I am not sure of it. My taxes are yet to pay." Later, he ominously wrote, "I am in debt." Even by the end of his first term in office his financial prospects were not much better. "I am always pressed for money and you must be as economical as you can for a while till my salary accumulates a little," he wrote Lizzie in 1885 while sending her $50. Bettie also lectured her about money: "Lizzie you must learn to take care of dimes and the dollars will be all right."[18]

George also experienced various health problems, most likely adding to his irritability. He had spent some two and a half years in Civil War prison camps, which were notorious for causing poor health. One of his ailments was an undisclosed nasal issue; he wrote Lizzie in 1887, "The doctor burnt my nose on Sunday with a wire—<u>white hot</u>. It didn't hurt me much." George also suffered from headaches; he was relieved when he could tell Bettie, "I am very well now. I am not having headaches at work." Unfortunately, they later came back. George told Bettie "My eyes particularly—work—have made this winter a great tire to me." Perhaps part of George's problems stemmed from either the need or the use of glasses. He told Bettie, "I have spectacles—with . . . glasses—one for reading and one for seeing at a distance." He also commented on his "inflamed eyelids."[19]

More ominously, George endured a severe case of eye infection near the end of his first term. "My eyes are improving all the time," he wrote Bettie in December 1884, but by March 1885 his right eye had turned blood red, "very much inflamed" as George described it. He had to resort to covering it with handkerchiefs. He did not sound very optimistic when he told Bettie, "I fear I am going to be troubled with my eye." By February 1887 he was still having trouble, telling her, "My eyes are not well. The doctor says they are better, but I am not sure but that he is too sanguine." Later in the month he wrote that the doctor said he was "a great deal better—in fact—nearly well, but I doubt—especially I doubt whether an apparent cure will be real or lasting." He also had periodic colds, and he normally experienced a lingering cough. Perhaps his smoking and tobacco use caused those problems. He told Bettie, "I am trying to quit smoking," but admitted, "I want to smoke every moment of my life."[20]

Travel back and forth to Washington from Mississippi was also hard on the aging couple, now in their mid to late sixties. He and Bettie, when she went, would take a roundabout route by rail to Chattanooga, where they would get a room in a sleeper for the trip to Washington. Numerous letters described how tired they were after the trips, and it only got worse as they aged.[21]

The best way George could keep his mind off his troubles was to work, and he did a great deal of that. He wrote Bettie after Christmas in 1884, "I have been busy all this week except Christmas [day]." On another occasion he commented that he was "glad for a short time to escape the worry of office seekers." In another letter he wrote, "I am anxious for this summer to come as I am very tired and want to be home with you and the children." The next sentence, however, stated, "I have to go to the capitol now to do some work." George was indeed a prodigious worker. He enthusiastically worked on a special committee investigating the relationship between labor and capital during his first term, and helped produce five large volumes of evidence and testimony. In addition, he offered no less than 155 bills, motions, and amendments in his first term, and spoke frequently on a variety of issues. Senator George Hoar of Massachusetts teased George one day, saying he was afraid George would spend all night thinking, "and will have more than fifty amendments tomorrow morning."[22]

George was not just busy in the Senate during the 1880s, however. He returned home several times to argue cases before the Mississippi Supreme Court, once in 1882 and again in 1885. He also supplied legal briefs for other cases. Perhaps the climax of his legal career came when he began to argue cases before the U.S. Supreme Court. Between 1881 and 1887 George was involved in six different cases before the high court. In three of the cases George was sole counsel. He argued two cases in 1881, two in 1884, and one in 1885, with a dismissed case coming in 1887. This was impressive work for a country lawyer schooled in his friend William Cothran's law office in 1846.[23]

George's main emphasis remained the Senate, however, where he supported many measures in his first term. Like all other senators, he had pet projects that he supported with zeal. One, of course, was a general defense of the South and a specific defense of Mississippi. His heated response to Dawes showed his love for his state and his willingness to confront an alleged wrong done to Mississippi. On numerous occasions George sustained the South as well as the Confederacy. To one senator he responded, "Sir, we acknowledge no inferiority; we confess no crime; we profess no repentance; we ask no forgiveness. But we acknowledge our defeat." On another occasion, when tension between Jefferson Davis and William T. Sherman spilled over into the Senate, George supported his former colonel, president, and fellow Mississippian. "I have no fear that anything in that judgement will be adverse to the honor or patriotism of Jefferson Davis," he told the Senate. But in all his defense of Mississippi and the South, George made clear that he was again an American, continuing his policy of reconciliation begun during Reconstruction. In one speech regarding the status of Ulysses S. Grant, George spoke clearly, "I tried to make that declaration [secession] good by all the means in my power. I deplored the loss of the cause to which I was attached." But, he reminded the Senate, that nation was gone, and he was now an American senator. "The Union has been restored," he spoke. "I am now here a senator from Mississippi in a restored Union. I determined when I took my seat on this floor that on all questions of mere sentiment connected with the late civil strife not adverse to the honor or substantial interest of the people whom I represent I would vote exactly as if I had been a Union man during the war." In stating his allegiance, he encouraged his fellow Southerners to let the past go as well.[24]

Another of George's major interests in the Senate was education. He had served on the board of trustees of the University of Mississippi and on the board of trustees of the Mississippi Agricultural and Mechanical College at Starkville, which he had been very influential in founding. He served on the Senate Education and Labor Committee and used his growing influence to promote public education for all people, not just those who could afford private schools. The deplorable state of Mississippi's schools ate at his conscience. George unsuccessfully advocated such issues as refunding Southern states' tariff receipts to be used for education as well as using proceeds from reclaimed western railroad public lands. He also supported a measure that would lessen the educational burden on Mississippi, the Blair Education Bill. Northern states presented what George termed an "offering" of money to Southern states in order to raise the standard of education. George supported this offer, despite objections from other Southern senators who protested the gift as an attack on Southern honor. George specifically debated with fellow Democrats John Tyler Morgan of Alabama and Isham G. Harris of Tennessee over the issue.

On this and other occasions, George spoke about the educational needs of poor blacks as well as poor whites. Although it is unknown how sincere George was in dealing with former slaves, he at least went on public record supporting education for black citizens in Mississippi. "I want to say, Mr. President," George told the Senate, "that I should like to have the colored people of Mississippi educated far beyond what they are likely to be, even if this bill passes." He also testified before the Senate to building at least two schools for blacks in Mississippi.[25]

Another of George's pet projects was a pension for Mexican War veterans, of whom he was one. George offered bills and amendments in almost every session to create such a pension. He reminded the Senate that relatively few veterans remained alive. Armies had not been that large to begin with, and most veterans would, by 1880, be over sixty years old. Thus George offered legislation that would provide a pension for veterans who could not support themselves by manual labor. Speaking on behalf of his fellow veterans, he reminded the Senate that the Union army had pensions. "I am willing so far as I am concerned, though I was on the other side, to vote them liberal pensions," he chided. After many defeats, George succeeded in getting this bill passed into law on May 19, 1886. The aging George received a pension of $8 a month, which he faithfully gave to a widow of a veteran. He also tried valiantly to increase the amount of the pension to $12, but he was not successful.[26]

One of George's major concerns was agriculture. One colleague in the Senate, in fact, remarked, "to him the bloom of the cotton plant was more beautiful than that of the rose." Back in Mississippi, George supported the new Agricultural and Mechanical College at Starkville in order to promote the study of agriculture in the state and provide scientific solutions to farmers' problems. In Washington, he served on the Agriculture and Forestry Committee, and his background as a plantation owner and farmer served him well. His state was full of poor farmers, suffering from overproduction, international competition, and declining prices. George pushed various measures on that committee, such as silk production to allow women more of a chance to enter the economy and the antioption bill, designed to stop dealing in agricultural futures. Similarly, George avidly pushed in the Senate what became known as the Hatch Act in early 1887. This law created agricultural experiment stations associated with the land-grant institutions. By attaching the stations to universities, George wanted the money spent for labor at the stations to be given to students to allow those who could not afford college a means of obtaining a higher education. George acted as floor manager for the Agriculture and Forestry Committee in the Senate, debating and passing many amendments involving dates, money, and wording. Because of George's work on the bill, modern agricultural historian William L. Giles has argued that if passed today, the legislation would carry the name Hatch-George Act. In order to give agriculture more influence in the government, George also championed the idea of making the U.S. Agricultural Bureau an "Executive Department," or a cabinet-level agency. George complained that the department as it stood was "very much like an experimental farm run by the Government of the United States." He desired real power for agricultural interests, but was repeatedly defeated in his first term. Ironically, the bill that finally passed was not George's at all, but a similar House bill that came over to the Senate. Because of all his agitation on the issue year after year, however, George is often credited with being the "Father of the Agriculture Department." For all his efforts, he was embraced by many farmers' alliances for his "manly effort" on behalf of agriculture.[27]

George also served on the Claims Committee, and he presented many petitions. In addition, he was appointed to several temporary committees, such as the funeral committee for Representative Robert M. A. Hawk of Illinois and the Select Committee on Woman's Suffrage, where in the Senate he opposed calling for a constitutional amendment for women's suffrage, even writing a minority report to legislation supporting a woman's right to vote. He was also a member of various harbor and river improvement committees. Perhaps the most time-consuming task was a vast correspondence, which included those petitioning for appointments and recommendations for offices.[28]

Many of George's senatorial activities had one common theme: they all promoted the interests of the common workingman or farmer. George saw in his defense of Mississippi a defense of the common Southern citizen. George stressed public education for the common people, and his efforts regarding pensions showed his desire to help those who could not help themselves. His work in agriculture also demonstrated his desire for relief for the common farmer as well as aid for students. George thus quickly gained the title of Mississippi's "Great Commoner."[29]

George's rhetoric demonstrated this concern. He often spoke of the need to "protect . . . employees and servants," or the common workers. He favored changing the appointment of judges and officials to elections "by the people." On other occasions George shunned "anything from the government of the United States that is denied to the great mass of the people of this country." George also spoke vehemently, if not eloquently, on behalf of debtors and bankruptcy victims, as well as regulating interstate commerce. At times George's concern produced more than rhetoric. During a major flood in 1882, he worked with the War Department to provide supplies to help relieve the victims.[30]

Even other senators admitted George's affection for the common people. One of George's archrivals in the Senate, Republican senator George Hoar of Massachusetts, accused him of being "a great friend of the laborers," cajoling that he would lose sleep over their plight. George responded, "I do not think it is any very great discredit to a man to be a friend of the laborers; and I do not think that I shall lose any more sleep in thinking about the laborers than my friend from Massachusetts will lose in thinking about corporations and that sort of interests in this country."[31]

Racial and even gender attitudes tempered this avid support for the common man, however. He was obviously a white supremacist, his record on race relations being hardly progressive. He was a former slave owner, and he had fought to separate from the Union mainly over the issue of slavery, as he had argued in the secession convention. His Reconstruction activities were likewise racially partisan. As late as 1887 he supported a petition by Mississippi blacks to pay them $100 each to emigrate to Liberia. In reality, George realized blacks were in Mississippi to stay, and thus worked to limit what he perceived as the African American race bringing down white society. He did see the need to help blacks, mainly in an effort to ease racial tensions and make a better overall Mississippi, but he did not support lifting them up to the status of equals with white people. He thus supported education for blacks, but it was less because he cared for the former slaves and more to make a white and black Mississippi better.[32]

And George's racial bias was not directed only toward blacks. In 1882 he supported the Chinese Exclusion Act. He favored such a law because the white people of the western states desired it on racial grounds. George called the Chinese "the inferior race." Also, immigrants from China would hurt white laborers' chances to gain and retain jobs, he insisted. He spoke of the common workingman, stating "the American laborer so far has been the greatest product of our free institutions."[33]

Thus, despite some tense moments of debate, George's first term in the U.S. Senate was marked by a sincere desire to help the common man of Mississippi. Although George had relatively little success in his first term, he nevertheless emerged onto the national scene. He rose from being an obscure junior senator to a well-known senior senator holding powerful positions on several important committees, such as the Agriculture and Forestry Committee and the Judiciary Committee. But George's first Senate term was only a launching point during which he prepared for coming duties.

CHAPTER 16

"The Demands on Me Are Incessant"

Second Senate Term, 1886–1890

J. Z. George wrote a friend in the spring of 1885 about his political future. The first-term senator did not have a tremendous record as yet, although he was now the state's senior senator. But George had done nothing in his years in Washington to make the people or the legislature of the state want him ousted. The only way George would not be returned to Washington was if he chose not to be reelected. And George did not decline reelection; he let it be known that he would serve at least another term. He bluntly wrote his friend Micajah Berry, "I desire to be returned to the United States Senate—this winter—as my own successor." George asked Berry for an appraisal of his standing around Jasper County, and around the state.[1]

The senator need not have worried, because the election brought him no opposition. The legislature unanimously reelected him on January 20, 1886. George's new term would run from March 4, 1887, to March 3, 1893.[2]

As a U.S. senator, George rubbed shoulders with some of the most famous Americans of the time. During his career in the Senate, he served under five different chief executives, and he at times wrote of them in letters to Bettie. "The Mississippians went to see the President this morning," he wrote, "and we found him in good condition and very pleasant." He also wrote her about cabinet appointments and the general work of the Senate, once stating, "the Senate is doing very little—and the President sends in but few nominations." Other times could be hectic; he wrote Bettie on another occasion, "The demands on me are incessant."[3]

George continued to miss his family dearly whenever they were not with him. He often wrote Bettie such lines as, "I want you to come in at as early a day as possible." The weariness and desire to be home can be heard in his voice when he wrote Bettie, "We are now almost within 2 weeks of the end of the session—They will be very long weeks to me for I am terribly tired of being away from home 2 years. I shall head home ... after Congress adjourns unless something extraordinary shall happen."⁴

Perhaps much of George's discontent was because of his quarters. He often lived in hotels and boardinghouses, which were not very homey. "There are many nice people at the hotel," he admitted to Bettie, but he also found the accommodations meager. Fortunately, George's living conditions improved over the years, taking at least one concern off his mind. "I am very pleasantly situated," he later wrote, "the only inconvenience is near-ness to the Capitol—whereby the inducement is taken away for exercise." He often wrote of his need for physical fitness because of some ailments "caused by a failure to take proper exercise." He happily told Bettie, "yesterday, however, and the day before I took long walks, but as yet I have experienced no good from them."⁵

In February 1886, when Bettie joined him for a time, he began looking at the possibility of moving away from the boardinghouses and obtaining a place of their own. He had been reelected in January, which assured him six more years in Washington. But the house hunt took a lot out of the aging George. "I have never seen your father so tired as he is," Bettie wrote to Lizzie. George eventually bought what he described as "a neat little cottage." He loved working in his library on the second floor.⁶

But George's reclusiveness outside of work did not change. He told Bettie, who by that time had returned to Mississippi, "my solitary life is such as to make me feel very keenly your absence." He did have a few friends, however, such as one acquaintance who invited him to Christmas dinner every year. "I was invited on that day ... as usual," he wrote Bettie. "We had a nice lunch and good egg nog and the company was agreeable and light." Never an optimist and always a hermit, he definitely did not thrive on the social aspects of the city. He was, of course, blunt as well, and was often troubled. "I always take the pessimist view," he admitted to Bettie, "I am never hopeful." George's negative mental state continued to affect his physical health, and the problems with his eyes and other issues lingered into the 1890s.⁷

Surviving family letters from Washington after 1887 indicate that Bettie spent most of her time there after his first term. But even with her there, George's life was still not perfect. Late in this second term George suffered from tongue cancer, the probable result of years of chewing tobacco. Mississippi historian Dunbar Rowland has described this as "excessive use." George's earliest extant records from the 1840s and 1850s indicate a heavy use of tobacco. One of the points of complaint he had during his prison tenure was his inability to get a steady supply of tobacco. And his usage only grew as he took on increasing responsibility after the war. Even in the Senate, his colleagues were mindful of his fondness for chewing.[8]

In 1892 George had to have the cancerous tumor removed. "The doctors claim they have cut out completely the cancer," he wrote a friend in April 1892. George could only trust the doctors, saying, "I can only say I hope they are right." George described the effect: "The wound inflicted by the cutting is not completely healed; that is, whilst there is no visible sore, there remains a feeling very much as like that of a scar in the mouth." Bettie said that he had told her that his tongue "feels like it had been scalded."[9]

Bettie was relieved at the outcome of the surgery, mostly that the doctors had gotten all the cancer. She was also pleased that the "bill [was] just one hundred dollars." Later tests revealed no cancer. "The last flesh cut from his tongue," Bettie wrote Lizzie later in the summer, "was found to be sound, healthy flesh." She confided, "I am not at all uneasy, but I think he is."[10]

Whether due to health scares or not, George joined a church and became a faithful member. In his earlier years, he had not joined Bettie's church in Carrollton, but not so much because he opposed religion; he often made comments in letters about his creator or other facets of God's presence in the world. He had allowed himself to be baptized in 1867, probably more for her than anything else. But he did not join the church at Carrollton and dive wholeheartedly into church work until later in life.[11]

Whether the volatile account of his baptism in 1867 was completely true is debatable. Nevertheless, something happened to George in the late 1880s, one newspaper relating that Bettie was "finally leading him to peace in trusting the Savior whom she had served for more than fifty years." Another noted: "By the way they say he has quit cursing and joined the Baptist Church." To be sure, George suddenly became an active and faithful member of the Carrollton Baptist Church. Several events had taken place that might explain such a move. George and Bettie had moved their official residence from Jackson back to Carrollton in the late 1880s, making their final home at Cotesworth. And George increasingly spent more time away from the Senate. Upon their return to Carrollton, Bettie immediately moved her church membership from her church in Jackson back to the Carrollton congregation. She rejoined the church she had attended all those years on November 25, 1888.[12]

George then joined the church, almost a year to the date after Bettie's return. The November 24, 1889, entry in the church minutes reads, "Brother James Z. George came forward and presented a certificate from

Elder Henry Pittman showing that he had previously been baptized by Brother Pittman upon his profession of faith in the Lord Jesus Christ, and on motion Brother George was received to membership." From that day onward, when he was in town, George was a faithful member of the church, no doubt much to Bettie's delight. This new religiosity quickly became evident. While making a political speech in Carrollton on a burning question of the day, he remarked, "If I were not a member of the church I would bet that such a thing is true." One of his supporters in the crowd yelled, "Bet a little anyhow, General." George retorted, "No, I see my pastor over there, and besides I am a Christian and would not bet anyway." George also continued his charity work. A pastor told of how he would ask the church deacons to send packages to the poor with the pastor's name on them so George would not get any credit. George also often reminded them, "Be sure not to forget [former slave] Jake."[13]

George also had another project to take his mind off Senate affairs while he was away from Washington. In 1887 he built a beautiful library on the grounds of Cotesworth. At first he had a library on the north side of the main house, connected by a breezeway, but that proved too noisy with all the grandchildren constantly around. He constructed a six-sided library in the front yard. This hexagonal outbuilding was a work of art, being one of the few six-sided buildings in the state. Atop the richly adorned, six-sided pitched roof sat a six-sided cupola that offered ample light into the office. A small porch provided access to the room through the doorway. Inside, the flooring radiated outward from the center of the room, with windows on each wall offering more light inside. Perhaps most novel, six large bookcases also branched out from the walls to the center of the room, connecting with the walls at each corner. Across the library from the door was a large fireplace, and George kept his desk in the center of the room. The library, of which George was immensely proud, contained numerous congressional volumes as well as other historical as well as fiction works. George had one of the finest libraries in the state, and it was his sanctuary while he was at home.[14]

Of course, George did not get to enjoy his new library or the church in Carrollton very often, because his presence was still required in Washington most of the time. There, in his second term, he reviewed, offered, and debated the numerous bills that came through the body during the late 1880s and early 1890s. Bettie admitted, "It keeps him busy to work up with the Republicans," and confessed, "They <u>have</u> some fiery <u>times</u> there sometimes."[15]

The vast majority of George's work was done in committee. Once again, he served on the Judiciary Committee, which met on Mondays, where he used his legal experience to form constitutional and historic arguments regarding legislation. George eventually became known as one of the great constitutional authorities of the Senate. Dunbar Rowland vouched for George's ability, saying, "I have great confidence in the Senator's accuracy of statement." The *New York Times* even stated, "He [is] . . . widely respected for his great erudition on legal and constitutional questions. Probably there has been no man in the Senate during the present generation who has made greater research into constitutional questions or could discourse more profoundly upon that instrument of government. Very few constitutional questions ever arose in the Senate that he did not participate in at length in their discussion, and he talked on comparatively few other topics." And George's ability was not lost on most senators. Many spoke of his "invincible and unanswerable argument[s]."[16]

George continued to serve on the Agricultural and Forestry Committee, meeting every Friday. His interest in education was evidenced in his reassignment to the Education and Labor Committee, and he served on the Railroads Committee as well. Later in his second term George would also serve on the Immigration and the Transportation Routes to the Seaboard committees, as well as a select committee on women's suffrage and numerous conference and death committees.[17]

George's efforts in the Senate, however, were limited by frequent interruptions. One was for the 1890 Mississippi constitutional convention, which took place late in his second term. But the majority of the interruptions were for health-related reasons. For instance, in October 1888 George asked the Senate to give him leave for the remainder of the session. He also asked to be excused "by the advice of a physician" from attendance during night sessions. The senator was getting older, and the grueling pace of political life was catching up with him. There were also trips, such as a sojourn in Florida in 1888, when he and Bettie and Lizzie spent time there with other Senate families. George told the *Washington Post*, perhaps jokingly, "next to Mississippi came Florida for a warm place in his heart."[18]

Despite his frequent absences, George was able to get a lot of work done in the Senate. Most of his work was mundane, such as many relief bills and applications for constituents. During his second term, he introduced bills for relief of Mississippi churches as well as individual citizens. Given his racial attitudes and his work on behalf of whites during Reconstruction, he also ironically offered a resolution to grant back pay to former

Mississippi senator Hiram Revels, an African American. George offered the resolution, he said, "to get some back pay by a former Senator."[19]

Unlike his earlier years in Congress, the maturing senator now spoke frequently on anything that captured his attention. He could at times, as was his nature, get into acrimonious debates with Northern senators, and at times he thought it necessary to revise and explain his comments to be sure no one took them out of context or to make sure no one thought he was leveling attacks on a specific individual. Speaking of "one sentence [that] is capable of an implication which I desire to disclaim," George assured his colleagues, "I have never had occasion to believe that any Senator gave support to any measure from other motives than his conscientious convictions of what is the public good. If a contrary implication can arise from what I said on the occasion alluded to I desire to disown it, and to express my regret that any language used by me in debate might be construed as reflecting upon any member of this body." He could also be self-deprecating; he once warned the Senate he would speak the next day instead of that afternoon, chiding that "after the very able and eloquent speech [about to be] made by the Senator from California, there will be little disposition on the part of the Senate to listen to anybody, and especially to me."[20]

While much of George's work was mundane, there were a few exciting ceremonial functions. He participated in counting the electoral votes in February 1893, and actually took Bettie to the House gallery to watch. Of course, the event was more exciting and notable to him because a Democrat, Grover Cleveland, was being elected for only the second time in three decades. Bettie was not so enthralled; "I do not care to see it again," she wrote, although she did "enjoy very much" attending the Senate debates as a spectator in the gallery. The Georges also participated in the various inaugural festivities.[21]

On several occasions George took part in debates concerning major issues facing the nation. Monetary policy, election reform, and trusts all captured his attention, and he gave long speeches for or against those major bills. In January 1889, for instance, he gave a strong defense of a low tariff and states' rights regarding trade. He derided the high protective tariff bill in the Senate, because appropriations bills were supposed to be started in the House, cajoling, "possibly it might be considered technically as an amendment to the House bill." George described the legislation as the "confessedly and avowedly highly, not to say enormously, protective [bill]."[22]

George began his tariff speech by stating his opposition to protective tariffs. "I believe a protective tariff to be unjust," he spoke. "I am opposed to a protective tariff further than such incidental protection as may result from a fair adjustment of revenue duties," he argued. The South was getting slighted; "agriculture is made to bear the burdens of this protective system."[23]

Yet George fully understood that the high tariff would pass, and thus he put his major effort into watering it down. He voted for several amendments while maintaining he would ultimately vote against the whole bill. "I oppose it with all my power; and yet when I see, when I am certain it will be adopted, I strive to make it less unjust, less unequal, and therefore less unconstitutional, but extending the benefits to those who are compelled to bear the burdens," he explained. Thus George issued what he termed his "doctrine"—that "if restitution for a wrong done be right, then this is right." Basically, he wanted the South compensated in the tariff, or, if not, then duties on certain agricultural items should be lowered.[24]

George's "doctrine" sparked a humorous exchange with a fellow senator, Republican Preston B. Plumb of Kansas. The senator asked George if he thought it was legal to pick another man's pocket after his own had been picked by a different person. George said no, but it was entirely just for a man to pick the pocket of the man who picked his and thus reclaim the lost goods. George turned back to seriousness as he drew to a close. An advocate of the New South, George described

> the devastation of war, the destruction of all the capital which had been accumulated in our section for one hundred years all gone; and now, in the struggle for resuscitation, when we want to establish factories with our limited means we find a bar in the shape of a high protective duty upon manufacturing machinery. I ask senators if that is right. In raising cotton we submit to all the taxation you impose upon us. We receive nothing in return. We want to manufacture. We are destitute to a large extent of capital necessary to compete with New England, and we ask that we may be allowed to introduce into our own section the instruments by which we may go into the manufacturing business.[25]

One of the biggest issues that George worked on during his second term was the Sherman Antitrust Bill in 1890, which sought to limit the effects of monopolies in business. Unlike most other Democrats, George became extremely involved, offering several amendments to make the legislation stronger, in his view. According to one government report, George "wrest[ed] control of the bill from Senator Sherman" and had it referred to the Judiciary Committee instead of the Commerce Committee, where George could personally oversee it. Eventually, Sherman agreed to include some of George's language, though not all of George's amendments were accepted. Nevertheless, when it passed, it had George's imprint and support. Such leading historians as Samuel Eliot Morison and Henry Steele Commager have referred to George as an actual coauthor of the legislation.[26]

George's efforts to lower the tariff and regulate corporations and monopolies demonstrated that he was indeed a commoner looking out for the masses in Mississippi. Many of the state's newspapers and politicians called him variations of the term "Great Commoner," such as "Old Commoner" or just plain "the Commoner." Most such comments said that George was Mississippi's commoner, as opposed to William Jennings Bryan, who was more well known nationally as the "Great Commoner."[27]

Some of George's other efforts in his second term fit into his states' rights position. One such major speech regarded pending election reform, a heated topic of the day in the face of Jim Crow segregation throughout the South, and particularly in Mississippi. As the Senate debated the Lodge Elections Bill regarding federal elections, which would basically return the nation to Reconstruction policies, also known as the Force Bill, George gave an extended speech in December 1890 on the subject. Foremost, he took the Senate down a historical walk through state sovereignty, going back all the way to the Declaration of Independence and Articles of Confederation to show how various states, particularly Massachusetts, where his major debate opponent hailed from, were very vocal about their sovereign rights. George then discussed the historic period under the Constitution, giving examples from many different states.[28]

George needled Massachusetts Republican senator George F. Hoar, who was one of the main supporters of the bill. This election reform, George argued, "will not affect the internal affairs of Massachusetts, but it has been so arranged that, whilst the Representatives from Massachusetts shall inflict the blow, it will fall only on the people of other States." He also argued, in light of his historical research, that many Northern states held their sovereignty dear, and "we have fallen on both strange and on evil times if great States shall disregard the teachings of the fathers and reverse their own traditions and principles in assuming a power which their teachings and their traditions and principles denounce as a mere political trick of a desperate political party." George concluded, "the bill is in direct conflict with the aims and purposes of the Constitution as explained by its framers." And, George argued, "it goes the whole length of that spoliation of the rights of the states."[29]

Warming to his subject, George argued that the bill "present[ed] very grave and important constitutional questions for our consideration." He attacked what the bill contained concerning credentials for canvassing boards, certificates of election, and appointments of election supervisors. George yielded at times to other senators, but as he began to draw to a close after hours on the floor he refused another senator's request to yield. "I am pretty nearly through. I feel like the weary traveler who is almost in sight of the promised land, and would like to make a landing," he said. After a few more minutes, George reported, "With these remarks, Mr. President, I submit this bill on my part to the consideration of the Senate."[30]

George played an important role in defeating for a time the legislation, not on an up or down vote, but on a brilliant procedural move. Democrats sided with Republican silver senators, who, together, had enough votes to call up a finance bill for consideration. If that happened, the Elections Bill would likely not return to the floor for consideration, effectively killing it. Thus Democrats and silver Republicans concocted a plan to have everyone there at a certain time when fewer Elections Bill Republican proponents would be in the chamber. A Democrat was also presiding at that specific time. At a prearranged moment, George, who had the floor, yielded to a silver Republican, who made a motion to bring up the finance bill. "For an instant there was absolute silence in the chamber," the *New York Times* reported. "Everybody knew what the motion meant." Force Bill author George Hoar of Massachusetts, his face "flushed until it was scarlet," jumped to his feet and objected, saying the silverites could not bring up another bill while George held the floor. George innocently responded, "But I yield for the Senator's motion." Hoar then argued George would have to give up the floor, but George stated he just yielded to allow another bill to be brought forward. Democrat Isham G. Harris, who was presiding while the Republican vice president was at lunch, quickly dismissed Hoar's argument, and the Elections Bill was pushed backward on the calendar. Although the Republicans were able to get the bill back to the floor later in January, a similar procedure killed it for good later in the month. The Force Bill, thus delayed by George's yielding, ultimately suffered an inglorious fate, killed by a procedural move rather than a vote. No doubt George was ecstatic at not only landing a mortal blow to the hated Force Bill but also to one of his least favorite colleagues, Senator Hoar of Massachusetts.[31]

Throughout his second term George remained a steadfast defender of states' rights and the old Confederacy. He defended a bill, ironically offered by a Northern senator, to allow former Confederates into the civil service. Likewise, in debating the use of the word "nation" in a bill, George defended the word, but added an antebellum states' rights caveat, saying, "I take my constitutional law on that subject from a great judge, Chief Justice Taney," the author of the famous Dred Scott decision in 1857.[32]

Perhaps his most telling states' rights speech came in the debate on inquests under national authority, which immediately triggered George's states' rights defense. "I had hoped that I would have no occasion whilst I had a seat in this body to say anything on the sectional questions which the debates during the present session have brought to bear." When he took his seat, he said, "It was my fixed purpose" that no one could say he had "in any degree contributed to the sectional bitterness." With his state's honor in jeopardy, however, he delivered a long and detailed speech regarding Northern state constitutions, the black suffrage question, and race relations. He adamantly stated that whites would "carry on the struggle for the preservation of their civilization."[33]

Despite his support of states' rights, George was not of the Bourbon opinion, excluding retaining white supremacy, that desired a return to the Old South ways. He had given the Confederacy all he had and never admitted its wrongs. But he did let go of the past and accepted federal authority after the war. He related, "the supreme authority of the Union has been recognized and obeyed," and continued, "I hope no such calamity may again befall any portion of the American people." George also stated he intended to vote "without reference to any position that I may have occupied in the late civil war. I have endeavored since the close of that war, since I took an oath of allegiance to the United States, to discharge my duty as an American citizen without reference to past conflicts, without reference to past jealousies and strifes." He also waxed eloquent in remembering a lifestyle gone but not forgotten:

> The world moves and we must move with it, keeping abreast with all the practical questions which may arise and seeking their solution for the interest and welfare of the people. I will not pass my life in a dreamy contemplation of the beauty and excellencies of obsolete theories, now mere abstractions, and in picturing the benefits and glories which would have come from their observance. It is enough to know that they are no longer potent for the good or evil of the Union. They

are gone, gone forever, and while I may indulge a tear over the tomb in which they are reposed, I will not pass my life in erecting altars to them or in ministering at altars erected by others.[34]

Despite the numerous clashes with Republicans, George's service in the U.S. Senate was by the last decade of the nineteenth century reaching respectable territory. He was no longer the quiet, timid, first-term junior senator. He was now a multiterm senior senator who had won the respect, if not friendship, of many colleagues. He had spoken on numerous issues, always with force and logic rather than overblown oratory, and fellow senators were coming to the conclusion that he was a gifted debater. In the middle of this second term, George would show that ability even more in perhaps his most notable action as a U.S. senator.

CHAPTER 17

"The Central Figure of the Convention"

Constitutional Convention, 1890

J. Z. George rose in the U.S. Senate on August 6, 1890, to ask for something fairly uncommon in that body—a long leave of absence. Short leaves were common, mostly for sickness or family issues. George himself had received a number of those. This would be a long-term absence, however, but to George it was necessary. "Mr. President," George drawled in his Mississippi accent, "it is necessary for me to be absent from the Senate for an indefinite time, and I ask leave." None of the senators present objected, so George's petition was granted.[1]

While George had been sick in the past, this new request was not for that issue; it was political. Mississippi was on the verge of writing a new constitution in 1890, and George was a major supporter of the effort. He wanted to be there in order to help sway the delegates, particularly on certain important issues.

The main problem for George and other Democrats in Mississippi was that the present constitution, created back in 1868 during the height of Reconstruction, was viewed as a thoroughly Republican and radical document that, along with the Fifteenth Amendment, allowed blacks the right to vote. Few Democrats had been part of that convention, which had been dominated by "carpetbaggers," "scalawags," and blacks. The Democrats even named it the "Black and Tan Convention." After 1875 and the purging of Republican power in the state in the years thereafter, Democrats sought to work within that old constitution to keep their power, sometimes through intimidation and extralegal means against black voters. One Mississippian described the effect as "simply drifting, and using all manner of extra legal schemes and contrivances."[2]

The idea of a new constitution for the state of Mississippi to legally (at least through state laws) keep masses of black voters disenfranchised had emerged in the early 1880s, although little had been done to promote the idea. By 1886 a bill calling for a convention meandered its way into the legislature, but was not adopted. In 1888 the state legislature passed a similar bill, but Governor Robert Lowry vetoed it. George was actually against the idea early on. He wrote Governor Lowry in 1888, "At my age I naturally shrink from movements tending to excitement or division among our people." But as the decade of the 1880s ended, more attention came to the issue, and George himself became one of the major supporters of the effort. One recent historian of Gilded Age Mississippi, Stephen Cresswell, has concluded that George's constituents changed his mind. The pending Elections Bill in the Senate also swayed him toward change.[3]

In 1889 the calling of a convention became the central focus of that fall's gubernatorial and legislative elections. George became deeply involved. He not only recruited friends to run for the legislative positions, but he also canvassed the state in support of the convention, speaking in favor of those candidates who supported it. He wrote open letters to newspapers, spoke to crowds all over the state, and even made a formal speech to a crowd in the House chamber of the capitol in Jackson. One particular speech illustrated George's sentiments: "The present constitution, though many of the original most obnoxious laws have been amended or thrown out, was the handiwork of the most corrupt government that ever disgraced any State of this Union, and I believe it is time it should disappear from the statute books, head, body, and soul."[4]

In taking such a stance, George was at odds with many of his fellow Democrats, but that was nothing new to the often-independent senator. "There are men who predict that no good can come from the Convention," George wrote Agricultural and Mechanical College president and future fellow delegate Stephen D. Lee in July 1890. Most notable among the opponents were L. Q. C. Lamar, now on the U.S. Supreme Court, and George's colleague in the Senate, Edward C. Walthall. Governor Lowry had also been against the idea, even vetoing the legislature's call for a convention in 1888. The divergence in Democratic thought, as exemplified by the differences between Senators George and Walthall, concerned the central issue of the new constitution: the race factor. Almost all Democrats were supportive of white supremacy and rule, but they differed on how to maintain it. George and his faction supported a new constitution that would disenfranchise blacks, thus reducing the need for voter manipulation and violence and thus legally, at least according to the state's constitution, and peacefully assure white control of state politics. The anticonvention side, including Lamar and Walthall, saw much danger in writing a new constitution, thinking it could only cause more problems that it would solve.⁵

Reasons for not wanting a new convention were many, with some arguing that the people of the state would not support a new document. "You are much mistaken in supposing that the people have rejected anything," George wrote Lee just before the convention. "They expect the Constitution to <u>save them</u> from negro <u>domination</u> and any plan that may be agreed on will be accepted by the people." The primary cause for concern was the reaction of federal agencies and officials to a new constitution. Much like during Reconstruction, there were many dominant Northern politicians just waiting for a chance to return Reconstruction policies to Mississippi and the other Southern states. The Elections Bill then pending in Congress was just such an example. For that reason, no other former Confederate state had tested the waters of creating a new constitution that would assure white rule. The main roadblock that worried Walthall and the anticonvention forces was the Fifteenth Amendment, which stated that no state could deny the right to vote because of race. Tampering with the state constitution in the effort to keep black Mississippians from voting might only bring the federal hand of disapproval and open up an unwanted crisis. Mississippi was doing just fine the way things were, opponents argued; there was no need to stir up emotions unnecessarily.⁶

George believed that a new state constitution was needed, however, and that a system of suffrage clauses could be put in place that would effectively keep the power in white hands even while working within the framework of the federal constitution and congressional opposition. He had candidly written to Governor Lowry in 1888 that any constitution needed to "give the political power of the State to the white race." Yet George was respectful of federal law; he had taken an oath after the war to always support it. "Our oaths to support those provisions," George wrote, "must be sacredly observed; and for one, whether in office or in private life, I propose to redeem this solemn pledge in letter and in spirit." In an open letter to the *Vicksburg Herald*, George wrote, "We must obey this Constitution or violate our oaths already taken. That the Constitution in any part of it may be wrong does not relieve us from this obligation. That any particular part of it was placed there by force, or fraud, does not relieve us so long as it remains a part of the Constitution." But there were ways around that constitution, George argued. In speaking to a crowd of citizens in the House chamber in October 1889, he related, "Our chief duty when we meet in Convention, is to devise such measures, consistent with the Constitution of the United States, as will enable us to maintain a home government, under the control of the white people of the State." To George, hard work and careful action could produce a legal yet white-tilted state constitution. And he expected to lead that effort.[7]

George reserved to the states the right to limit the right of suffrage, which had been done for centuries (and is still being done today—as with age, for example). Issues such as age, property ownership, mental state, gender, and others had been used to decide who could vote throughout the years. George made it plain that blacks in Mississippi had rights as citizens, but he thought that they were not capable of knowing for whom or what they were voting, as were many whites, or of running the government. Thus George began to toy with the idea of restricting voting rights that would actually disenfranchise many whites as well as blacks. One contemporary described George making "a patriotic appeal to the white men of the State to make a sacrifice, if necessary, in order to elevate and purify the electoral body of the State."[8]

The hard work paid off, one historian arguing that George's support guaranteed the movement's success. The 1889 election was a landslide in favor of the convention. A majority of state representatives and senators elected that fall supported the convention, and the new governor, John M. Stone, who had served in the same office back in the 1870s, also approved of it. In February 1890 the legislature passed, and the governor signed, legislation for the convention to convene at noon on August 12, 1890.[9]

Statewide election of the 134 delegates took place in July. One black contemporary, John Roy Lynch, remembered in his memoirs: "In order to take no chances and run no risks, the senator [George] had himself nominated and elected a member of the convention." George was elected as the Fourth District's at-large delegate, and was easily the convention's most prominent member. His knowledge of Washington politics and the law would certainly be beneficial to the delegates as they worked, supposing as they did that some in Congress and the courts would question the document produced at the convention.[10]

The main issue was suffrage, and much as during Reconstruction when he had to walk a fine line between stopping the black vote and bringing down the wrath of the federal government on Mississippi, so again George had to tread lightly. He knew that there was a larger audience watching. Whatever he and the other delegates did in Jackson would have to be acceptable to Congress and probably the Supreme Court in Washington. George thus began his convention work even before he left Washington.[11]

George wrote out suffrage clauses to take with him to Jackson. Perhaps he was thinking of Lamar and his prewriting of the secession ordinance before that convention even began in January 1861. But George had additional reasons for going ahead and writing his proposals. There were cracks developing in the Democratic facade over how to proceed with disenfranchising blacks, and several prominent plans concerning apportionment had already been put forward. Most consideration went to two ideas, one of which became known as George's plan while the other came from George's friend and old ally for decades, Josiah A. P. Campbell. George discussed the apportionment issues over the summer, but he kept his larger franchise ideas to himself for the time being.[12]

George was thinking in the largest context of all. Before he left Washington, he had several of the most prominent and respected members of the U.S. Senate look at his ideas on paper. He was testing the waters, knowing full well he might have to defend the new constitution upon his return. Senator David Turpie of Indiana remembered George's careful action:

> Some time before he left Washington on this service he had, after long reflection, and upon great consideration, drafted a proposed clause in the constitution upon the right of suffrage. This draft he submitted, for inspection and examination, to a few of his Senatorial colleagues, upon the single question of its constitutionality, whether there was anything in its terms in conflict with the Constitution of the United States. Receiving for answer, without dissent, that the clause in question was not in conflict with the Federal Constitution, he carried the draft of it with him upon his journey home.[13]

It was a reunion of sorts when George walked into the House chamber in Jackson that August 12. Almost thirty years earlier, he had attended the state's secession convention in that same chamber with some of the very men present at this 1890 convention. Delegates John A. Blair, Walter L. Keirn, and Thomas D. Isom had been minor players in the secession convention. Two more prominent members of the earlier convention were also there, including George's former law partner, Wiley P. Harris. James L. Alcorn, the Whig leader in the antisecession movement and Reconstruction Republican governor and senator, was also there amid all the lifelong Democrats. Alcorn always had a way of being whatever he needed to be at the time, which raised George's ire. Also present were other state luminaries, such as Edward Mayes, with whom George had recently had the spat over education. David Thomas Guyton, who had been one of George's bunkmates at Johnson's Island during the Civil War, was also a delegate. Former Confederate generals William T. Martin, Winfield S. Featherston, and Stephen D. Lee were there as well. Tellingly, only one African American and only a handful of Republicans were delegates.[14]

George's role in the convention has been debated over the years. One contemporary Mississippi member of Congress reported he was "easily the leading spirit in this convention composed of many of our ablest men." A recent historian has echoed those sentiments, saying George was the "most influential member of the coming convention." A newspaper journalist of the 1960s labeled George "The Father of Mississippi's Constitution." Many go so far as to claim that George was the actual author of the entire document. On the other hand, Mississippi historian Dunbar Rowland has written that George was "an able and influential delegate to the convention, but did not dominate it, as sometimes asserted." Perhaps all are right. George was extremely influential, but he chose to serve in a reserved manner. His main focus, after all, was black suffrage, but he did not demand a hearing on that issue immediately. One observer noted, "He had wisely . . . refrained from proposing at the outset any particular scheme, or plan, for regulating the suffrage, and accordingly, he occupied a position in respect to the subject in which he could use his influence in any direction, and according to the exigencies of the occasion." A U.S. senator marveled at his timing, stating George "at the proper time offered it [his prewritten clauses] as a section in the new constitution."[15]

George's behind-the-scenes power was seen immediately, after the organization and election of officers. The elected president, S. S. Calhoon, appointed the standing committees. Despite the fact that Calhoon was unhappy because George had voted for his opponent for president, he nevertheless put George on the suffrage committee. The senator thus had the clear way to sway the action as it moved through the Elective Franchise, Apportionment and Elections Committee.[16]

Although George chose to work behind the scenes on the suffrage effort, he was openly active in the other deliberations of the convention, sometimes showing his quirkiness at refusing to vote on certain issues and making sure a statement as to why he did so appeared in the record. His Senate colleagues were well acquainted with his detailed eccentricity, and now his fellow delegates saw it, too. He served on several committees besides the franchise body, such as the committees dealing with the public printer, militia, temperance and liquor traffic, and rules. The militia committee was made up of such former general officers as George, Alcorn, Lee, Featherston, and Martin. George also offered resolutions on matters such as seating in the convention, rules, the legislature, meeting times, a bill of rights, and the judiciary, including the state supreme court. He also made a motion to allow Senator Walthall to attend the convention, and Walthall was "very cordially greeted."[17]

Other than the franchise, the major arena in which George participated was in regulating corporations within the state, an obvious outgrowth of his work on the Sherman Antitrust Act in the U.S. Senate. George offered a series of six sections to get the debate started in the deliberations, and later provided numerous provisions and amendments to the committee's work on the issue. One historian of the convention has gone so far as to say his "views dominated the convention's actions in regard to corporations."[18]

By far, however, George's main effort concerned the black vote, and he worked within the committee to deal first with apportionment. Opponents of the prevailing ideas said the committee gave more representation to white counties than black. A major debate thus occurred because white delegates from black counties were not interested in giving up their power. George brokered a deal by which the legislature would be increased in size, with the extra delegates all coming from white counties. Voting representation would be allotted according to voting population rather than total population, which gave white areas more representation. Several white areas in black counties were also gerrymandered into new districts.[19]

Apportionment did not receive much national attention because everyone understood at that time that the way a state established its districts was entirely up to the state itself. No one would question that provision. But not so with the next item. At just the right time in the deliberations, when the ideas on what to do seemed to be deadlocked, George offered his thoughts as a compromise. The central piece, in addition to a poll tax that had been in operation previously, was the new idea of an "understanding clause." One Mississippi congressman stated it "was devised by the genius of Senator George as a compromise, and without it it may be doubted whether any agreement could have been reached by the convention." One of George's fellow senators related how "it was adopted, after full debate, in very nearly the text and terms of the original draft, and is now a part of the organic law of the State."[20]

The clause itself read: "Sec. 244. On and after the first day of January, A. D., 1892, every elector shall, in addition to the foregoing qualifications, be able to read any section of the Constitution of this State; or he shall be able to understand the same when read to him, or give a reasonable interpretation thereof. A new registration shall be made before the next ensuing election after January the first, A. D., 1892." Basically George argued that a voter had to know what he was voting on and how that related to the state's law. The unstated idea was that most blacks were not competent enough to understand the constitution, while most whites were. Even more clandestine was the idea that the official doing the testing had wide latitude in passing or failing any particular applicant; he could easily give unfair questions to blacks or unfairly grade them. It was ingenious and vague, but it was constitutional, George believed, and made it possible to eliminate most black voters while keeping white ones.[21]

George swayed many in the convention no doubt through back-room negotiation, but he also gave a two-hour speech concerning suffrage on September 16. One Mississippian noted how he "explained to them the grave necessity of protecting the future of the State by new constitutional enactments." George laid out his plan, and proceeded to back it up with logic and argument. "The Negro has guaranteed rights," George concluded his speech to great applause, "but one of these is not the right of destroying the civilization of Mississippi." "When he concluded that memorable address," one observer noted, "opposition had vanished, and unity of purpose had taken the place of difference and discord." Newspapers applauded the effort, one saying, "It is conceded that he rose to the height of the occasion. Senator George is the central figure of the Convention."[22]

But not everyone was enthusiastic about the new idea. Several opposition newspapers in Mississippi decried the understanding clause. Likewise, not all delegates gave in to George, and some even challenged him. After George spoke somewhat harshly against the Judiciary Committee's recommendation regarding the Supreme Court's jurisdiction, which one newspaper reported had the Judiciary Committee "squirming under the lash," one of the members of that committee, J. W. Fewell, stated George was "seeking popularity at the expense of his professional brethren." An incensed George rose quickly and stated he was not at all judging his brethren or seeking popularity, and that he was proud of his profession. "Everything I have achieved in life," he stated, "I owe to my connection with the legal fraternity." George resumed his seat, but Fewell accused George again. One newspaper reported, "here Senator George, livid with rage, rose again and said, 'I denounce it; I denounce the statement.'" Chaos broke out as "the members gathered near the disputants, expecting a physical encounter," the newspaper reported. Fewell stated there would be no quarrel and asked that "I . . . be permitted to proceed without further interruption." George responded, "Well, let me alone then" as he resumed his seat. The chamber erupted in laughter.[23]

The convention ended on November 1, with George fittingly making the last motion to print the president's address to the delegates along with the journal of the convention. When George left the capitol, he did so knowing that the easy part had been done. Now he had to go back to Washington and defend the new constitution, and its understanding clause, before the Congress or the Supreme Court, or both. He realized the real work was just beginning.[24]

CHAPTER 18

"I Will Correct Them at the Proper Time"

Defense, 1890–1891

When the Mississippi constitutional convention ended in early November, Senator George went home to Carrollton for a few days before returning to Washington and the political battles that awaited him. While at Cotesworth, he oversaw Lizzie's wedding to Dr. Thomas R. Henderson, which took place on November 12, 1890. There George showed his abrasiveness yet again. The wedding was to take place at "high noon," and the bride-to-be and others were hurriedly preparing for the affair while guests and relatives gathered. George asked Lizzie when she was going to get "old Jake," George's former slave who had remained on the plantation and had been a steady friend through the years. George was partial to the old man, who had buried the family silver during the war and had helped care for Bettie and the children while he was away. Lizzie told him she did not have time to go see him, whereupon George scolded, "You will take time! There has never been a wedding in my house at which old Jake has not carved and to which he has not been bidden, personally, by the bride." A distraught Lizzie hurried to Jake's place nearby and impatiently waited while the old man shined his shoes and brushed his dress coat. The wedding did not take place at high noon, but neither Jake nor the senator seemed too distressed about it.[1]

After the wedding festivities, George and Bettie hurried to Washington for the start of the next session of Congress in early December. George had missed much of the first session of the Fifty-first Congress because of his participation in the constitutional convention. As expected, as soon as the second session of that Congress convened in December 1890, the new Mississippi constitution became a favorite target. The main reason it was so prominent was because the Senate was debating the famed Federal Elections Bill, also known as the Force Bill. As noted earlier, George made his thoughts known in a long speech on the Force Bill in mid-December.

He listened with growing impatience as Republican after Republican senator castigated the new Mississippi constitution, using it as an example of why election regulation reform was needed. Having heard all he could stand, George decided to defend his state and its new constitution. He alerted his enemies, "Go on with your mistakes and I will correct them at the proper time."[2]

George took the floor on December 31, 1890, in the first of three long days of defending the constitution. He began by acknowledging the "acrimonious debate and severe criticism" the Republican senators had heaped on the document, and laid the foundation for his argument by asserting first that Mississippi was equal to the other states. "Sir," George began, "Mississippi is a State in the Union. She stands to-day on an equal footing with any other State in the American Union. She has the same rights, the same faculties, the same powers of local self-government that any other State has." He also asserted that suffrage regulation was entirely a state issue as long as it was not in violation of the federal constitution.[3]

With that groundwork done, George examined the historic as well as modern constitutions of every state except New York, for which he had no data at the time. He demonstrated that each state had deprived blacks of voting and other rights until recent times. He illustrated how property, legal, social, and monetary issues were used to keep voting rights in white hands. It was not by choice, but only the Fifteenth Amendment, he insisted, that had caused these states to allow blacks to vote. George lambasted what he called the hypocrisy of the Northern senators now wanting to tell Mississippi how to regulate suffrage.[4]

As George reached each state, the effect could be seen throughout the chamber. If those states' senators were not on the floor, they soon appeared. George kept them on the defensive by engaging them in debate and asking them about the history of their own constitutions. Most could not answer his questions, tacitly admitting that George knew more about their own state constitutions than they did. Admittedly George caught each senator off guard, but it nevertheless evidenced that George knew what he was talking about. More than a few senators came back later and asked George to recognize them, allowing them to supply some date or action George had requested of them. The debate soon took on the look of pupils doing their homework and reporting back to the teacher what they had found. George was in firm control.[5]

As George went through state after state, several senators engaged him, mostly Northern Republican senators Joseph R. Hawley of Connecticut,

George F. Hoar of Massachusetts, James F. Wilson of Iowa, John C. Spooner of Wisconsin, George F. Edmunds of Vermont, and Joseph N. Dolph of Oregon. George remained unruffled, and got under the skins of some of them. He seemed to take special delight in needling Connecticut's senator Hawley, saying he respected Connecticut, which was "great in intelligence, great in virtue, great in everything in the world except its territory." Later in the debate George asserted that Connecticut was not fair in its apportionment, saying, "I suppose they do not count votes but they weigh votes up there," an obvious slap at the rotund Hawley. At another time George got Hawley to admit that Connecticut people were involved in the slave trade, Hawley acknowledging that some people will sell anything that other people will buy. George retorted, "especially will a man from New England do that thing." Hawley responded, "I think I shall get even on that after a while," to which George responded, "I reckon you will. It is not very hard, Mr. President, to get even with me."6

George worked hard to show that Northern states historically had no justification for criticizing Mississippi's race relations in terms of electoral suffrage. One Northern senator fought back: "The Senator seems determined to prove that Mississippi has got up to where New England was one hundred years ago. We will admit that." George acidicly responded, "I have sometimes thought it would be better for the country if New England was where she was one hundred years ago. Not all advance is progress; not all movement is improvement." Similarly, when Senator Wilson of Iowa debated George, the Mississippian quipped, "We have wasted enough time upon Iowa."7

George soon finished the history part of his lecture, which, he admitted, was done "with some prolixity and some weariness to myself and I fear also to the Senate." But he was hardly through. Convinced he had clearly established that Northerners believed in "the utter incapacity of this unfortunate [black] race for self-government," George moved beyond the Fifteenth Amendment. He then dealt with the two major problems mentioned by Northern senators about Mississippi's constitution: one, it was vague and could allow fraud and, of course, black disqualification from voting, and two, that the understanding clause was in the subjective hands of a single registrar.8

George sought to show that there was just as much laxity, vagueness, and possibility for fraud in other constitutions as in Mississippi's. For example, Minnesota's and Wisconsin's constitutions required a court to find voters of mixed blood competent. Vermont's constitution required voters to be "of quiet, peaceable behavior." "It is all right, all fair, all in accord with the Constitution of the United States, all in strict accord with the grand principles of free American institutions for Minnesota to have a court to determine upon the competency of a voter," George thundered. "But if Mississippi should take a step in that direction it is treason to the Constitution of the United States; it is a fraud." George then hit again his favorite target, Connecticut, which brought the absent Hawley to the floor once more. Connecticut required voters to be of "good moral quality." The two debated Connecticut's history again, with Hawley trying to make George seem less convincing by saying, "The Senator is a very promising young student, but he needs a little guidance occasionally." George jabbed back, "I like to be guided." At one point after Hawley had explained something that favored George's argument, he responded, "So much the better, Mr. President." On another occasion, he quipped, "Now the distinguished Senator helps me out again."[9]

George also targeted Hawley on his second point, since the Connecticut senator had been loud about chastising the Mississippi constitution for allowing a single registrar to decide whether the potential voter understood the constitution. George challenged him to find anywhere in the new document where a registrar had that power. George asserted that Hawley erred "from a misconception, from hurry and haste, and from taking the slanders of the enemies of Mississippi, he assumes as a fact that which has no foundation whatever." To further weaken Hawley's position, George then went into a tirade about gerrymandering, which had had its birth in Connecticut and was often used to keep Republicans in power.[10]

Connecticut was not George's only target, however. Vermont's senator Edmunds had complained that Mississippi's constitution had not been put to the people of Mississippi for a vote, but George showed that several of Vermont's constitutions had not either, nor had the U.S. Constitution. "Now, if the people of Vermont could frame a constitution without submitting it to the people, I submit that the people of Mississippi have the same right," George argued.[11]

After George had spent several hours on his feet, he determined to finish the next day. Senator Edmunds asked him to yield, and George responded, "I am very much used up by fatigue and shall be glad to hear the Senator." He did so with the understanding that he would have the floor back the next day. But the Republicans switched pending bills on him, bringing up the "Financial Bill." George gave way out of custom, but also probably because he had felt ill for several days, and the break would give him more time to recover. Bettie, in fact, wrote Lizzie in early January, "Your father is not well atall and is taking medicine."[12]

The first opportunity George had to renew his Mississippi constitution speech came during the Democratic filibuster of the Force Bill on January 19, 1891. He took the floor and summarized his argument of several weeks earlier, that Northern states had denied blacks the right to vote, serve in the militia, and serve on juries. It took the Fifteenth Amendment, not state choice, to change that. He also summarized how some Northern states' constitutions had fewer guiding principles than Mississippi's in determining who could vote. From that point, George continued to show how Northern states were biased and prejudiced in their modern constitutions, obviously covering new ground he had researched in the intervening weeks. He brought gerrymandering up again, this time in New Jersey, New York, and Massachusetts. He then pointed out the most recent vague constitution to be adopted, that of Idaho, which had recently passed through Congress. George quoted how voters in Idaho could not be "idiotic or insane," which left a lot of room for maneuver. There were also stipulations about bigamy or polygamy. "What a wide field," George argued.[13]

After disposing of the state constitutions, George turned to the vagueness in the Reconstruction acts and amendments. For example, the Fourteenth Amendment disqualified anyone who had "given aid" to the Confederacy. George asked who would decide who had given aid. George then made the point that Mississippi's 1868 constitution had not allowed appeal from disenfranchisement, which the 1890 document did. George also looked at Reconstruction-era speeches and insisted that famous Republicans such as Preston King, Thaddeus Stevens, William Seward, and even President Abraham Lincoln, among others, had not wanted black suffrage.[14]

After several more hours on his feet, George once again began tiring, and he gave the floor to Senator Walthall, who engaged Hawley. Feeling rested, George returned and closed his arguments for the day, meeting charges that he was "the author of this alleged devilment." He argued that Mississippi's constitution was no more lax, unfair, or problematical than those of many other states. "You have assailed her, you have made her the object of your ridicule, you have made her the object of your poisoned darts of calumny and defamation," George declared, but through it all he maintained that the Mississippi constitution actually "is an enlargement of the right to vote, and not a restriction upon it." In explanation, he maintained that many constitutions, including Mississippi's old document, required people to be able to read; now this one stated that people who could not read but who could understand the constitution could vote. With that, the tired senator gave up the floor with the understanding he would have it again the next day.[15]

On January 20 George returned to the attack. He summarized his speech of the day before, stating again that the constitutions of Connecticut, Vermont, and Idaho were more vague on suffrage requirements than Mississippi's and that Reconstruction laws and "pet constitutions" set up in Southern states had been so as well. He again insisted that senators had told lies about the Mississippi constitution, saying "the Senators on the other side who have ignorantly—I measure my words on this subject—who have ignorantly, without understanding or attempting to understand the constitution of Mississippi, seen proper to cast reflections." George thus spent a great deal of time again refuting what he considered lies about the constitution, asking that the entire document be printed verbatim in the record, "and not in the fine type in which extraneous matter is usually printed," which "nobody will read." George threatened to read the entire document into the record if there was objection to including it in larger type. No one objected. George concluded that "if anything is plain it is plain that every single criticism made upon that constitution is founded in error."[16]

To conclude his three days of speaking, George touted the best parts of the new constitution, "which ought to commend it to the favorable consideration of the people of Mississippi and of all persons who take an interest in good constitutional enactments." George noted such advances as the inclusion of the denial of the right to secede, the right to bear arms, no double jeopardy, and many other attributes.[17]

George then finished by saying that the Mississippi constitution was a matter "so purely personal; or, rather, I will not say personal, but so purely a matter which concerns a State which I have the honor in part to represent." He went on: "I have endeavored to do my duty to that noble State in asserting her right to make her own constitution; but I suppose, sir, that still misrepresentation, abuse, vilification is to go on." When George argued that the larger Force Bill was a travesty, he stated, "Well, you may go on. I can not control you; I can only do my duty." Senator Hoar responded, "If the Senator will pardon me for suggesting it, the difficulty is to have somebody to control him." Keeping the focus on the Force Bill, however, George stated the "clamor" about Mississippi's constitution "serve[d] no other purpose except to gild the bitter pill which the majority of this chamber propose[s] to administer to the American people in the shape of the bill now under consideration." Then George ended: "Mr. President, I have but very little more to say. I have done my duty, as I understand it."[18]

Reaction to George's speech varied, but most observers hailed the ability and logic of his thoughts. Senator Turpie from Indiana described George's effort as "one of the ablest and clearest ever heard here upon any occasion. Objection was silenced. The attack failed and has never since been renewed." A Mississippi congressman agreed that George's speech "was so convincing and complete that all attacks were silenced." Backing up George's claims was the fact that the only black representative in the convention had supported it wholeheartedly, and there was no outcry from Mississippi's black leaders, including former senator Blanche K. Bruce. Further diminishing the storm surrounding the document was the later 1898 U.S. Supreme Court case (*Williams v. Mississippi*), in which the court found the state constitution in adherence with federal law.[19]

Clearly George's activities during the convention and his subsequent defense of the state's constitution in the Senate demonstrated that he viewed blacks as inferior, and that the entire reason for limiting their suffrage was because he and other white Mississippians believed they were not capable of good government. He had stated he would support the convention if "the majority of the white people decide in favor of it." George also wrote about "the majority [black] race being wholly incapable of forming or administering a constitutional government," and used the Reconstruction years as proof. It is telling that George both began and ended his speech with admonitions that the Anglo-Saxon race was dominant. "He must be made a good citizen," George spoke of blacks, "and must be taught to live and reverence the name and character of the State as we do. He must also be taught to rely on the State, as white men do, for protection in all his rights. He has political rights which cannot be denied him, and these rights impose upon him the proper performance of political duties. He must be taught to perform aright these political duties, of which he is lamentably ignorant."[20]

George's understanding clause worked just as he envisioned, disenfranchising thousands of black Mississippians for decades. And it had major ramifications throughout the nation. The example of the Mississippi constitution allowed other Southern states to move confidently toward legally segregating their own states, ushering in the era of segregation and Jim Crow. Much as George's Mississippi Plan in 1875 had been an example for other Reconstruction-era states, so also was his work in 1890. In Mississippi itself, the understanding clause remained on the books for decades, serving its purpose of disenfranchising blacks through the civil rights era of the 1960s. In fact, it was further strengthened in 1965 by a segregationist Mississippi legislature. But the clause, as well as most of the other premodern issues such as the poll tax, finally met its end in 1975, when the famous Section 244 was repealed from the state's constitution. Obviously, George was a major factor in his day and in the succeeding decades, but his policies, much like his fame, have been surpassed by a more progressive Mississippi.[21]

CHAPTER 19

"Seems to Be Worn Out"

Third Senate Term, 1892–1897

Large numbers of Mississippi Democrats were unhappy with Senator J. Z. George by 1892. No matter that he had led the effort to throw off Republican rule during Reconstruction, or that he was one of the state's top leaders, or that he had built up seniority in the Senate, or that he was a chief player in drafting the new 1890 state constitution and then later its chief defender. When a new issue developed that saw George take an opposing position, a major wing of the state Democratic Party turned against him and sought his replacement.

The major dissatisfied bloc was made up of farmers. George was a planter, but it did not matter. It also did not matter to them that George had championed farmers' issues during his terms, much more so than Lamar or Walthall. George was sympathetic to the Mississippi farmers' plight, even becoming a favored member of the Farmer's Alliance. Indeed, George worked hard for farmers, serving on the Agricultural and Forestry Committee in the Senate and championing such ideas as regulating railroads so farmers could ship goods more cheaply and lowering the protective tariff so farmers could mechanize. He was, after all, Mississippi's "Great Commoner."[1]

None of that mattered, however, when George came out against the Farmer's Alliance's favored subtreasury scheme. One of the major issues of the day in Mississippi was agricultural monetary policy. In a day of falling farm prices, farmers favored a subtreasury in each county that would allow them to deposit their crops for a partial advance on payment, the treasury holding the crops until the prices rose and the farmers could sell at better prices. George was very much against this measure, writing an open letter to the Carroll County Alliance denouncing the subtreasury. One newspaper reported, "Old, life-long friends dropped away from him." Yet he stood firm in his convictions, arguing in a major speech, "If they [farmers] desire to commit suicide, I shall decline to be an abettor in self murder. I will not hold the poisoned chalice to the lips of my countrymen, though they, themselves, insist that I should do so."[2]

The farmer wing of the Mississippi Democratic Party, which would soon elsewhere morph into the Populist Party, sought to have a more supportive representative elected to the Senate to replace George. Perhaps his support for industrialization and economic collusion with the North, which had always made the farmers nervous but had not in itself constituted enough of a concern to turn on him, added to their animosity. Led by anti-George newspaper editor Frank Burkitt of the *Chickasaw Messenger*, the farmers nominated Ethelbert Barksdale, George's old ally during the 1875 fight and recently a member of the U.S. House of Representatives. National Populist leaders even traveled to Mississippi to help unseat George. In a hard-fought campaign, in which the state newspapers fell into dirty personal attacks, George politicked for his seat, meeting Barksdale in debates across the state. The Democratic Party nominated George nevertheless, but that was not the deciding body. When the state legislature voted on January 20, 1892, George won seventy-seven to Barksdale's forty votes in the House, with one vote going to James L. Alcorn. A similar tally came in the state senate, with George getting twenty-four of thirty-seven votes over Barksdale. Thus George was set to embark on a third term, beginning in March 1893.[3]

Senator Walthall presented George's credentials for reseating to the Senate in March 1892. Although that was very early, George nevertheless had his administrative paperwork taken care of well before the new Congress met in March 1893. At that time, George was present for the second inauguration of President Grover Cleveland. With a Democrat in the White House and both houses of Congress under Democratic leadership for the first time in decades, George no doubt thought the time had finally come to get things done in Washington.[4]

George was entrenched in his committee assignments, once more serving on Agriculture and Forestry, Education and Labor, Transportation Routes to the Seaboard, and his favorite, the Judiciary Committee. He also served on temporary committees such as the committee "To Investigate the Condition of the Potomac River Front at Washington," for which he served as chairman, and the committee on women's suffrage. George had his personal secretary, his grandson James Z. George Jr., appointed to the clerkship of his Potomac River Front Committee. At perhaps the apex of his power, George was the ranking majority member on the Senate Agriculture and Forestry Committee and thus served as chairman during the

Fifty-third Congress, the only Congress during his tenure in which Democrats held a majority in the Senate.[5]

As was his custom, George was prickly about his image. He occasionally corrected wrongs in the printed record and met head-on any complaint about his actions. On one such occasion in April 1894, he took the floor to correct the singular use of "United States" that was printed in the record. Always the states' righter, George informed the Senate that this matter was "of a very material character in my opinion." He stated that he always used the words in the plural, and offered constitutional testimony that he was right. Several Northern senators confronted George, with one asking if "E pluribus unum" was plural and another stating, "for myself . . . I consider this country to be one Government, one nation, one people."[6]

On another occasion in 1895, when a newspaper reported George had rudely denied a request for another senator's bill to go ahead of his bankruptcy bill, George took the floor to defend himself. "I mention this to show that I have not been guilty of any discourtesy whatever," he spoke. One senator responded, "The Senator from Mississippi is forceful at times, very direct and pungent in his utterances, but I have never noticed either in public or in private that he has been disposed to be discourteous to any fellow-Senator."[7]

George's service as chairman of the Agriculture and Forestry Committee put him at the height of his power. One of the group's tasks was to report periodically to the Senate on agriculture, prices, futures, and the state of the business. George concentrated his efforts on cotton growers, of whom, of course, he was very knowledgeable. He took testimony all over the South at such places as St. Louis, Memphis, and New Orleans, and he sent out a circular letter to farmers. The Democratic majority on the committee gave detailed reasoning as to why cotton prices were so low, although some of the Republicans offered a minority opinion.[8]

George blamed a lot of the agricultural problems on monetary policy, and he used that platform to back the silver issue. He advocated the remonitization of silver, seeing it as he almost always did in light of his common constituents back home. He had farmers in mind when he spoke on behalf of silver in September 1893, arguing that inflation of the monetary supply would raise the price of farm products and also help farmers who were in debt. "The present hopeless condition of the farmer," George argued, required silver as a medium of exchange that could be readily obtained and kept. "Death, sir, is the end of the trouble [for the farmer], it would seem; but not so, the inheritance of debts and ruinous finances he leaves to his children, perpetuates through them the horrors from which he has escaped." George said that the lowered costs of production had not kept up with the fall in prices. And taxes were also still as high as ever. He argued for "the wants of the American farmers, for an increased coinage, and the ability of that want, with others, to keep silver at a parity with gold." George also launched into an attack on all types of coinage, mostly company coins, or "sham money" as he called it, usable only at company stores. After George described what was on the face of one particular coin, another senator asked about "in God we trust." "No sir," replied George. "They were not trusting in God over there, they were trusting in the other power." "I think if we had a good honest silver dollar it would be better," George argued. In supporting free silver, George was again at odds with many Democrats, most notably his president, Grover Cleveland.[9]

Another major issue of the day was the blossoming Populist Party. George was universally harsh against those he considered defectors from the Democratic Party. In one exchange with Populist senator William V. Allen of Nebraska, George was adamant that "about the only thing in the Populist platform that is of any value was taken from the action and declaration of the Democrats." Soon George brought up the subtreasury scheme, which prompted Allen to respond: "I thought the Senator from Mississippi would reach the subtreasury scheme very soon." George soon gave up when Allen notified the Senate he would yield for questions but not debate, causing George to chide, "Then I understand the Senator's permission to interrupt him is simply this, that I am to ask questions and accept his answers without comment. Is that the idea?" When Allen replied that George could respond on his own time, not Allen's, George argued, "Very well. Then I decline to interrupt the Senator. That is a one-sided affair, and I do not care to enter into a controversy with my distinguished friend, able as he is, when he is to have all of the talk and I am only to interrogate him."[10]

George also continued defending Mississippi, its people, and its rights. He was instrumental, along with Senator Walthall, in eulogizing former senator Lamar in the U.S. Supreme Court at his death in 1893. Ever the states' rights supporter, George also agreed and worked with Senator Walthall as well as Governor John M. Stone on the state's auditor warrants. These had been printed in St. Louis but were seized by federal officials, who said they were against federal statute. The case was to go to trial in St. Louis, but George and others argued that it should be heard in Mississippi. Holding the case "many hundreds of miles from our State Capital," George argued, "is flagrantly unjust and can subserve no other purpose than to vex and harass the State and her officials." He went on, "I regard the proceeding from beginning to end, as insulting to the State." He frequently met and corresponded with Secretary of the Treasury J. G. Carlisle on the issue, and "express[ed] in the strongest terms, my protest against the action of your Department." George insisted that nothing had been done illegally, and even if it had, it had not been done intentionally.[11]

George rarely spoke on foreign affairs, the exception being the fisheries treaty, diplomatic appointments and recalls, and the treaty to annex the Hawaiian Islands. George supported both treaties, offering detailed historical lectures on why the Senate should ratify them.[12]

As always, George spent a lot of time dealing with constituents and office seekers. To one desiring a consulship, he wrote, "get up your endorsements." He warned, however, that there had been "over 100 applicants for the same position, but I will do what I can for you." Even in the midst of the trying office seekers, George was ever mindful of how he was viewed at home and in the press. He sent home copies of speeches he gave on the floor of the Senate, writing that one in particular on railroad regulation had "made a great stir." He wrote constituents, "I am glad to find in your letter an embodiment of the views expressed in my speech."[13]

In Washington, society was still not George's highest priority. He had never been a socialite and was especially reclusive when Bettie remained in Carrollton. Money was also tight for the senator and his family. "Your father is about the poorest man I ever saw," Bettie wrote Lizzie in 1892. When Bettie was in town, the couple did attend some functions and occasionally had dinner with some of the Mississippi couples in Congress such as the Moneys, Hookers, Walthalls, Catchings, and Singletons. Bettie especially enjoyed seeing other Mississippi wives. George much preferred private carriage rides. One day George was driving Bettie and fellow Carrolltonian and U.S. representative Hernando Desoto Money and his wife when, while trying to miss a hole in the road, he turned the carriage over. No one was seriously hurt, although Bettie described to Lizzie how "Mr. Money fell on your father and I on Mrs. Money." She was able to laugh about it, though, saying, "We had the best natured crowd you ever saw."[14]

The senator's routine remained fairly fixed in Washington. He would eat breakfast before heading to a long day at the capitol. He came home around five or six in the evening and "seems to be worn out," Bettie wrote to one of the children. He took walks every morning and had massages every evening. Most of his leisure time, especially later in his Senate career, was taken up with grandchildren who lived with them in Washington. Bettie described, on one occasion, how "your father was dancing last night to show how much better he was."[15]

In his later years George increasingly desired to spend more time at home, but he had difficulty getting away from his national duties even in Carrollton. He often spoke around the state. George thus cherished the relaxing time he spent at Cotesworth. One Senate colleague remembered that "one of his social delights was to tell of his country home near Carrollton, Miss., where his cattle browsed and his lambs skipped around him." His new library continually beckoned him, as did other tasks around Cotesworth, Carrollton, and Runnymede. When not in Washington, George was most active in his newfound religion and church. Once he gave in to his wife and the church, George spent an increasing amount of time on religious work. As a faithful member of the Carrollton Baptist Church from the time he joined in 1889, George served in various capacities, such as a delegate to the Yazoo Baptist Association's annual meeting in 1895 and as a delegate to the state Baptist convention held in Starkville in 1896. He served on a five-man committee to oversee the church's parsonage, the committee recommending and the church voting to sell it to raise money for a new sanctuary. He also served on the building committee tasked to "advise as to the proper course to proceed, contract for, and superintend the building of a new Baptist Church." George was very involved in the effort, even buying the old church building that sat across town from the site of the new church. When time came to build the new building and to gather proceeds for it, George apparently gave a lot of the money for the construction of the new church. The story is told, although unsubstantiated, that in one particularly long business meeting a member of the church, after looking around to see who was there, offered somewhat vainly to match any contribution made that day. Having not seen George slumping in the back, the man was quite surprised when the senator raised up and replied, "I'll pay the other half. Let's go home."[16]

George had other issues on his mind as well, such as the marriage of his children and his growing horde of grandchildren. Pink and Joseph, as well as Lizzie, married in the 1890s. His farming operations also took his time, as did his sons who were taking over the agricultural efforts and needed guidance. He was still dispensing advice as late as 1895, calling for diversification of family crops from cotton. As chairman of the Senate Agriculture and Forestry Committee, George certainly knew what he was talking about.[17]

Despite appeals from some citizens that he seek a fourth term, and from some newspapers in Mississippi even calling on him to run for president, George let it be known in 1895 that he was retiring to Cotesworth to study and hopefully finish a manuscript on the political history of slavery in the United States. There were other issues as well. Bettie, an invalid since 1892, made the trips to Washington despite her paralysis, but these trips were growing harder on her. George was also apparently dissatisfied with the Democratic Party. Although he would not say so publicly, he told his son, "The administration (or something else) has succeeded in knocking the life out of the Democratic Party. I never saw it darker—not even in Reconstruction days."[18]

In particular, George was unhappy with Grover Cleveland. The feuding became so bad that George even felt obliged to shun any leadership by the president. In writing that George's "most notable trait was independence," one newspaper described George's anger with Cleveland when the president withheld nominations in order to twist senators into voting his way. Once when Cleveland summoned him to the White House, George responded: "You tell the big beef from Buffalo that it is no nearer from the Capitol to the White House than from the White House to the Capitol. I get up at 5 o'clock every morning, eat my breakfast, come down here and go to work. If he wants me he knows where to find me." Later, George opposed one of Cleveland's Supreme Court nominees, resulting in his falling out of favor with the president even more and Walthall getting most of the patronage for Mississippi. George confided in 1894 to a constituent, "my endorsement is not worth anything with the present Administration."[19]

George was evidently tiring of politics on the state level as well. As early as 1888 he confided to Winfield S. Featherston that "I know less of the inside working of Mississippi politics than any man who was ever elected to the Senate from the State," adding that the political bosses in Mississippi "rather tolerate than support me." The backlash against him in 1892 by the farmers no doubt added to his ambivalence. And he was even seeing himself as a has-been in Carrollton. "I can't even promise you the support of my old County," he wrote Featherston, who was seeking the governor's chair. He noted that in the years since he left, many of his old friends were dead. "Young men have come to the front," he declared, "Some of them entire strangers to me and some even prejudiced against me." He even admitted that he was concerned he would be considered an "intruder" when he returned.[20]

Despite his retirement declaration, a rumor started during the summer and fall of 1895 that George would allow himself to be elected again. A reporter in Carrollton went out to Cotesworth to get the scoop. "Senator George, ... out at his pleasant old country home two miles from here," the newspaper reported, "is annoyed by these reports, and told *The Times-Democrat* correspondent so, when the latter went out there to get an authoritative denial of the rumor." George stated that it certainly would not be fair to jump in the race now that other men had already put a lot of time and energy in the canvass.[21]

A spat over the election also developed between George and Governor Anselm McLaurin in 1895. A newspaper reported that McLaurin had approved a report charging George with waiting until McLaurin announced his candidacy for reelection as governor before announcing his own retirement from the Senate, thus knocking McLaurin out of the Senate race. The paper called this a "neat little trick" played on McLaurin. George wrote the governor denying the charge, saying he had "ceased to be a factor in active politics" after his retirement announcement. George also said that he did not think the governor believed he had done this, and asked him to print a correction. McLaurin wrote back a very nice letter but failed to promise to correct the slight. George wrote again, but little ever came of the affair. An ever-mellowing George nevertheless showed his hatred of any personal feuds, saying he was "anxious to close my political career without becoming entangled with mere personal politics."[22]

In 1896 the state legislature elected George's friend and fellow Carrolltonian H. D. Money to take the Senate seat in 1899, when George's third term ran out. Unfortunately, Senator George's health would not allow him to finish out his third term. He often missed meetings of the Senate in his later years, and commented on the floor that he welcomed interruptions because "I am becoming fatigued." In the winter of 1896 he became very ill, prompting his remaining at home at Cotesworth until he recovered; he was not able to attend the opening of the second session of the Fifty-fourth Congress in December 1896. Senator Walthall took the floor as soon as the session began and asked unanimous consent that George be granted a leave of absence. "I desire to state that my colleague [Mr. George] is absent on account of sickness. I ask that he be granted an indefinite leave of absence." Unfortunately, George was not able to return to the Senate, and Walthall had to perform the same duty when the Fifty-fifth Congress began in March 1897. "I ask that an indefinite leave of absence be granted to my colleague [Mr. George], who is absent on account of sickness," Walthall spoke. There was, of course, no objection.[23]

There was hope George would recover and fill out his term. He rebounded, in fact, several times, and even made his way to Washington to return to work, but again fell into the throes of sickness. Unfortunately, as time would tell, he would never take his seat in the U.S. Senate again.

◆ ◆ ◆

When J. Z. George ended his Senate career, he had spent some sixteen years in that body, and he was Mississippi's longest-serving senator to that date. What were his accomplishments? What was the final tally concerning his service to the state and nation? George obviously never reached the lofty status of a Calhoun, Clay, or Webster, and his years were marked with relatively few major successes. The fact that he was a relatively low-ranking Democrat in a series of Republican-dominated Congresses tells much of the tale. Indeed, Republicans had the Senate majority in seven of the eight Congresses during his tenure, the Fifty-third Congress being the only one in which Democrats had a majority in the Senate, and that was a slight four-vote margin. Within that national framework, George could not be expected to turn out much national legislation. In that context, one of his Northern Senate colleagues remarked, "the man was greater, far greater, than his opportunities." In fact, he served mostly as the loyal opposition.[24]

Yet he did take an active part in the Senate, offering an average of forty-four bills and amendments per two-year Congress. These bills ranged in scope from small relief actions on the part of everyday citizens to larger efforts that created great bureaucracies. Most never passed, although George offered them nearly every session. There were others that passed and became national law, however. George was also active in the workings of the Senate, sitting on committees and participating in conferences and other organizations. He also frequently made motions, and often engaged in debate. Some senators insisted they could always tell if George was going to get involved in a debate and offer amendments on any certain day when he first appeared on the Senate floor. If his ruddy hair was straight and neat, he would be silent that day. If it was disheveled, they knew he had been up much of the night wrestling with whatever question was at hand and that he would be prepared to take action the next day, unkempt hair and all.[25]

By all accounts George was not a great orator. One Mississippian wrote,

> As a popular orator Senator George was not a success. His speech was low and often indistinct. He rarely used gesture and his language was without embellishment or adornment. As a speaker he seldom resorted to the employment of wit or humor, never quoted poetry and never indulged in classical allusions. His style and manner of address were better adapted to the bar than the forum, although he never failed to secure the interest of Senators who wished for solid information and enlightenment. His peculiar intellectual force was that of analysis, in which he was rarely gifted.

Dunbar Rowland has written, "Strong, cogent reasoning, plain but deep sense were the leading characteristics of his eloquence." He went on to say, "The flow of his oratory was in perfect keeping with the rugged simplicity of his character. His neglect of the ornamental had something stern and imposing about it, he seemed to stand like the top of some majestic mountain that scorned to be beautiful and adorned by the wild flowers and vines at its base." Rowland summed George up as "a man who was speaking for a purpose and not for display . . . to persuade not to entertain, to instruct, not to please." Another contemporary stated George "was as near the rank of a great orator as a deficient imagination would allow him to go."[26]

Perhaps George's major hallmark in the Senate was his independence. He was never afraid to support unpopular issues. He favored the 1883 civil service bill, which Democrats did not heartily endorse. Likewise, he found himself on the opposite side of issues with other Democrats on matters such as the antitrust bill and the silver issue. The most notable event, of course, was his defiance of his beloved farmers in the subtreasury debate, which could have cost him his Senate seat. He once remarked, with apparent truthfulness judging from his record, "I shall not therefore, compromise my principles, not advocate what I know will injure the people, for the poor privilege of occupying a conspicuous place among those who have aided in destroying what I have always endeavored to preserve and advance—the welfare of my countrymen." Thus, even within the Democratic Party, George was also sometimes the loyal opposition. He himself admitted to an office seeker during President Cleveland's second term that he could not help him: "for the reason that my relations are such with The Hon. Hoke Smith,—that I would not—I could not with any self respect,—ask anything of him at all. Even if I could, my endorsement,—I very much regret to say—is utterly worthless with this Administration." One of George's colleagues, Democrat David Turpie of Indiana, remarked that even when the Democrats held the majority in the Senate during the Fifty-third Congress, George was still in the minority.[27]

Such independence produced a senator who is difficult to explain to modern readers. George fits into no major category except white supremacist, and even what would be thought of as his major attributes have questionable or ironic parts. For instance, one writer has tried to fit George into the contemporary Democratic wings of Mississippi politics of the Gilded Age. Was he a Bourbon or a liberal? In 1881 the *New York Times* described him as "a thoroughly representative Bourbon Democrat." On the other hand, May Spencer Ringold has concluded that George actually took liberal positions and wrote that he "does not fit neatly into the pattern of Mississippi Bourbonism." In fact, his mantra of commoner, while questioned by some, is justifiable. Despite living on a plush plantation with a mansion and library, George usually sided with the common people of his state, and was very much identified with them through his dress, mannerisms, and attitudes even in Washington. Ringold has concluded, with convincing research, that George's commoner status was real; he often used words such as "mass," "toilers," "people," and "workers." He supported regulation of businesses, railroads, and banks, once arguing that Lincoln had not said "government of the banks, by the banks, for the banks." He supported, Ringold argued, legislation that "confers a great boon on those who need it most, the great mass of our people, the workers, the toilers, by whose muscle, intelligence, and energy we have achieved the grand material results of our present civilization." "Such protestations are common enough, it is true, among politicians," Ringold continued. "But when bill after bill, amendment after amendment and argument after argument are offered by a politician for the benefit of the laborer, the farmer, the consumer, one should hesitate to question the sincerity of his utterances. Senator George's record on economic issues reveals him as keenly alive to the needs of the masses." His support of the Agricultural and Mechanical College also fits that pattern. And no doubt his deepest political hurt came when his beloved farmers turned against him in 1892, seeing him as a villain. Yet, and this is what is so ironic, George was a multithousand-acre plantation owner, had been an elite plantation and slave owner in antebellum times, was one of the top lawyers of the state, and was involved in many industrial ventures such as railroads, even owning stock in the

Mississippi Central. One historian has surmised that George's ability to relate to both the common people and the aristocracy helped weld a major political machine in Mississippi that ruled for the last quarter of the nineteenth century. Such a thesis also helps explain how a disheveled, outspoken, brusque, introvert like George got himself reelected time after time.[28]

George's personality in the Senate was perhaps the cause of his nonconformism. Throughout his entire life George had questioned authority, gone out on his own, and taken stances that were sometimes unpopular with others. Even his rebellious appearance turned heads. One Mississippi contemporary remembered, "He carried his rural plainness to the Senate Chamber and could not be induced to change the comfort of his store clothes for the agony of high collars and evening dress." His quirks of a brusque personality, quick anger, and country mannerisms enlivened the Senate during his terms. Many cool exchanges appear in the record, such as: "I have stated—as the Senator would have known if he had paid attention," or when a colleague said, "I will not cavil with the Senator about that. I am inclined to think that he is right." George responded, "Certainly, I am right." George often got extremely excited in debate and forgot the rule that he had to address the chair at all times. He often directly addressed other senators and had to be reminded by the chair that all debate should be directed toward the presiding officer. George was also resolute in his actions, perhaps too much so sometimes. In one episode when he was grilling a fellow senator, George stated, "That is not an answer to my question. . . . I am not going to hedge, but I propose to hold the Senator to the record." He later confided, "I do not intend to allow him to get away from the point."[29]

Contemporaries of George frequently recalled his curt personality. In eulogizing him at his death, the *New York Times* quipped that "Senator George was well liked in the Senate, notwithstanding a rather brusque manner. Those who knew him realized fully that beneath the outward crust was hidden a kind and gentle disposition." A contemporary, in writing of George's career in 1903, summed up his manner well:

> Personally Senator George was a man without polish or the lighter accomplishments of polite society. He was, in fact, a diamond in the rough. His dress was exceedingly plain, he was simple in his habits and unostentatious in manner. He was rugged and courageous in character, rather blunt in address and somewhat brusque in demeanor. He was sometimes impatient of opposition and was inclined to overbear those

who sought to thwart his plans. However, this was more the fault of his manner than of his heart, and he was known to express great regret that he had unintentionally wounded the feelings of a colleague.[30]

Not everyone gave George the benefit of the doubt, however. One Northern newspaper, while admitting his ability, described George as a senator who "takes his shoes off when he feels like it, props his feet on his desk, talks aloud to anyone whenever he wants to, stamps about the chamber, goes to sleep when he feels inclined, snorts at speeches he does not like, and does not care what anyone thinks about him." The writer went on to say he acted like an "educated hog," but one Republican took exception, saying "Great Scott! . . . Who in all this world has ventured to call that man 'educated'?"[31]

Thus a combination of George's personality, status in the Senate, and complex views on issues led to him having a sometimes volatile career in the U.S. Senate. He was in the minority most of the time, but George was nevertheless heard on most issues that interested him and Mississippi. In the end, George was not a dynamic Senate leader, but he did what Mississippi sent him to do—represent the state faithfully during a time of troubled national and state affairs.[32]

CHAPTER 20

"Death Came Very Peacefully"

Death, 1897

Mississippi's junior senator Edward C. Walthall had mixed feelings in August 1897. Obviously, he and the senior senator from Mississippi had never been on intimate terms, although they had grown closer during their numerous years together in the upper chamber of Congress. Walthall later admitted that he and George had seen some "intermediate interruptions" in their friendship, although, he said, "for nearly [the last] twenty years our relations were most cordial." Nevertheless, George and Walthall agreed on most issues, and Walthall respected George. As the senior senator lay dying, however, Walthall could not help but realize that with George's passing, he would obviously move up the ladder. He would become the state's senior senator, as well as de facto leader of Mississippi's Democratic Party. Still, there was a bit of sadness as Walthall wrote his sister in mid-August that he planned to go see George, "who can not live long, it seems."[1]

George had been unwell for nearly a year, in addition to the eye and mouth problems he had experienced in the last decade. The seventy-year-old senator had nevertheless kept up a grueling pace in the mid-1890s, Bettie saying to Lizzie that he was "as well as I ever saw him." His fast pace continued into 1896, serving in the Senate as well as on numerous other bodies such as the Resolutions Committee of the Democratic Party and the board of trustees of the Mississippi Agricultural and Mechanical College, the annual meeting of which he attended in June 1896. He continued his practice, as described by another member of Congress at the time, of rising "with the sun, and although he went to bed almost as early as the lark, he counted it no strange or unusual thing to sit at his desk studying, reading, examining, annotating—working persistently, working cheerfully, working untiringly, day by day, nine, ten full hours each day." Bettie likewise continued to be as active in social aspects of Washington as she could with her disability. By the fall of that year, however, both George and Bettie began to have serious medical complications.[2]

The senator had attended the first session of the Fifty-fourth Congress through June 1896, and Walthall commented on his "robust appearance." But then his major sickness began as early as August 1896, when one newspaper reported he had issues "of both heart and throat." He recovered somewhat and recuperated at Cotesworth before suffering a setback in October, which forced him to cancel speaking engagements. Another recovery brought George enough strength to return to Washington in early January 1897. The trip obviously took a lot out of him, and doctors put George into Washington's Garfield Hospital immediately upon his arrival on January 5. His situation became so alarming, in fact, that the doctors called Bettie and his children from Carrollton to Washington because they feared he was dying. The *New York Times* reported George was "suffering from a complication of diseases, bronchial catarrh causing him the greatest annoyance. During the past week his heart has become involved in the general complications, and it is from this source that the greatest fears are now entertained." Three of the area's best doctors expressed "the gravest fears of his recovery."[3]

By late January George's health was so precarious that the family, all who could, traveled to Washington to be with him. Two grandchildren, a daughter, and four sons were there, but not Bettie. Her age was catching up with her as well, and she had suffered another paralyzing stroke at Cotesworth and was bedridden. Meanwhile George was able to sit in an invalid chair at the hospital once in a while, but most of his time was spent bedridden. He remained conscious, though, and recognized his children and other visitors.[4]

George wrote his last will and testament in Washington on January 28, with Senator Walthall and Senator-elect Money as his witnesses. In the will, George left Cotesworth and Runnymede to Bettie, with everything else split evenly between the nine surviving children. Upon Bettie's death, George stipulated, Cotesworth and his political library would go to his grandson and namesake, James Z. George Jr. To his son Joseph, a budding lawyer, George left his papers and legal library. He appointed his four sons to be the executors of the will, with specific instructions not to fight over the results: "I desire to particularly warn them and my other children against any litigation concerning the distribution of my estate." He left in place a system in which the sons could resolve any misunderstanding by majority vote, and, if tied, Cothran was to cast the deciding vote.[5]

Fortunately, George soon recovered enough to move back to Carrollton to be with his beloved wife; doctors realized the benefit of his being with his mate, so they ordered the move. Most astute observers recognized that he would never again return to Washington, much less enter the Senate chamber again. Rumors began that he intended to resign his seat. He nevertheless held his own throughout the spring, despite the fact that Cotesworth was now an invalid home for both George and Bettie. One observer was touched by the way he cared for her; "it was wondrously moving to see the gentleness, the solicitude, the marvelous tenderness with which this big brained, big-hearted man, with the leonine head and thunderous voice, though himself smitten with death, ministered to his aged and invalid wife."[6]

One event in May strengthened the senator more than any other. On May 27 he and Bettie celebrated their fiftieth wedding anniversary with a large party at Cotesworth. Their children, grandchildren, and great-grandchildren were there, along with many guests. One of them commented on George and Bettie sitting at the "head and foot of the table . . . [their] white locks showed that many winters had passed over their heads." The tables were decorated with golden ribbon. After the event, George remarked that he "was stouter and felt better than at any time since his illness." During the event, congratulations from the state legislature, then in session, arrived for the happy couple.[7]

Apparently George's appetite never waned as he recovered through the spring and summer. One newspaper reporter traveled to Cotesworth to interview George. The senator would not speak on the record, but the reporter got plenty of information. He told his readers, "the following will not be believed, but it is the truth." The reporter found the senator in his library, George declining to talk because he was "feelin' ve'y po'ly, ve'y po'ly, indeed, suh. Hain't had a well day for a week." George nevertheless invited the reporter to lunch. The stunned reporter described the affair: "After grace was said he reached for a dish of boiled cabbage and heaped his plate with it. This he drowned in vinegar and devoured with eagerness. Two glasses of rich buttermilk followed the cabbage. There was apple pie on the table and he took half a pie. Over it he poured a pitcher of honey. It disappeared. Then he went to the front gallery and stretched himself in a rocking-chair."[8]

George continued to gain strength over the summer, and was well enough to take walks around the grounds of Cotesworth as well as ride his horse for a mile or so. His doctors gave their permission for the short rides, knowing they would probably aid in his recovery. But the rebellious George exceeded his doctors' orders. "Thinking he was strong enough," his son Alfred noted in July, "he rode double the distance allowed by his doctors. From that he got a setback, from which he has been unable to recover." George rarely left the house thereafter.[9]

The major turn for the worse came in late July, however, when Bettie died. She had been such a part of his life that he could hardly live without her. All through his life he had been miserable away from her, whether in Jackson as court reporter prior to the Civil War, in a Northern prison camp during the war, or in Washington serving in the Senate. Once she died, George seemed to give up. In fact, the *New York Times* reported later that he had "failed much in strength and health since the death of his wife, on July 29."[10]

A Jackson paper reported Carrollton was "wrapped in gloom" after Bettie's death. Her funeral service took place at the Baptist church in Carrollton on July 30, and newspapers reported the church "was filled to overflowing by sympathizing friends." Afterward, she was laid to rest in Evergreen Cemetery, in the same plot where her two young sons were buried. Many applauded her life, with one newspaper claiming George "acknowledge[d] her as the most potent factor in his life's success."[11]

George's sorrow was evident when his former slave and friend Jake came to see him a couple of days after her passing. "Good morning, Jake," George said. "Good morning, master," Jake replied. With tears streaming down his face, George began to tell his old friend how she had died. "Jake, she fell asleep as an infant seeks to rest upon its mother's bosom."[12]

Bettie's passing necessitated a change in the will, which George made on July 31. He took out everything pertaining to his wife as well as his grandson, who "has informed me that he intends to follow a profession that would require his residence in some city." Thus he had no need for Cotesworth. George therefore gave Cotesworth to Cothran, and stipulated that upon his death it should go to one of his descendents "in good standing, of the Baptist Church." He also added modest payments to his stepsisters, daughters of his mother and Seaborn Durham.[13]

The senator soon became so depressed and ill after Bettie's death that it looked as though he might not live much longer. Walthall described him as "lonely in the midst of family and friends, desolate with loving hearts around him." George's sons determined they should try to move him to a better climate, getting him away from his memories of Cotesworth and Bettie. The Mississippi Gulf Coast was a wonderful spot for rehabilitation. George's sons took him to Mississippi City in early August, hoping the change would do him some good.[14]

Meanwhile, with George's repeated bouts of sickness, calls for his senatorial resignation increased. The *Natchez Democrat* was especially vocal, but many other papers came to George's defense, dismissing the Natchez rhetoric as the stuff of "the most bitter and violent gold-standard paper in the State." The *Jackson Weekly Clarion Ledger* defended George as "the man who has done more for Mississippi than any other man, living or dead. . . . To him she is largely indebted for white supremacy." The editor stated that George should not be stripped of his position even at death, and argued that he could not do much in the Senate anyway since he was paired with a Republican, which would cancel out his vote.[15]

George was probably oblivious to all this talk. And the change of location did little to help him; his health continued to slip. Friends and family attended him, including his children and grandchildren as well as Senator Walthall and other politicians. They kept political officials as well as family members apprised of the situation. Briefly, it looked like George might gain some strength. On August 14, however, he began to go down quickly. When word that he was in his final hours reached Washington, the *Post* announced the reports caused "a general feeling of sorrow as the news spread throughout the city."[16]

On the afternoon of August 14, George slipped into unconsciousness, and an hour or so later he passed away, at 2:40 P.M. "Death came very peacefully," the *Washington Post* announced. The contemporary description of George's fatal condition was "fatty degeneracy of the heart."[17]

There was no doubt he would be brought home to Carrollton and placed beside Bettie and the two children. The family wanted the funeral to be held in the Carrollton church where he was an active member, with the pastor, John L. Johnson, officiating.[18]

George's body traveled by train northward from the coast to Jackson; two special coaches were attached to the regular train, one for the body and one for the dignitaries and military escort. The *New York Times* stated the "family consented, in deference to the wishes of the public, that his body should lie in state at the seat of the Government for twenty-four hours before being carried to Carrollton for internment." Thus George returned one final time to the building where he had served so many times. It was there that he had held an office as court reporter before the war and there where he had attended the secession convention in 1861. He had held court in that very building as chief justice of the state supreme court, and then had helped form Mississippi's 1890 constitution there. He had made other speeches there as well. Now he was making his final appearance.[19]

When the remains arrived at 2:00 P.M. on August 15, an "immense crowd of citizens" met the body and accompanied it to the statehouse. The official greeters were the governor and staff, along with several state militia units and official pallbearers such as former governors John M. Stone and Robert Lowry, Senator Walthall, various state officials, and several of George's close associates such as Josiah A. P. Campbell. The throng escorted the casket to the rotunda of the statehouse, where it sat under military guard for twenty-four hours.[20]

Once in the capitol rotunda, the casket sat atop a "flowery bier," and the lid of the coffin was removed, allowing those filing by to look upon the body. A "ceaseless throng of people passed in line to view for the last time the face of the great statesman," the *Washington Post* reported. A Jackson paper continued, "There are very few people in Jackson, white or black, who did not visit the capitol during the twenty-four hours the body of Senator George laid there in state." A funeral service took place at noon on August 16, with the president of local Millsaps College, W. B. Murrah, presiding.[21]

After the ceremony in Jackson, escorts took the remains back to the railroad station and placed the coffin on the train for the trip north to Winona. Station after station along the rail line was draped in mourning. As the train sped past the station at Vaiden, where George had first lived as a boy, the businesses were closed, and the people stood hatless on the platform. At Winona, where a huge funeral arch sat on the railroad station platform, the remains were transferred to another rail line for the short trip westward to Carrollton. Arriving at the depot on the afternoon of August 16, George's body made the familiar trip up the hill to Carrollton. One paper reported that the town's houses and businesses, along with the "big brick courthouse in the middle of the square," were "tastily draped in black." All businesses were closed. George's body lay in state in the Baptist church during the night, guarded by the military escort.[22]

George's funeral services took place at eleven o'clock on the morning of August 17. Many of the state's and nation's leaders were there, although one newspaper declared that it was difficult to get a political representation together in such a short time during the recess, "with Senators widely scattered and the place of funeral remote." Nevertheless, all who could, including many representatives and Senators Walthall, William Bate of Tennessee, Edmund Pettus of Alabama, and Thomas Turley of Tennessee, and Senator-elect Money, gathered at what one witness described as "one of the prettiest churches in a country town the size of Carrollton you will see anywhere." In addition, a newspaper reported, "the whole population [of Carrollton] had turned out." Also attending were many black people, including George's former slaves, particularly his "body servant" Jake, who continually stood "next to his bier as one of the chief mourners at the funeral." During the service, Jake sat with the family, and afterward told an attendee, with tears streaming down his cheeks, "I have lost my best friend."[23]

The service took place in the new church George had been so instrumental in building and funding. His pastor, John L. Johnson, gave the funeral sermon, in which he talked about George's full life, using Job 5:26 as his text: "Thou shalt come to thy grave in a full age, like a shock of corn cometh in in his season." The reference was especially fitting for George since he was a planter. Johnson described George's life, statesmanship, and family, but he was most impressed with George's Christianity. Recounting the story of George being baptized after the war, Johnson said that the senator's "increasing love, and his interest in the church has steadily grown." He also noted, "This building is largely the result of his concern to see his own people credibly domiciled, and his contributions to its erection were liberal."[24]

Johnson also remarked that George had recently confided to him his "deep regret in later years that he had not given greater emphasis to his Christian life and walk." It occurred to him, Johnson said, that "the less now had needed to be done if he had done more." Nevertheless, Johnson was convinced George was enjoying his eternal reward in heaven, and ended with, "Let us go now and bury him—the soldier, the citizen, the Christian."[25]

"The immense concourse of people of all classes and conditions and from many quarters of the State who followed his remains to the public cemetery from the Baptist Church at Carrollton," one observer noted, "attested [to] the esteem and affection in which he was held by those who had known him longest and knew him best." The crowd made its way down the hill, across the creek in which he was probably baptized, and out the old road toward Cotesworth. George had made the trip many times. At Evergreen Cemetery, George's friends laid him to rest beside Bettie, James, and Frank.[26]

But time moved on. Once George was resting peacefully beside his dear Bettie, political activities returned. Mississippi's governor appointed Senator-elect H. D. Money to finish George's term, which expired in 1899. Money was the logical choice, because the state legislature had already elected him to replace George when the senator let it be known he would not return to Washington after his third term.[27]

The official notification to the Senate of George's death came from Senator Walthall. He stated that Mississippi had "lost her most useful and distinguished public servant, the Senate one of its ablest and conspicuous members, and the masses of the people throughout the land an earnest and powerful champion and defender." After issuing condolences to the family, the Senate adjourned for the day "as a further mark of respect." That same day Mississippi congressman John M. Allen announced George's death in the House of Representatives. That body likewise adjourned out of respect.[28]

Obituaries filled newspapers across the nation, with most providing the standard biographical treatment found in the various congressional directories of the day. But not all were positive. The *Ohio State Journal* in Columbus, for instance, admitted that George was a brilliant constitutionalist, but that his states' rights positions nullified his ability. "He was so radical and set in his opinions," the paper reported, "that he did not assume the leading place in the Senate to which his talent and long term of service entitled him." The paper went on to say, "In his death the most charitable thing to be said of him is that he did his duty as he understood it."[29]

Many memorials soon followed. Various Mississippi towns held special memorial services, the one at nearby Greenwood being organized by James K. Vardaman. George's former law partner Robert W. Williamson spoke at that meeting. The Carrollton Baptist Church erected a "memorial window to the memory of our beloved Brother and Sister James Z. George and Bettie Young George," while son Alfred donated a "pulpit Bible" in honor of his mother. The George family also set up an endowed scholarship at the Mississippi Agricultural and Mechanical College. In November 1897 George's son Cothran gave the college $250 annually for the "J. Z. George Scholarship."[30]

Most of the memorials were political in nature. In January 1898 the Mississippi legislature passed a series of resolutions in memory of George, describing him as "an eminent citizen, an unselfish patriot, a farseeing statesman, a wise and safe counselor, and an intrepid leader." They also "rejoiced to know that he passed away not only ripe in years and in honors, but rich in the strong assurance of another and better life." The legislature also stated that his life "recalled the earlier and better days of the Republic." The state supreme court likewise eulogized its former chief justice.[31]

The U.S. House and Senate held special days of eulogy: the Senate on April 7 and the House on May 25, 1898. Senators and representatives of both parties paid tribute to George, including many from Mississippi, with each house adjourning after its tributes as "a further mark of respect."[32]

Almost to a man, the speakers spoke in positive terms of George, something that would be expected at such an event. The Mississippians in Congress were most intimate in their eulogies, calling him "Jim," as he was known to his friends around Carrollton. However, this was no lovefest. Fellow Mississippian Edward C. Walthall admitted he and George had not always seen eye to eye. He also spoke of how he was "impatient of opposition." Yet Walthall readily admitted that George was not one for "brooding or repining" when defeated; he went on to the next issue and gave it his all.[33]

In all the overblown rhetoric, almost all the speakers concentrated on several parts of George's life, and the themes seemed to recur repeatedly. One was his shortness and brusque manner. A fellow Senate Democrat spoke of his "brusque and rather rugged nature." Senate Republican Henry M. Teller of Colorado called him "combative, but not quarrelsome." Democrat George Gray of Delaware stated he "did not cultivate as much as others, or perhaps as much as he ought, the social side of his nature" and "often repelled those who were prepared to admire his abilities." He noted George also "often offended without being conscious of his offense." Fellow Carrolltonian H. D. Money remarked, "few men knew him as well and none loved him better than I," but stated George "regarded his enemies with little consideration and was prone to express his sentiments toward them with great frankness." Another stated, "he was not without faults, and, no doubt, at times his prejudice misguided his judgment, but no one ever doubted his sincerity."[34]

Another issue raised by most of the speakers was his plainness. Senator William Bate stated, "The simplicity of dress and manners of Senator George was a key to his nature, as it was an indication of his politics and his idea of government." Another spoke of "no glitter, no tinsel," while others stated that Washington did not spoil him, and he did not "cultivate the social side of his nature." Numerous speakers referred to him as Mississippi's "Great Commoner" or "Old Commoner."[35]

Many others remarked on his ability, character, and firmness. Senate Democrat David Turpie of Indiana stated, "I do not think there has ever been a fairer disputant or debater than our late colleague." Senator Teller said, "he was not a trimmer. Right with him was right, and the consequences of such support did not concern him." Perhaps Republican senator Redfield Proctor of Vermont summed George up best when he defined him as "An Honest Man."[36]

The attribute that all remarked upon most frequently, however, was his brilliance, especially concerning the law and the Constitution. Many described him as a "legal gladiator." One Missouri representative caught up in the occasion described George as "one of the greatest constitutional lawyers ever in the Congress of the United States in the whole history of the Republic." Another stated his speeches "compare favorably with the best speeches of Calhoun or Webster," and he also described George's "massive brain."[37]

Such rhetoric can be dismissed as partisan politics, but the eulogy given by an opponent, Republican senator Orville H. Platt of Connecticut, was obviously sincere. "I think he was perhaps a man not easy to become acquainted with," Platt began. "It is fashionable to lament that there are no longer Websters, or Clays, or Calhouns, or Benton's in the Senate of the United States; and yet, in view of my observation of the late Senator from Mississippi, I am convinced that if he had lived and been a member of the Senate fifty years ago, he would have taken rank, in the estimation of the people, among the most wise and able Senators who have adorned the Senate." He went on to state, "The term 'great lawyers' is so often used that it comes to mean very little, and yet I think I can say, and say truly, that Senator George was a great lawyer, and that is great praise." Perhaps most telling, Platt confessed: "When he came to the Senate I think his career in his own State during reconstruction times had created in my mind a prejudice against him. But as I came to know him and understand his character I formed a juster estimate of the man and came to be one of his admirers."[38]

In the end, that is all George would have wanted: to be judged fairly on his actions. He was confident of the results.

Conclusion

J. Z. George's fame in Mississippi continued to increase after his death. Numerous contemporaries who worked on histories of the Civil War and Reconstruction years, and his Senate career, portrayed him in glowing terms. In an age of segregation and white supremacy, George was a hero to white Mississippians.[1]

The publication of George's manuscript on politics, slavery, and reconstruction also publicized his name, this time as a historian. George's successor in the Senate, H. D. Money, took the mostly finished manuscript and toiled with it for several years before giving it up due to bad eyesight. Then, George's son-in-law William H. Leavell published it in 1915 with the Neale Publishing Company of New York as *The Political History of Slavery in the United States*. Reviews of the states' rights work in the days of segregation were not critical, although most reviewers acknowledged that George did not provide any new information. James W. Garner, a historian of Reconstruction, wrote in the *Mississippi Valley Historical Review* that "it can hardly be said that the work adds anything to our knowledge of the political history of slavery." He did, however, say that the already-known information was condensed into a convenient venue for students and that "the cause of the South is defended with considerable ability." A reviewer in the *Journal of Negro History* stated, "the chief value of the work consists in its being an expression of the opinion of a distinguished man who participated in many of the events narrated."[2]

More memorials to George also came about in later years. The nearby Greenwood United Daughters of the Confederacy (UDC) group took the name J. Z. George Chapter. George's daughter Lizzie was a charter member and president, later becoming president of the national organization. The Mississippi Department of Archives and History placed George in the state's Hall of Fame in 1908, and the family presented a portrait on the occasion. In 1911 the George family provided another portrait of the senator to the George School in Jackson, with Senator John Sharp Williams addressing the crowd. In observation of his efforts on behalf of education, two of the state's major universities honored the deceased senator by naming buildings for him on their campuses. At the Mississippi Agricultural and Mechanical College, the college's military company was also named for George (the George Rifles) during World War I.[3]

George's children were also a memorial to him in certain ways. Many continued his work in law, education, and politics. Son Joseph W. George became a noted Mississippi lawyer, and he and Alfred served several terms in the Mississippi legislature around the turn of the century. One of George's granddaughters married the chancellor of the University of Mississippi, Andrew A. Kincannon, while Joseph served on the board of trustees of the University of Mississippi. Cothran served on the board of trustees of the Agricultural and Mechanical College.[4]

The state also memorialized George, naming a new county after him in 1910. The greatest honor, however, came in June 1931, when the Mississippi legislature chose him as one of two Mississippians to honor in the National Statuary Hall Collection in the nation's capitol. Each state was given the opportunity to place statues of its two most distinguished citizens in the nation's capitol building, and Mississippi chose Jefferson Davis and James Z. George.[5]

Augustus Lukeman, the sculptor of Georgia's Stone Mountain Confederate Memorial, created the two statues, and the state dedicated them in Washington, D.C., on June 2, 1931. Speeches by leading Mississippians and an unveiling by each man's descendants highlighted a day of music, oratory, and celebration. Mississippi senator Hubert D. Stephens and University of Mississippi law professor Stone Deavours gave speeches regarding George's life and contributions, while Katy Boyd George, the senator's granddaughter, unveiled the statue.[6]

Had the ambitious George known his statue would one day reside in Statuary Hall as one of Mississippi's two favorite sons, he would no doubt have been proud. That he was there with his old commander, president, and friend Jefferson Davis would have been especially heartening to him. In speaking of George, Senator Stephens pointed out that George had served under Davis in two wars and that George had sat in Davis's Senate seat. "In life they walked together," Stephens stated. "In death they are not separated. The statue of each is here." George would have liked that.[7]

◆ ◆ ◆

If George's fame spread rapidly in the first several decades of the twentieth century, it has disappeared in the last seventy years. If every "school boy" in

Mississippi could "unhesitatingly" identify the state's "Great Commoner" around the turn of the century, as Dunbar Rowland stated, it would not be overstating it to say that over 90 percent of today's school boys and girls in Mississippi could not answer the question, who was James Z. George? Obviously, with the demise of his racial attitudes and disenfranchising accomplishments, George's fame has diminished. As Mississippi has become more modern in terms of race relations, George's theories, and his fame, have been relegated to the past.[8]

Yet there remain subtle hints that James Zachariah George once lived, and that he was important. In Washington, his statue still resides in the capitol. Likewise, his portrait hangs in the old Mississippi statehouse, now known as the Old Capitol, where George performed so much work and then laid in state. As a member of the Mississippi Hall of Fame, his portrait hangs in the supreme court chamber. And his beloved Cotesworth is still an active plantation, owned by his descendents. His mansion, furniture, portraits, papers, and library are all still there, not that much different than when he left them in August 1897.[9]

But George is not a well-known statesman today. He is almost unheard of outside of Mississippi, and younger generations of Mississippians outside Carroll County know nothing of him. Even many Carroll County residents only know the name as the title of the public school in Carroll County established in 1920. But even in the honor of naming a school after George, his statesmanship has been somewhat reduced. The school's mascot was once the Senators, but that has been changed to the more vicious Jaguars in recent years.

Perhaps most ironic is the fact that J. Z. George High School today is 60 percent black, and George was such a champion of white Mississippi. Yet it is also fitting because George was a vocal advocate of education. And although a supporter of white rule, he was also, at times in opposition to his own allies, a sponsor of African American education. Of course, such support was not intended to heighten the status of blacks but to make Mississippi a better place altogether, but such irony illustrates the complex and difficult-to-understand personality and policies of J. Z. George; it also illustrates his habit of standing up for issues that were unpopular or even unwinnable. One writer has labeled George a "Man of Spine." The often-rebellious George, whatever may be said of him, was certainly that.[10]

Notes

Preface

1. Dunbar Rowland, *Political and Parliamentary Orators and Oratory of Mississippi* (Harrisburg, Pa.: Press of Harrisburg, 1901), 393. For an example of the lessening of George's fame, see the developing confusion over his career. He has repeatedly been labeled a Confederate general while he was only a general officer in state service. His highest Confederate rank was colonel. See W. L. Cabell, "Living Generals of the Confederate States Army," *Southern Historical Society Papers* 20 (1892): 39; W. L. Cabell, "Confederate Generals Yet Living," *Confederate Veteran* 2, no. 1 (January 1894): 28; Nicholas Lemann, *Redemption: The Last Battle of the Civil War* (New York: Farrar, Straus and Giroux, 2007), 127.

2. Margaret Armstrong, "James Zachariah George: Champion of White Supremacy" (master's thesis, University of Alabama, 1938), 9.

3. J. Z. George to Bettie, undated, Undated Folder, James Z. George Papers, Mississippi Department of Archives and History (hereafter cited as MDAH).

4. Willie D. Halsell, "The Bourbon Period in Mississippi Politics, 1875–1890," *Journal of Southern History* 11, no. 4 (November 1945): 524; *Memorial Addresses on the Life and Character of James Z. George (Late a Senator from Mississippi) Delivered in the Senate and House of Representatives* (Washington, D.C.: Government Printing Office, 1898), 18, 20; J. Z. George to Bettie, January 2, 1856, and undated, James Z. George Papers, MDAH.

5. Stephen Cresswell, *Rednecks, Redeemers, and Race: Mississippi After Reconstruction, 1877–1917* (Jackson: University Press of Mississippi, 2006), 89.

Chapter 1

1. Joseph W. George File, July 2, 1829, Probate Judge's Office, Monroe County Courthouse; Joseph W. George Estate Records, Ordinary Annual Returns, Book B, Probate Court Records, Monroe County Courthouse, 175–177.

2. Joseph W. George Estate Records, Ordinary Annual Returns, Book B, Probate Court Records, Monroe County Courthouse, 175–177.

3. Dunbar Rowland, *Courts, Judges, and Lawyers of Mississippi, 1798–1935* (Jackson, Miss.: Harderman Bros., 1935), 99.

4. Lawrence E. Noble, "The Georgia Background of James Zachariah George," April 1999, MDAH, 5, 10, 11, 15, 34; Armstrong, "James Zachariah George," 3–4.

5. Noble, "Georgia Background," 24, 26, 34.

6. Joseph Warren George and Mary Chambliss Marriage Record, December 27, 1825, Marriage Book A, Probate Court Records, Monroe County Courthouse, 29a; Noble, "Georgia Background," 30, 34–35, 37; "Monroe County—A Good Place to Live," *Monroe Advertiser*, September 3, 1931.

7. "The Estate of James Z. George, Minor," 1830, Ordinary Annual Returns, Book B, Probate Court Records, Monroe County Courthouse, 272; Noble, "Georgia Background," 37–38.

8. *Memorial Addresses on the Life and Character of James Z. George*, 49; Noble, "Georgia Background," 37.

9. "Estate of James Z. George, Minor," 1830, 272–275; Noble, "Georgia Background," 28–29.

10. Joseph W. George Estate Records, Ordinary Annual Returns, Book B, Probate Court Records, Monroe County Courthouse, 176; Noble, "Georgia Background," 30–32; 1830 Georgia Census, Monroe County, Slave Schedules, National Archives and Records Administration (hereafter cited as NARA), 187.

11. Mary George Bond, September 1, 1828, Record of Bonds, Book A, 1825–1854, Probate Court Records, Monroe County Courthouse, 161–162; Seaborn Durham Deed, May 4, 1830, Deed Book G, Superior Court Records, Monroe County Courthouse, 16; "The Estate of James Z. George, Minor," 1830–1840, Ordinary Annual Returns, Book B, Probate Court Records, Monroe County Courthouse, 272–275; Noble, "Georgia Background," 38.

12. Mary George et al., Bond, August 6, 1832, Administrators and Guardians Bonds, Book A, Probate Court Records, Jones County Courthouse, 70–71; "James George Sr. Estate," December 31, 1832, Ordinary Annual Returns, Book J, Probate Court Records, Jones County Courthouse, 5–19; Noble, "Georgia Background," 11–12, 15, 25–26. George's other grandfather, Zachariah Chambliss, would live to be ninety-nine, dying in 1874, so no inheritance from that side would be forthcoming in George's younger years.

13. Joseph W. George Estate Records, Ordinary Annual Returns, Book B, Probate Court Records, Monroe County Courthouse, 175–177; "The Estate of James Z. George, Minor," 1830, Ordinary Annual Returns, Book B, Probate Court Records, Monroe County Courthouse, 272–275; Noble, "Georgia Background," 14, 16, 42.

14. John Hal Shanks, "The Early Career of James Z. George" (master's thesis, University of Mississippi, 1938), 3; Noble, "Georgia Background," 41.

15. May Spencer Ringold, "Some Liberal Aspects in the Senatorial Policies of James Zachariah George during the Period 1881–1890" (master's thesis, University of Mississippi, 1950), 1; Shanks, "Early Career of James Z. George," 3. Seaborn and Mary would move on again after several years, this time back south and eastward, finally settling in Attala County at Kosciusko.

16. Dunbar Rowland, *Mississippi; Comprising Sketches of Counties, Towns, events, Institutions and Persons, Arranged in Cyclopedic Form*, 3 vols. (Atlanta: Southern Historical Printing Association, 1907), 1:373; For Carroll County, see William Franklin Hamilton, "History of Carroll County," undated, Carroll County Library; and Bingham Duncan, "A History of Carroll County from 1871" (master's thesis, University of Mississippi, 1933). For Leflore, see Allene De Shazo Smith, *Greenwood Leflore and the Choctaw Indians of the Mississippi Valley* (Memphis, Tenn.: C. A. Davis, 1951).

NOTES   191

17. Seaborn Durham Deeds, November 22 and December 23, 1837, Deed Book B, Carroll County Courthouse, 247–248, 679; Rowland, *Mississippi*, 2:663; Shanks, "Early Career of James Z. George," 3; Seaborn Durham Petition, November 1840 Term, Probate Court Record Book A, 1834–1841, Carroll County Courthouse, 209–210; Armstrong, "James Zachariah George," 5; 1840 Mississippi Census, Carroll County, Slave Schedules, 31, NARA. For Seaborn Durham's annual reports on his guardianship, see Probate Court Record Book B, 1841–1845, Carroll County Courthouse, 1–2, 11, 41, 115, 117, 179, 228, 243.

18. "Estate of James Z. George, Minor," 272–275; *Acceptance and Unveiling of the Statues of Jefferson Davis and James Z. George* (Washington, D.C.: Government Printing Office, 1932), 47; Shanks, "Early Career of James Z. George," 3; Armstrong, "James Zachariah George," 6; Ringold, "Some Liberal Aspects," 2; *Memorial Addresses on the Life and Character of James Z. George*, 91; "Famous Mississippians: Senator James Z. George, the Great Commoner of His Commonwealth," *Memphis Commercial Appeal*, October 5, 1902,; "Speech by Hon. John Sharp Williams on James Z. George, The Man and Speech by Dr. Dunbar Rowland on James Z. George, the Statesman," 4, copy in J. Z. George File, Greenwood-Leflore Public Library.

19. Shanks, "Early Career of James Z. George," 4; *Memorial Addresses on the Life and Character of James Z. George*, 96; Ringold, "Some Liberal Aspects," 2; "Senator George Dead," undated newspaper clipping, J. Z. George Scrapbook, Cotesworth; "The Late Senator J. Z. George," undated newspaper clipping, J. Z. George Scrapbook, Cotesworth; Undated and untitled newspaper clipping, J. Z. George Scrapbook, Cotesworth. Another newspaper reported George also later taught school for a time.

20. "Famous Mississippians"; Shanks, "Early Career of James Z. George," 4.

21. Seaborn Durham Deed, April 1, 1843, Deed Book E, Carroll County Courthouse, 354; J. Z. George Indictment and Sentence, October 11 and 16, 1845, Circuit Court Record Book D, 1845–1848, Carroll County Courthouse, 46, 84; Seaborn Durham Annual Report and Final Settlement, December 1845 and January 5 and November 3, 1846, Probate Court Record Book C, 1845–1848, Carroll County Courthouse, 56, 58, 148; Seaborn Durham Annual Report, September 1844, Probate Court Record Book B, 1841–1845, Carroll County Courthouse, 228.

22. William Cothran Marriage License, July 11, 1839, Marriage Book A, 1834–1853, Carroll County Courthouse, 182; 1850 Mississippi Census, Carroll County, NARA, 230; Hamilton, "History of Carroll County," 11.

23. Lucy Henderson Horton, *Family History* (Franklin, Tenn.: Press of the News, 1922), 136–140; J. Z. George to Bettie, January 15, 1858, James Z. George Papers, MDAH; Lizzie George Henderson, "The Wife of Gen. J. Z. George," *Jackson Clarion Ledger*, April 16, 1908. A copy of Henderson's article can be found in J. Z. George Subject File, MDAH. One source indicates Elizabeth was raised in Hardin County, Tennessee. See "Famous Mississippians."

24. Seaborn Durham Final Settlement, November 3, 1846, Probate Court Record Book C, 1845–1848, Carroll County Courthouse, 148.

25. *Laws of the State of Mississippi Passed at a Regular Biennial Session of the Legislature Held in the City of Jackson in January, February and March, A.D. 1846* (Jackson, Miss.: C. M. Price and G. R. Fall, 1846), 428; *Journal of the House of Representatives of the State of Mississippi at a Regular Session Thereof, Held in the*

City of Jackson (Jackson, Miss.: Price and Fall, 1846), 4, 545; *Journal of the Senate of the State of Mississippi at a Regular Session Thereof Held in the City of Jackson* (Jackson, Miss.: Price and Fall, 1846), 526. The bill read: "Be it enacted by the Legislature of the State of Mississippi, that James Z. George, minor of Carroll County, be, and he is hereby released from the civil disabilities of minority: and he is hereby authorized to receive from, and receipt for all his estate now in the hands of his guardian, and to do and perform all acts for himself, as fully and lawfully as if he had attained the age of majority prescribed by law."

26. Seaborn Durham Final Settlement, November 3, 1846, Probate Court Record Book C, 1845–1848, Carroll County Courthouse, 148.

Chapter 2

1. John Seigenthaler, *James K. Polk* (New York: Times Books, 2003), 131–132.
2. For an overview of the Mexican War, see K. Jack Bauer, *The Mexican War: 1846–1848* (New York: Macmillan, 1974).
3. Dunbar Rowland and H. Grady Howell Jr., *Military History of Mississippi: 1803–1898, Including a Listing of All Known Mississippi Confederate Military Units* (Madison, Miss.: Chickasaw Bayou Press, 2003), 19.
4. W. F. Hamilton and Betty Wiltshire, *Military Annals of Carroll County, MS, Expanded* (Carrollton, Miss.: Pioneer, 2004), 3.
5. Shanks, "Early Career of James Z. George," 6.
6. J. Z. George Mexican War Compiled Service Record, First Mississippi Infantry, NARA; William C. Davis, *Jefferson Davis: The Man and His Hour, a Biography* (New York: Harper Collins, 1991), 132–133; "List of Mississippians in 1st and 2nd Regiments of Mississippi Riflemen," undated, MDAH. For a history of the regiment, see Joseph E. Chance, *Jefferson Davis's Mexican War Regiment* (Jackson: University Press of Mississippi, 1991).
7. "Roll of 'Carroll County Volunteers,'" *Carrollton Democrat*, June 10, 1846; Carnot Posey to George Gordon, July 5, 1846, Carnot Posey and Family Letters, MDAH.
8. James C. Browning Diary, July 22 and 27 and August 3, 1846, MDAH; J. Z. George Mexican War Compiled Service Record, First Mississippi Infantry, NARA; Davis, *Jefferson Davis*, 134, 136; Hamilton and Wiltshire, *Military Annals of Carroll County*, 3; Carnot Posey to George Gordon, July 5, 1846, Carnot Posey and Family Letters, MDAH.
9. Hamilton and Wiltshire, *Military Annals of Carroll County*, 3.
10. James C. Browning Diary, August 21, 1846, MDAH; Hamilton and Wiltshire, *Military Annals of Carroll County*, 3.
11. Jefferson Davis to John A. Quitman, September 26, 1846, Mexican War Documents, MDAH; Bauer, *Mexican War*, 96; James C. Browning Diary, September 1846, MDAH; Chance, *Jefferson Davis's Mexican War Regiment*, 44–47.
12. Daniel R. Russell to Jefferson Davis, September 26 and October 18, 1846, Mexican War Documents, MDAH.

13. Ibid.; "From the Carroll Volunteers," Carrollton *Mississippi Democrat*, October 21, 1846.

14. "From the Carroll Volunteers."

15. Ibid.; Davis, *Jefferson Davis*, 220.

16. J. Z. George Mexican War Compiled Service Record, First Mississippi Infantry, NARA; Shanks, "Early Career of James Z. George," 8.

17. Davis, *Jefferson Davis*, 155; Joseph Allan Frank and George A. Reaves, *Seeing the Elephant: Raw Recruits at the Battle of Shiloh* (Westport, Conn.: Greenwood Press, 1989).

18. *Memorial Addresses on the Life and Character of James Z. George*, 118; Armstrong, "James Zachariah George," 8. Armstrong states George joined the offices of "Neill and Cothran."

19. J. Z. George Family Bible, Cotesworth; James Z. and Elizabeth George Marriage License, May 30, 1847, Book A, Carroll County Courthouse, 709; J. Z. George to Bettie, December 27, 1855, and January 15, 1858, James Z. George Papers, MDAH; Henderson, "Wife of Gen. J. Z. George."

20. J. Z. George to Bettie, January 19, 1855, James Z. George Papers, MDAH.

21. Carrollton Baptist Church Minutes, October 25, 1849, Book 1, 1833–1861, Carrollton Baptist Church, 138.

22. J. Z. George to Bettie, January 2 and 10, 1856, and undated, James Z. George Papers, MDAH.

23. J. Z. George Family Bible, Cotesworth; J. Z. George Deed, October 27, 1849, Deed Book J, Carroll County Courthouse, 590; J. Z. George Deed, November 15, 1849, Deed Book J, Carroll County Courthouse, 360; 1850 Mississippi Census, Carroll County, Slave Schedules, NARA, 705; 1850 Mississippi Census, Carroll County, NARA, 230.

24. 1850 Mississippi Census, Carroll County, NARA, 230; 1850 Mississippi Census, Carroll County, Agricultural Census, NARA, 161–162.

25. 1850 Mississippi Census, Carroll County, NARA, 230. See the tombstones in the Oakwood Cemetery in Carrollton for death dates.

Chapter 3

1. William W. Freehling, *The Road to Disunion: Secessionists at Bay, 1776–1854* (New York: Oxford University Press, 1990); William W. Freehling, *The Road to Disunion: Secessionists Triumphant, 1854–1861* (New York: Oxford University Press, 2007).

2. *Journal of the Senate of the State of Mississippi at a Regular Session Held in the City of Jackson, 1856* (Jackson, Miss.: E. Barksdale, 1856), 5; Rowland, *Courts, Judges, and Lawyers*, 258; J. Z. George to Bettie, February 1, 1856, James Z. George Papers, MDAH; Collection Description, Watkins-Walton Family Papers, MDAH; Norma Wilkins, "Robert W. Williamson," Robert W. Williamson Subject File, MDAH; J. Z. George to Sir, December 11, 1856, Lockhart-Weir Family Papers, MDAH; *Proceedings of the Grand Royal Arch Chapter of the State of Mississippi at Its Thirty-third Annual*

194   NOTES

Convocation, held at Jackson, February 7th and 8th, 1881 (Jackson, Miss.: Clarion Steam Book Publishing House, 1881), 90; William Martin Walton, *An Epitome of My Life: Civil War Reminiscences* (Austin, Tex.: Waterloo Press, 1956), 14.

    3. J. Z. George to Bettie, January 23, 1855, James Z. George Papers, MDAH. This data is gleaned from the Lexis-Nexis Academic Universe legal database. It is extremely difficult to pinpoint the exact number of cases George argued because records are not clear. For example, George was sometimes listed as J. Y. George, and at other times as just George. These simple listings of George no doubt refer to him, however, because all the cases arose in Carroll County. George's transcripted treatment in the legal records became much more standard when he himself became the recorder in 1855.

    4. Lexis Nexis, "21 Miss. 281; 1850 Miss."

    5. J. Z. George to Bettie, January 6, 1856, James Z. George Papers, MDAH; Lexis Nexis, "32 Miss. 260; 1856 Miss."; Shanks, "Early Career of James Z. George," 60.

    6. J. Z. George Indictment and Sentence, December 5, 1855, Circuit Court Minute Book, 1855–1857, Carroll County Courthouse, 103, 155; Lexis Nexis, "32 Miss. 469; 1855 Miss."; J. Z. George to Bettie, January 19, 1855, James Z. George Papers, MDAH.

    7. J. Z. George to Bettie, May 29, 1852, and December 27, 1855, James Z. George Papers, MDAH.

    8. J. Z. George Family Bible, Cotesworth; J. Z. George to Bettie, May 29, 1852, and December 27, 1855, James Z. George Papers, MDAH.

    9. J. Z. George to Bettie, May 29, 1852, James Z. George Papers, MDAH.

    10. J. Z. George to Bettie, May 29, 1852, and January 23, 1855, James Z. George Papers, MDAH.

    11. J. Z. George to Bettie, May 29, 1852, January 19 and December 22, 1855, and January 22, 1858, James Z. George Papers, MDAH.

    12. J. Z. George to Bettie, May 29, 1852, James Z. George Papers, MDAH; 1860 Mississippi Census, Carroll County, Agricultural Census, NARA, 16; 1860 Mississippi Census, Carroll County, Slave Schedules, NARA, 304; James Z. George Deed, December 2, 1850, Deed Book J, Carroll County Courthouse, 449; Slave Deed, December 7, 1853, Deed Book L, Carroll County Courthouse, 44; James Z. George Deed, January 1853, Deed Book L, Carroll County Courthouse, 182; James Z. George Deed, June 27, 1854, Deed Book L, Carroll County Courthouse, 183; James Z. George Deed, October 27, 1854, Deed Book L, Carroll County Courthouse, 276; James Z. George Deed, August 19, 1854, Deed Book L, Carroll County Courthouse, 286; James Z. George Deed, November 13, 1856, Deed Book M, Carroll County Courthouse, 424; James Z. George Deed, November 24, 1860, Deed Book P, Carroll County Courthouse, 323; Mississippi Central Rail Road Company Records Collection Description, MDAH.

    13. C. S. Tarpley to Robert Armstrong, July 5, 1852, W. S. Barry to J. Z. George, October 23, 1855, and J. Z. George to Bettie, December 27, 1855, and January 2, 1856, all in James Z. George Papers, MDAH.

    14. "Police Court Minutes," 1853, Carroll County Courthouse, 486.

    15. James Z. George Deed, January 6, 1853, Deed Book L, Carroll County Courthouse, 182; James Z. George Deed, June 30, 1854, Deed Book L, Carroll County Courthouse, 183.

    16. *Memorial Addresses on the Life and Character of James Z. George*, 33; Shanks, "Early Career of James Z. George," 11.

NOTES   195

17. *Journal of the House of Representatives of the State of Mississippi at a Regular Session Thereof, Held in the City of Jackson, 1854* (Jackson, Miss.: Barksdale and Jones, 1854), 165–166; V. A. Griffith, "Mississippi Reports and Reporters," *Mississippi Law Journal* 22, no. 1 (December 1950): 37–58.

18. John Ray Skates, *A History of the Mississippi Supreme Court, 1817–1948* (Jackson: Mississippi Bar Foundation, 1973), 21; *Journal of the House of Representatives of the State of Mississippi at a Regular Session Thereof*, 3, 165–166.

19. *Laws of the State of Mississippi Passed at a Regular Session of the Mississippi Legislature Held in the City of Jackson January, February, and March, 1850* (Jackson, Miss.: Fall and Marshall, 1850), 109–111; Skates, *History of the Mississippi Supreme Court*, 22.

Chapter 4

1. J. Z. George to Bettie, December 22, 1855, James Z. George Papers, MDAH; *Journal of the House of Representatives of the State of Mississippi* (Jackson, Miss.: E. Barksdale, 1859), 4, 67; J. Z. George Court Reporter Commission, Register of Commissions, 1858–1864, 1.

2. James Z. George, *Reports of Cases Argued and Determined in the High Court of Errors and Appeals for the State of Mississippi—Volume XXX—Volume I, Containing Cases Determined at the December Special Term, 1855, and a Part of the April Term, 1856* (Philadelphia: T. & J. W. Johnson, 1857), ix–x.

3. James Z. George, *Reports of Cases Argued and Determined in the High Court of Errors and Appeals for the State of Mississippi—Volume XXXI—Volume II, Containing Cases Determined at a Part of the April Term, 1856, and a Part of the October Term, 1856* (Philadelphia: T. & J. W. Johnson, 1858); James Z. George, *Reports of Cases Argued and Determined in the High Court of Errors and Appeals for the State of Mississippi—Volume XXXII—Volume III, Containing Cases Determined at a Part of the October Term, 1856* (Philadelphia: T. & J. W. Johnson, 1858); James Z. George, *Reports of Cases Argued and Determined in the High Court of Errors and Appeals for the State of Mississippi—Volume XXXIII—Volume IV, Containing Cases Determined at the April Term, 1857, and a Part of the October Term, 1857* (Philadelphia: T. & J. W. Johnson, 1859); James Z. George, *Reports of Cases Argued and Determined in the High Court of Errors and Appeals for the State of Mississippi—Volume XXXIV—Volume V, Containing Cases Determined at a Part of the October Term, 1857, and a Part of the April Term, 1858* (Philadelphia: T. & J. W. Johnson, 1859); James Z. George, *Reports of Cases Argued and Determined in the High Court of Errors and Appeals for the State of Mississippi—Volume XXXV—Volume VI, Containing Cases Determined at the April Term, 1858, and a Part of the October Term, 1858* (Philadelphia: T. & J. W. Johnson, 1860); James Z. George, *Reports of Cases Argued and Determined in the High Court of Errors and Appeals for the State of Mississippi—Volume XXXVI—Volume VII, Containing Cases Determined at a Part of the October Term, 1858, and a Part of the April Term, 1859* (Philadelphia: T. & J. W. Johnson, 1860); James Z. George, *Reports of Cases Argued and Determined in the High Court of Errors and Appeals for the State of Mississippi—Volume XXXVII—Volume VIII, Containing Cases Determined at a Part*

of the April Term, 1859, and a Part of the October Term, 1859 (Philadelphia: T. & J. W. Johnson, 1860); James Z. George, *Reports of Cases Argued and Determined in the High Court of Errors and Appeals for the State of Mississippi—Volume XXXVIII—Volume IX, Containing Cases Determined at a Part of the October Term, 1859, and a Part of the April Term, 1860* (Philadelphia: T. & J. W. Johnson, 1861); *Memorial Addresses on the Life and Character of James Z. George*, 10.

4. J. Z. George to Bettie, January 6 and 26, 1856, and January 2, 1858, James Z. George Papers, MDAH.

5. J. Z. George to Bettie, January 19, 1855, and January 26, 1856, James Z. George Papers, MDAH.

6. J. Z. George to Bettie, January 19 and December 22, 1855, January 10, 1856, and January 22, 1858, James Z. George Papers, MDAH.

7. J. Z. George to Bettie, December 22, 1855, James Z. George Papers, MDAH; J. Z. George Family Bible, Cotesworth.

8. J. Z. George to Bettie, January 19, 1855, January 1 and 10 and February 1, 1856, and January 2, 1858, James Z. George Papers, MDAH.

9. J. Z. George to Bettie, January 19, 1855, and January 26, 1856, James Z. George Papers, MDAH.

10. J. Z. George to Bettie, January 19, 1855, January 6, 1856, and (no month given) 4, 1858, James Z. George Papers, MDAH.

11. J. Z. George to Bettie, December 27, 1855, and January 26, 1856, James Z. George Papers, MDAH.

12. J. Z. George to Bettie, February 1, 1856, James Z. George Papers, MDAH.

13. J. Z. George to Bettie, January 26, 1856, James Z. George Papers, MDAH.

14. J. Z. George to Bettie, January 23 and December 27, 1855, and January 10 and February 1, 1856, James Z. George Papers, MDAH.

15. J. Z. George to Bettie, January 10, 1856, James Z. George Papers, MDAH.

16. J. Z. George to Bettie, January 26 and February 1, 1856, and January 19, 1858, James Z. George Papers, MDAH.

17. J. Z. George to Bettie, January 22, 1858, James Z. George Papers, MDAH.

18. J. Z. George to Bettie, January 23, 1855, January 1, 1856, and January 13, 1858, James Z. George Papers, MDAH.

19. J. Z. George to Bettie, January 23, 1855, and January 15, 1858, James Z. George Papers, MDAH.

20. J. Z. George to Bettie, January 13, 1858, James Z. George Papers, MDAH.

21. J. Z. George to Bettie, January 8, 1857, James Z. George Papers, MDAH.

22. J. Z. George Family Bible, Cotesworth; J. Z. George to Bettie, undated letter, May 29, 1852, and January 23, 1855, James Z. George Papers, MDAH.

23. J. Z. George to Bettie, undated letter, May 29, 1852, and January 23, 1855, James Z. George Papers, MDAH.

24. J. Z. George Accounts, 1845, 1847, 1850, and 1855, James Z. George Papers, MDAH; Cotton Receipt, undated, J. Z. George to Bettie, February 1, 1856, J. S. Johnson to J. Z. George, January 25, 1858, and J. Z. George to Whalen, February 5, 1859, all in James Z. George Papers, MDAH.

25. 1860 Mississippi Census, Carroll County, Agricultural Census, NARA, 16; 1860 Mississippi Census, Carroll County, Slave Schedules, NARA, 304; 1860

Mississippi Census, Carroll County, NARA, 790; J. Z. George to Bettie, October 1, 1864, James Z. George Papers, MDAH.

Chapter 5

1. J. Z. George Family Bible, Cotesworth.
2. Percy L. Rainwater, *Mississippi: Storm Center of Secession, 1856–1861* (Baton Rouge: Louisiana State University Press, 1938), 178.
3. Ibid., 179.
4. Ibid., 198.
5. Ibid., 179.
6. *Journal of the House of Representatives of the State of Mississippi: Called Session* (Jackson, Miss.: Ethelbert Barksdale, 1860), 13; Rainwater, *Mississippi*, 179, 182. For Pettus, see Robert W. Dubay, *John Jones Pettus, Mississippi Fire-eater: His Life and Times, 1813–1867* (Jackson: University Press of Mississippi, 1975).
7. "Alphabetical List of Members of the Mississippi State Convention," Box 8, Secession Convention Folder, Power Family Papers, MDAH; Rainwater, *Mississippi*, 196, 207; Alexander Clayton, "The Secession Convention," undated, J. F. H. Claiborne Papers, University of North Carolina (hereafter cited as UNC).
8. Clayton, "Secession Convention"; *Journal of the State Convention and Ordinances and Resolutions Adopted in January, 1861, With an Appendix* (Jackson, Miss.: E. Barksdale, 1861), 9–13; Rainwater, *Mississippi*, 208; J. L. Power, *Proceedings of the Mississippi State Convention, Held January 7th to 26th, A.D. 1861. Including the Ordinances, as Finally Adopted, Important Speeches, and a List of Members, Showing the Postoffice, Profession, Nativity, Politics, Age, Religious Preference, and Social Relations of Each* (Jackson, Miss.: Power and Cadwallader, Book and Job Printers, 1861), 7.
9. Thomas H. Woods, "A Sketch of the Mississippi Secession Convention of 1861—Its Membership and Work," in *Publications of the Mississippi Historical Society*, 13 vols., ed. Franklin L. Riley (Oxford: Mississippi Historical Society, 1902), 6:94–95; William R. Barksdale to Ferrell, January 18, 1861, William R. Barksdale Papers, MDAH; "Reminiscences of J. A. Orr," J. A. Orr Papers, MDAH; Ralph A. Wooster, "The Membership of the Mississippi Secession Convention of 1861," *Journal of Mississippi History* 16, no. 4 (October 1954): 251.
10. Power, *Proceedings of the Mississippi State Convention*, 11–13, 46.
11. Hugh R. Miller to George, January 14, 1861, Miller Family Papers, MDAH; *Journal of the House of Representatives of the State of Mississippi: Called Session, January 1861*, 146; Power, *Proceedings of the Mississippi State Convention*, 16, 19, 58.
12. Power, *Proceedings of the Mississippi State Convention*, 58–59.
13. *Journal of the State Convention and Ordinances and Resolutions Adopted in January, 1861*, 42, 64–69, 126–132, 136, 138–141; D. C. Glenn, "Memoranda," 1861, J. F. H. Claiborne Papers, UNC; Power, *Proceedings of the Mississippi State Convention*, 33–36; William R. Barksdale to Ferrell, January 18, 1861, William R. Barksdale Papers, MDAH; Cresswell, *Rednecks, Redeemers, and Race*, 90.
14. *Journal of the State Convention and Ordinances and Resolutions Adopted in January, 1861*, 24–25, 83–84; Power, *Proceedings of the Mississippi State Convention*, 41–42.

15. *Journal of the State Convention and Ordinances and Resolutions Adopted in January, 1861*, 3–5, 88.

16. Power, *Proceedings of the Mississippi State Convention*, 19, 43.

17. Ibid., 44.

18. *Journal of the State Convention and Ordinances and Resolutions Adopted in March, 1861* (Jackson, Miss.: E. Barksdale, 1861), 21–36.

19. Ibid., 3–4, 30, 39, 43–44, 46, 48, 77–78, 84–86, 94–95; Woods, "Sketch of the Mississippi Secession Convention," 102.

20. *Journal of the State Convention and Ordinances and Resolutions Adopted in March, 1861*, 48.

21. J. Z. George Deed, June 20, 1861, Deed Book P, Carroll County Courthouse, 331–333. Many sources list different dates for George's purchase, with the earliest, family lore, as 1847. Others mention 1850. See Shanks, "Early Career of James Z. George," 9. Unfortunately, most writers do not list their sources. Obviously, the deed books contain the best information.

22. "National Register of Historic Places Inventory—Nomination Form," November 30, 1977, Cotesworth Subject File, MDAH.

23. J. Z. George Deed, April 6, 1861, Deed Book P, Carroll County Courthouse, 322; J. Z. George Deed, June 19, 1861, Deed Book P, Carroll County Courthouse, 331–333.

Chapter 6

1. Bruce S. Allardice, *More Generals in Gray* (Baton Rouge: Louisiana State University Press, 1995), 99.

2. Company C, Twentieth Mississippi Muster Roll, April 19, 1861, Twentieth Mississippi Infantry Regiment, MDAH; Bruce S. Allardice, *Confederate Colonels: A Biographical Register* (Columbia: University of Missouri Press, 2008), 330; Rowland and Howell, *Military History of Mississippi*, 235, 376; J. Z. George Civil War Compiled Service Record, Twentieth Mississippi Infantry, NARA; Jerry Causey, ed., "Selected Correspondence of the Adjutant General of Confederate Mississippi," *Journal of Mississippi History* 43, no. 1 (February 1981): 39. Apparently, the first organization of the Carroll Guards in April had been for only three months, because the company was again enrolled in June, this time for the entire war. The officers remained the same.

3. Rowland and Howell, *Military History of Mississippi*, 236; J. Z. George Civil War Compiled Service Record, Twentieth Mississippi Infantry, NARA.

4. William Cothran to J. Z. George, August 28, 1861, J. Z. George to Bettie, July 22 and 23, 1861, and Unknown to J. Z. George, August 5, 1861, all in James Z. George Papers, MDAH.

5. Unknown to J. Z. George, August 5, 1861, and J. Z. George to Bettie, July 22, 1861, both in James Z. George Papers, MDAH.

6. Rowland and Howell, *Military History of Mississippi*, 236; J. Z. George Civil War Compiled Service Record, Twentieth Mississippi Infantry, NARA; *War of the Rebellion: A Compilation of the Official Records of the Union and Confederate Armies*, 128 vols. (Washington D.C., 1880–1901), Series 1, 4:383 (hereafter cited as *OR*).

7. J. Z. George to Bettie, August 27, 1861, James Z. George Papers, MDAH; Douglas Southall Freemen, *R. E. Lee: A Biography*, 4 vols. (New York: Charles Scribner's Sons, 1934), 1:593.

8. J. Z. George to Bettie, August 27 and September 16, 1861, James Z. George Papers, MDAH; "Carrollton in Gloom," *Jackson Weekly Clarion Ledger*, August 5, 1897; Henderson, "Wife of Gen. J. Z. George." According to one of their daughters, Bettie even cut up her carpets in blanket-size portions to send to the soldiers.

9. J. Z. George to Bettie, September 16, 1861, James Z. George Papers, MDAH.

10. J. Z. George to Bettie, October 6, 1861, James Z. George Papers, MDAH.

11. *OR*, 1, 5:900; J. Z. George to Bettie, October 6 and 12, 1861, James Z. George Papers, MDAH. George also stated that he had nothing to read, "except the Bible."

12. J. Z. George to Bettie, August 27 and October 6, 1861, James Z. George Papers, MDAH; Cothran George to J. Z. George, October 6, 1861, J. Z. George Letters, Cotesworth.

13. *OR*, 1, 5:901; J. Z. George to Bettie, November 4, 1861, James Z. George Papers, MDAH.

14. J. Z. George to Bettie, November 4 and 12, 1861, James Z. George Papers, MDAH.

15. *OR*, 1, 5:996; J. Z. George to Bettie, November 12, 1861, James Z. George Papers, MDAH; W. A. Rorer to Susan, December 5, 1861, W. A. Rorer Letters, Duke University (hereafter cited as DU). Copies of the Rorer letters are in MDAH.

16. J. Z. George to Bettie, November [date torn], 1861, and Fayette Durham to J. Z. George, December 2, 1861, both in James Z. George Papers, MDAH.

17. J. Z. George to Bettie, November [date torn], 1861, and January 22, 1862 [mislabeled 1861], James Z. George Papers, MDAH; Rowland and Howell, *Military History of Mississippi*, 237; *OR*, 1, 5:1000; J. Z. George Civil War Compiled Service Record, Twentieth Mississippi Infantry, NARA.

18. J. Z. George to Bettie, January 18, 1862, James Z. George Papers, MDAH.

19. J. Z. George to Bettie, January 18 and 22, 1862 [mislabeled 1861], James Z. George Papers, MDAH.

20. Allardice, *Confederate Colonels*, 330; *OR*, 1, 7:379; Shelby Foote, *The Civil War: A Narrative*, 3 vols. (New York: Random House, 1958), 1:200. For Fort Donelson, see Benjamin F. Cooling, *Forts Henry and Donelson: The Key to the Confederate Heartland* (Knoxville: University of Tennessee Press, 1987).

21. *OR*, 1, 7:379.

22. Ibid., 338, 379.

23. Ibid., 339, 380.

24. Ibid., 339, 380; W. J. Hardee, *Rifle and Light Infantry Tactics; For the Exercise and Manoeuvres of Troops When Acting as Light Infantry or Riflemen*, 2 vols. (Philadelphia: J. B. Lippincott, 1861), 1:5. Companies B, G, K, E, and H would have been the left five companies according to the formation prescribed in *Hardee's Tactics*, and this is backed up by Brown's report, which mentioned several of the wounded officers and their companies from this firefight, all coming from those companies.

25. *OR*, 1, 7:381.

26. Ibid.

Chapter 7

1. Cooling, *Forts Henry and Donelson*, 209.
2. *OR*, 1, 7:381.
3. Francis Marion Baxter to Rit, undated, Francis Marion Baxter Papers, MDAH; Foote, *Civil War*, 1:212; *OR*, 1, 7:380; W. A. Rorer to Susan, April 22, 1863, W. A. Rorer Letters, DU.
4. "Fort Donelson," February 16, 1862, "Confederate States Army Casualties: Lists and Narrative Reports, 1861–1865," Microfilm #4682, MDAH; Foote, *Civil War*, 1:213; *OR*, 1, 7:380; Armstrong, "James Zachariah George," 13–14.
5. *OR*, 1, 7:341, 381, 383.
6. J. Z. George Civil War Compiled Service Record, Twentieth Mississippi Infantry, NARA; David S. Heidler and Jeanne T. Heidler, eds., *Encyclopedia of the American Civil War: A Political, Social, and Military History*, 5 vols. (Santa Barbara, Calif.: ABC-CLIO, 2000), 3:1078–1079.
7. Heidler and Heidler, *Encyclopedia of the American Civil War*, 3:1078–1079. For a partial list of George's fellow prisoners, see J. Z. George Prisoner of War Autograph Book, University of Mississippi (hereafter cited as UM).
8. Edward T. Downer, "Johnson's Island," in William B. Hesseltine, *Civil War Prisons* (Kent, Ohio: Kent State University Press, 1997), 99, 101.
9. Ibid., 101, 103.
10. Ibid., 99.
11. Ibid., 101–103. For a list of money and goods of the Carroll Guards, see List of Carroll Guards Money Spent, June 1862, J. Z. George Letters, Cotesworth.
12. Downer, "Johnson's Island," 103, 106.
13. J. Z. George to Bettie, July 8, 1862, November 9, 1863, and April 10, 1864, James Z. George Papers, MDAH.
14. J. Z. George to Bettie, July 8, 1862, James Z. George Papers, MDAH.
15. J. Z. George to unknown, undated scrap, Undated Folder, James Z. George Papers, MDAH; Downer, "Johnson's Island," 104; Thomas Babington Macaulay, *Critical and Historical Essays Contributed to the Edinburgh Review*, vol. 3 (Leipzig: Bernhard Tauchnitz, 1850), book found in James Z. George Papers, MDAH.
16. *Memorial Addresses on the Life and Character of James Z. George*, 12; Shanks, "Early Career of James Z. George," 56–57; Armstrong, "James Zachariah George," 15; "Famous Mississippians."
17. J. Z. George to Bettie, July 8, 1862, Mary Durham to J. Z. George, July 9, 1862, and J. T. Young to J. Z. George, June 1, 1862, all in James Z. George Papers, MDAH.
18. Mary Durham to J. Z. George, July 9, 1862, James Z. George Papers, MDAH.
19. J. Z. George to Bettie, July 8, 1862, James Z. George Papers, MDAH.
20. "Military Prison General Registers of Prisoners, 1862–1864," Microfilm Roll 3308, MDAH; J. Z. George Civil War Compiled Service Record, Twentieth Mississippi Infantry, NARA; J. Z. George to Bettie, July 8, 1862, James Z. George Papers, MDAH.

Chapter 8

1. J. Z. George Civil War Compiled Service Record, Twentieth Mississippi Infantry, NARA.
2. Ibid.
3. Ibid.; Dunbar Rowland, ed., *Jefferson Davis, Constitutionalist: His Letters, Papers and Speeches*, 10 vols. (Jackson: Mississippi Department of Archives and History, 1923), 5:351.
4. John J. Pettus to J. Z. George, October 15, 1862, T. C. Tupper to J. Z. George, October 28 and November 3 and 6, 1862, and R. W. Memminger to J. Z. George, December 15 and 27, 1862, all in "1862" Folder, Correspondence of Various Mississippi Officers and Military Staff Members, 1861–1865, MDAH; Shanks, "Early Career of James Z. George," 35.
5. J. Z. George to Bettie, November 19, 1862, James Z. George Papers, MDAH.
6. J. Z. George to John J. Pettus, November 3, 1862, Governor John J. Pettus Correspondence and Papers, 1859–1863, MDAH.
7. Ibid.; *OR*, 1, 17, 2:745.
8. J. Z. George to Bettie, November 19, 1862, and July 4, 1863, James Z. George Papers, MDAH.
9. Petition to John J. Pettus, February 12, 1863, Governor John J. Pettus Correspondence and Papers, 1859–1863, MDAH; Edwin C. Bearss, *The Vicksburg Campaign*, 3 vols. (Dayton, Ohio: Morningside House, 1986), 1:51.
10. J. Z. George to John J. Pettus, December 25, 1862, Governor John J. Pettus Correspondence and Papers, 1859–1863, MDAH.
11. J. Z. George to Bettie, December 20 and 25, 1862, James Z. George Papers, MDAH.
12. Green L. Blythe to J. Z. George, January 29, 1863, and T. C. Tupper to J. Z. George, January 27, 1863, both in "1863" Folder, Correspondence of Various Mississippi Officers and Military Staff Members, 1861–1865, MDAH; J. Z. George to John J. Pettus, December 29, 1862, and January 2, 1863, Governor John J. Pettus Correspondence and Papers, 1859–1863, MDAH.
13. J. Z. George to John J. Pettus, January 12, 1863, Governor John J. Pettus Correspondence and Papers, 1859–1863, MDAH.
14. J. Z. George to John J. Pettus, January 27, 1863, J. M. Powell to John J. Pettus, February 15, 1863, and Petition to John J. Pettus, February 12, 1863, all in Governor John J. Pettus Correspondence and Papers, 1859–1863, MDAH; Petition to John J. Pettus and Petition to J. Z. George, both dated February 19, 1863, Third Regiment Minute Men Folder, Box 297, Series 390, MDAH. The petitioner who asked that no action be taken nevertheless added, "I take occasion, however, to say that this command will never be satisfied until their grievances in the subject of furloughs are redressed."
15. J. Z. George to John J. Pettus, March 4, 1863, Governor John J. Pettus Correspondence and Papers, 1859–1863, MDAH.
16. Ibid.
17. Ibid.
18. Ibid.

19. Ibid.

20. J. Z. George to John J. Pettus, March 4 and 7, 1863, Governor John J. Pettus Correspondence and Papers, 1859–1863, MDAH.

21. C. D. Fontaine to John J. Pettus, March 9, 1863, Governor John J. Pettus Correspondence and Papers, 1859–1863, MDAH; *OR*, 1, 24, 3:667; Allardice, *More Generals*, 99.

22. *OR*, 1, 24, 3:622, 636.

23. Ibid., 669–670, 673, 683, 691, 693, 695, 701, 709; J. Z. George to Bettie, April 10, 1863, James Z. George Papers, MDAH.

24. J. Z. George to Bettie, November 19, 1862, James Z. George Papers, MDAH.

25. *OR*, 1, 24, 3:765–766.

26. J. Z. George to John J. Pettus, April 23, 24, and 25, 1863, Military Telegrams, Pettus, 1860–1863, MDAH.

27. J. Z. George to John J. Pettus, April 29 and May 2, 3, 4, 10, and 11, 1863, Military Telegrams, Pettus, 1860–1863, MDAH.

28. *OR*, 1, 24, 3:689, 691, 693, 695, 923, 925; *OR*, 1, 52, 2:453; J. Z. George to John J. Pettus, May 3, 1863, Military Telegrams, Pettus, 1860–1863, MDAH.

29. J. Z. George to John J. Pettus, May 3, 10, 12, 22, and 28, 1863, Military Telegrams, Pettus, 1860–1863, MDAH; J. Z. George to John J. Pettus, March 11, 1863, Governor John J. Pettus Correspondence and Papers, 1859–1863, MDAH.

30. J. Z. George to John J. Pettus, April 4 and May 26, 1863, and John J. Pettus to J. Z. George, May 28, 1863, all in Governor John J. Pettus Correspondence and Papers, 1859–1863, MDAH.

31. J. Z. George to Bettie, May 30 and July 4 and 16, 1863, James Z. George Papers, MDAH; W. A. Goodman to J. Z. George, July 21, 1863, James Z. George Papers, MDAH.

32. Richard M. McMurry, *Two Great Rebel Armies: An Essay in Confederate Military History* (Chapel Hill: University of North Carolina Press, 1989), 35.

Chapter 9

1. J. Z. George to Bettie, June 4 and July 4, 1863, James Z. George Papers, MDAH.

2. J. Z. George to Bettie, May 30, June 4, and July 4, 1863, James Z. George Papers, MDAH; *OR*, 1, 24, 3:925, 934; Bearss, *Vicksburg Campaign*, 3:1103–1104; *The Official Records of the Union and Confederate Navies in the War of the Rebellion*, 30 vols. (Washington, D.C.: Government Printing Office, 1894–1922), Series 1, Volume 25, 116.

3. J. Z. George to Bettie, May 30 and June 4, 1863, James Z. George Papers, MDAH.

4. J. Z. George to Bettie, November 19, 1862, and July 4, 1863, James Z. George Papers, MDAH; J. Z. George Family Bible, Cotesworth; *A Thousand American Men of Mark of To-day* (Chicago: American Men of Mark, 1917), 95.

5. *OR*, 1, 24, 3:962–965.

6. J. Z. George Special Order, June 27, 1863, Third Regiment Cavalry, Mississippi State Troops, MDAH; *OR*, 1, 24, 2:491, 501, 503–507.

7. J. Z. George to John J. Pettus, July 4, 1863, Military Telegrams, Pettus, 1860–1863, MDAH; *OR*, 1, 24, 2:506; *OR*, 1, 24, 3:995–997.

8. J. Z. George to Bettie, June 4 and July 4, 1863, James Z. George Papers, MDAH.

9. W. A. Goodman to J. Z. George, July 21, 1863, James Z. George Papers, MDAH; *OR*, 1, 24, 3:1004–1005, 1006, 1009, 1020, 1022–1023, 1027, 1035; *OR*, 1, 31, 3:829.

10. J. Z. George Special Orders, July 23, 1863, and J. Z. George Parole of James M. Carson, August 27, 1863, both in James Z. George Papers, MDAH; *OR*, 1, 30, 4:635; Special Orders Number 118, August 8, 1863, James Z. George Papers, MDAH; J. Z. George Civil War Compiled Service Record, Fifth Mississippi Cavalry, NARA.

11. H. H. Chalmers to J. Z. George, August 8, 1863, James Z. George Papers, MDAH; J. Z. George to Bettie, September 9, 1863, James Z. George Papers, MDAH; *OR*, 4, 2:707; *OR*, 1, 31, 3:580; Special Orders Number 134, August 31, 1863, James Z. George Papers, MDAH; J. Z. George Civil War Compiled Service Record, Fifth Mississippi Cavalry, NARA. For more on the Fifth Mississippi Cavalry, see the Fifth Regiment Cavalry, MDAH. All of the documents in the regiment's records are post George's command.

12. *OR*, 1, 30, 2:757, 761, 787, 793–794; *OR*, 4, 2:928. The *Official Records* contains a curious piece of correspondence attributed to George in late September. See *OR*, 1, 30, 2:658–659. According to this document, George and the Fifth Mississippi Cavalry were in Tennessee, being assigned to Colonel Daniel W. Holman's brigade of Joseph Wheeler's cavalry. Colonel George and his men became engaged in a small fight near Winchester, Tennessee, on September 26, in which Colonel Holman and several other officers and men were captured when the command was attacked in the rear. Colonel George took over and promptly reported to Wheeler the facts of the situation. Writing from Boonshill, Tennessee, Colonel George reported, "the command is here without any person with proper authority to take command. I shall endeavor to hold it together until I can hear from you or some other proper authority." Colonel George did note, however, that "the command is increasing rapidly from both volunteers and soldiers left behind on the retreat of our army. I believe we will soon have a command of 1,500 or 2,000 good, effective men, mounted, armed with such arms as can be found through the country. We are deficient in ammunition." This account does not fit with other records, particularly that the regiment was still unorganized at that point, and Mississippi's leading military unit expert, Dunbar Rowland, discredited it and did not include it in the regiment's history. Apparently, the organizers of the *Official Records* mistakenly attributed the correspondence to George of Mississippi when it probably came from another George.

13. *OR*, 1, 31, 3:580, 728, 747; Rowland and Howell, *Military History of Mississippi*, 415; J. Z. George Civil War Compiled Service Record, Fifth Mississippi Cavalry, NARA.

14. *OR*, 1, 31, 3:605; *OR*, 1, 31, 1:247.

15. *OR*, 1, 31, 1:251–252; J. Z. George to Bettie, November 5, 1863, James Z. George Papers, MDAH.

16. J. Z. George to Bettie, November 5, 1863, James Z. George Papers, MDAH.

17. Ibid.

18. *OR*, 1, 31, 1:252, 245, 252; J. Z. George to Bettie, November 4 and 5, 1863, James Z. George Papers, MDAH; Armstrong, "James Zachariah George," 14. Some fifty years later, George's arms were returned to the family.

19. *OR*, 1, 31, 1:248, 252.

20. J. Z. George to Bettie, November 4, 5, and 9, 1863, James Z. George Papers, MDAH.

21. J. Z. George to Bettie, November 4, 1863, James Z. George Papers, MDAH; J. Z. George to his sister, November 7, 1863, James Z. George Papers, MDAH.

22. J. Z. George to Bettie, December 25, 1862, James Z. George Papers, MDAH.

Chapter 10

1. *OR*, 1, 31, 1:243, 245.

2. J. Z. George to Bettie, November 4, 1863, James Z. George Papers, MDAH.

3. Ibid.

4. J. Z. George to Bettie, November 4 and 9, 1863, James Z. George Papers, MDAH; Henderson, "Wife of Gen. J. Z. George."

5. J. Z. George to Bettie, November 9, 1863, James Z. George Papers, MDAH.

6. J. Z. George to Bettie, November 7 and 9, 1863, James Z. George Papers, MDAH.

7. *Journal of the House of Representatives of the State of Mississippi: December Session of 1862, and November Session of 1863* (Jackson, Miss.: Cooper and Kimball, 1864), 139.

8. *OR*, 2, 7:1278; *OR*, 2, 8:131; J. Z. George Civil War Compiled Service Record, Fifth Mississippi Cavalry, NARA; *OR*, 1, 32, 1:334; *OR*, 1, 32, 2:585; *OR*, 1, 32, 3:605; *OR*, 1, 39, 2:779.

9. J. Z. George to Bettie, January 31 and February 22, 1864, James Z. George Papers, MDAH; J. Z. George Prisoner of War Autograph Book, UM.

10. J. Z. George to Bettie, January 31, February 22 and 28, September 11, and October 1, 1864, James Z. George Papers, MDAH.

11. J. Z. George to Bettie, March 6, May 1, and June 26, 1864, James Z. George Papers, MDAH.

12. J. Z. George to Bettie, March 8 and 29, May 22, and June 12, 1864, James Z. George Papers, MDAH.

13. J. Z. George to Bettie, March 6, April 10, and May 29, 1864, James Z. George Papers, MDAH.

14. J. Z. George to Bettie, June 5 and 12 and November 20, 1864, and April 22, 1865, James Z. George Papers, MDAH.

15. J. Z. George to Bettie, January 31, February 28, March 14 and 29, April 10, and May 22, 1864, James Z. George Papers, MDAH.

16. J. Z. George to Bettie, June 12, 19, 26, and 30, and July 18, 1864, and J. Z. George to J. F. Sessions, October 2, 1864, all in James Z. George Papers, MDAH.

17. J. Z. George to Bettie, September 18, October 1 and 5, and December 4, 1864, James Z. George Papers, MDAH.

18. J. Z. George to Bettie, January 8 and 19 and February 5, and 12, 1865, James Z. George Papers, MDAH.

19. J. Z. George to Bettie, January 31, February 22, March 8, April 3 and 10, May 1, June 5, and October 23, 1864, and February 5 and 15, and April 9, 1865, James Z. George Papers, MDAH.

NOTES

20. J. Z. George to Bettie, October 16, 1864, James Z. George Papers, MDAH.

21. J. Z. George to Bettie, January 31, April 3, June 12 and 23, and July 18, 1864, and January 8, 1865, James Z. George Papers, MDAH; "Register of Express Packages Received for Prisoners and Examined, 1865," Microfilm Roll 4248, MDAH.

22. J. Z. George to Bettie, October 5 and December 4, 1864, and April 22, 1865, James Z. George Papers, MDAH; James Z. George, *The Political History of Slavery in the United States* (New York: Neale, 1915), xi.

23. J. Z. George to Bettie, August 14, 1864, James Z. George Papers, MDAH; George, *Political History of Slavery*, xi–xii.

24. J. Z. George to Bettie, January 31, February 28, April 10, May 1 and 22, June 12, and September 16, 1864, and April 22, 1865, James Z. George Papers, MDAH.

25. J. Z. George to Bettie, April 10, May 29, and June 12 and 30, 1864, James Z. George Papers, MDAH.

26. J. Z. George to Bettie, September 16 and October 1 and 5, 1864, James Z. George Papers, MDAH.

27. J. Z. George to Bettie, October 5, 1864, James Z. George Papers, MDAH.

28. J. Z. George to Bettie, May 7 and 14, 1865, James Z. George Papers, MDAH.

29. Amnesty Roll, Microfilm 4248, MDAH; J. Z. George Civil War Compiled Service Record, Fifth Mississippi Cavalry, NARA.

Chapter 11

1. Henderson, "Wife of Gen. J. Z. George."
2. J. Z. George to Bettie, May 1, 1865, James Z. George Papers, MDAH.
3. J. Z. George to Bettie, May 7 and 14, 1865, James Z. George Papers, MDAH.
4. J. Z. George to Bettie, May 7, 1865, James Z. George Papers, MDAH.
5. Ibid.
6. Ibid.
7. J. Z. George to Bettie, May 7 and 14, 1865, James Z. George Papers, MDAH; Allardice, *Confederate Colonels*, 399–400.
8. J. M. Dyer to J. Z. George, May 7, 1867, James Z. George Papers, MDAH; J. Z. George Receipt Book, 1869–1870, Cotesworth. See George's Reconstruction-era receipt book for tax stamps on transactions as well as a glimpse into George's purchases at the time. They include numerous items such as tuition for the children, farm implements, carriages, and household items.
9. For Reconstruction, see William C. Harris, *Presidential Reconstruction in Mississippi* (Baton Rouge: Louisiana State University Press, 1967); William C. Harris, *Day of the Carpetbagger: Republican Reconstruction in Mississippi* (Baton Rouge: Louisiana State University Press, 1979); William C. Harris, "The Reconstruction of the Commonwealth, 1865–1870," in *A History of Mississippi*, 2 vols., ed. Richard A. McLemore, (Hattiesburg: University and College Press of Mississippi, 1973), 1:542–570; David G. Sansing, "Congressional Reconstruction," in McLemore, *History of Mississippi*, 1:571–589.
10. J. Z. George to J. T. Mitchell, October 27, 1870, James Z. George Papers, MDAH; J. Z. George to L. Q. C. Lamar, April 15, 1874, L. Q. C. Lamar and Edward

Mayes Papers, MDAH; Fred M. Witty, "Reconstruction in Carroll-Montgomery Counties," in Riley, *Publications of the Mississippi Historical Society*, 10:130. For George's cases, see the legal data found in Lexis Nexis.

11. *Memorial Addresses on the Life and Character of James Z. George*, 64.

12. J. Z. George to Bettie, January 9, 1867, James Z. George Papers, MDAH.

13. J. Z. George to Sir, May 4, 1872, J. Z. George Letters, Cotesworth; J. Z. George Family Bible, Cotesworth.

14. J. Z. George Family Bible, Cotesworth.

15. Carrollton Baptist Church 175th Anniversary Program, October 26, 2008, author's collection; Undated and untitled newspaper clipping, J. Z. George Scrapbook, Cotesworth, original in *New York Tribune*, August 24, 1897; Armstrong, "James Zachariah George," 9.

16. "Tribute to Gen. George," undated newspaper clipping, J. Z. George Scrapbook, Cotesworth; J. Z. George to Bettie, November 4, 1863, James Z. George Papers, MDAH.

17. "James Z. George: The Great Commoner of Mississippi," George Family File, Monroe County Historical Society; "Tribute to Gen. George," undated newspaper clipping, J. Z. George Scrapbook, Cotesworth; Undated and untitled newspaper clipping, J. Z. George Scrapbook, Cotesworth.

18. "Senator J. Z. George," undated newspaper clipping, J. Z. George Scrapbook, Cotesworth.

19. Shanks, "Early Career of James Z. George," 8; James Z. George, *Reports of Cases Argued and Determined in the High Court of Errors and Appeals for the State of Mississippi—Volume XXXVIII*; James Z. George, *Reports of Cases Argued and Determined in the High Court of Errors and Appeals for the State of Mississippi—Volume XXXIX—Volume X, Containing Cases Determined at February and October Terms, 1860, April and October Terms, 1861, and April Term, 1863* (Philadelphia: T. & J. W. Johnson, 1867); "Letter From the Chairman of the Democratic Conservative Election Committee on the Subject of Common School Legislation," J. Z. George Scrapbook, Vol. 1, Box 2, James Z. George Papers, MDAH. For the newspaper articles, see various copies of his works in the J. Z. George Subject File, Mississippi Supreme Court.

20. J. Z. George to O. J. E. Stewart, April 6, 1870, James Bull Smith Dimitry Papers, DU; James Z. George, *A Digest of the Reports of the Decisions of the Supreme Court and of the High Court of Errors and Appeals of the State of Mississippi, From the Organization of the State, to the Present Time* (Philadelphia: T. and J. W. Johnson, 1872); Shanks, "Early Career of James Z. George," 61; "George's Digest," *Jackson Weekly Journal*, October 10, 1872.

21. George, *Digest of the Reports*, iii.

22. Ibid., i.

23. For J. Z. George deeds, see Deed Book R, 251, Deed Book S, 124, 180, 252, 310, 535, Deed Book T, 195, 281, 451, 455, 585, 587, Deed Book U, 152, 351, Deed Book V, 166, 362, 450, Deed Book W, 391, 471, 647, 663, 739, Deed Book Y, 483, Deed Book Z, 69, 746, Deed Book 1, 330, 331, Deed Book 3, 396, and Deed Book 5, 412, all in Carroll County Courthouse.

24. J. Z. George Deeds, July 1868, Deed Book E, 598, February 21, 1874, Deed Book 2, 783, and September 25, 1879, Deed Book 8, 435, with a correcting deed of August 1883, Deed Book 10, 187, all in Leflore County Courthouse; Runnymede Description, Runnymede Subject File, MDAH.

25. 1870 Mississippi Census, Carroll County, NARA, 24; "Mess. George and Henderson Accounts," 1888, James Z. George Papers, MDAH; Richardson and May to J. Z. George, June 22, 1888, James Z. George Papers, MDAH.

26. J. William Harris, *Deep Souths: Delta, Piedmont, and Sea Island Society in the Age of Segregation* (Baltimore: Johns Hopkins University Press, 2001) 43; John William Wade, "Lands of the Liquidating Levee Board through Litigation and Legislation," in Riley, *Publications of the Mississippi Historical Society*, 9:288.

27. J. Z. George Cases, Chancery Court Minute Book, 1872–1888, Carroll County Courthouse, 2, 220, 222; J. Z. George Cases, Circuit Court Minute Book K, 1871–1881, Carroll County Courthouse, 298, 476; Wade, "Lands of the Liquidating Levee Board," 288–289; Lexis Nexis, "47 Miss. 713; 1873 Miss."; Lexis Nexis, "47 Miss. 725; 1873 Miss."

28. *Mississippi in 1875: Report of the Select Committee to Inquire into the Mississippi Election of 1875, With the Testimony and Documentary Evidence*, 2 vols. (Washington, D.C.: Government Printing Office, 1876), 2:1121; J. Z. George to Sir, May 4, 1872, J. Z. George Letters, Cotesworth; Norma Wilkins, "Robert W. Williamson," Robert W. Williamson Subject File, MDAH; Shanks, "Early Career of James Z. George," 61; Woods, "Sketch of the Mississippi Secession Convention," 94–95; "Wiley P. Harris," *Dictionary of American Biography* (New York: Scribners, 1932), 8:325; Wiley P. Harris, "Autobiography," in Rowland, *Courts, Judges, and Lawyers*, 259–260, 328; George, *Political History of Slavery*, xii; J. Z. George to Ridgley C. Powers, July 26, 1873, Governor Ridgely C. Powers Correspondence and Papers, 1871–1874, MDAH; Clayton Rand, "They Built the South," *New Orleans Times Picayune*, January 30, 1944, copy in James Z. George Biographical Vertical File, Louisiana State University. See the Lexis Nexis database for the George-Harris cases.

29. "Testimonial to Gen. J. Z. George by His Old Neighbors," *Jackson Weekly Clarion*, January 16, 1873.

Chapter 12

1. Shanks, "Early Career of James Z. George," 63. For more on the Radical Reconstruction context, see Eric Foner, *Reconstruction: America's Unfinished Revolution, 1863–1877* (New York: Harper Collins, 1989); Harris, *Day of the Carpetbagger*.

2. "Our Poliot What Should It Be?" *Canton American Citizen*, April 4, 1868; "The Speaking Tuesday Night," *Jackson Weekly Clarion*, October 17, 1872; "Mass Meetings of the Friends of Greeley and Brown," *Jackson Weekly Clarion*, September 26, 1872; "Canvass on the Sea Coast," *Jackson Weekly Clarion*, October 31, 1872.

3. J. Z. George to Bettie, January 10, 1867, James Z. George Papers, MDAH.

4. Ibid.; Harris, "Reconstruction of the Commonwealth," 549; J. Z. George Apprentice Application, December 23, 1865, Probate Court Minute Book, 1862–1866,

Carroll County Courthouse, 503–504; J. Z. George Apprentice Document, January 24, 1868, Probate Court Minute Book, 1867–1870, Carroll County Courthouse, 30–31.

5. W. N. Goodman to J. Z. George, February 14, 1867, J. Z. George to Bettie, January 9, 1867, and J. Z. George to J. T. Mitchell, October 27, 1870, all in James Z. George Papers, MDAH.

6. J. Z. George to Bettie, January 9, 1867, James Z. George Papers, MDAH. George would later eulogize Brown at his death in 1880. See "The Late Hon. A. G. Brown," J. Z. George Scrapbook, Vol. 4, Box 3, James Z. George Papers, MDAH; James Byrne Ranck, *Albert Gallatin Brown: Radical Southern Nationalist* (New York: Appleton-Century, 1937), 295–298.

7. "James Z. George and L. Q. C. Lamar and Their Citizen Leadership in Mississippi during the Reconstruction Period," undated, Box 3, Folder 6, Annie E. Cody Papers, Tennessee State Library and Archives; "Senator J. Z. George of Mississippi," undated, Rare Book and Special Collections, LC.

8. J. Z. George to L. Q. C. Lamar, April 15, 1874, L. Q. C. Lamar and Edward Mayes Papers, MDAH.

9. Frank Johnston, "The Conference of October 15, 1875, Between General George and Governor Ames," in Riley, *Publications of the Mississippi Historical Society*, 6:65; J. Z. George to L. Q. C. Lamar, April 15, 1874, L. Q. C. Lamar and Edward Mayes Papers, MDAH.

10. "James Z. George and L. Q. C. Lamar and Their Citizen Leadership," 580–581.

11. "James Z. George and L. Q. C. Lamar and Their Citizen Leadership"; Frank Johnston, "The Public Services of Senator James Z. George," in Riley, *Publications of the Mississippi Historical Society*, 8:202; Shanks, "Early Career of James Z. George," 73; Johnston, "Conference of October 15, 1875," 66; J. S. McNeily, "Climax and Collapse of Reconstruction in Mississippi, 1874–1876," in Riley, *Publications of the Mississippi Historical Society*, 12:336–337; Edward Mayes, *Lucius Q. C. Lamar: His Life, Times, and Speeches, 1825–1893* (Nashville, Tenn.: Publishing House of the Methodist Episcopal Church, South, 1896), 319; "Democratic Conservatism," *Jackson Daily Mississippi Pilot*, May 22, 1875; "Democratic-Conservative Convention," *Jackson Weekly Clarion*, August 4, 1875.

12. Johnston, "Conference of October 15, 1875," 76.

13. Johnston, "Public Services of Senator James Z. George," 208; Johnston, "Conference of October 15, 1875," 68–69; Dunbar Rowland, "Rise and Fall of Negro Rule in Mississippi," in Riley, *Publications of the Mississippi Historical Society*, 2:193–194.

14. "James Z. George and L. Q. C. Lamar and Their Citizen Leadership"; J. Z. George to L. Q. C. Lamar, May 3, 1874, L. Q. C. Lamar and Edward Mayes Papers, MDAH; "The Clinton Riot," Campaign Document No. 2, Democratic Executive Committee, 1875, MDAH. For Lamar, see James B. Murphy, *L. Q. C. Lamar: Pragmatic Patriot* (Baton Rouge: Louisiana State University Press, 1973).

15. M. D. Leggett to Rutherford B. Hayes, March 12, 1877, Rutherford B. Hayes Papers, Rutherford B. Hayes Presidential Center (hereafter cited as RBHPC).

Chapter 13

1. Johnston, "Conference of October 15, 1875," 67–69; Sansing, "Congressional Reconstruction," 1:585, 587; *Mississippi in 1875*, 1:lxxvi, 382–383, 385.

2. Johnston, "Conference of October 15, 1875," 67–69; Sansing, "Congressional Reconstruction," 1:585, 587; *Mississippi in 1875*, 1:382–383, 385.

3. Johnston, "Conference of October 15, 1875," 67–69; Sansing, "Congressional Reconstruction," 1:585, 587; *Mississippi in 1875*, 1:382–383, 385.

4. "Letter from the Chairman of the Democratic State Executive Committee on the Subject of Common School Legislation," J. Z. George Scrapbook, Vol. 1, Box 2, James Z. George Papers, MDAH; Shanks, "Early Career of James Z. George," 85; Johnston, "Conference of October 15, 1875," 67–68; James W. Garner, *Reconstruction in Mississippi* (New York: Macmillan, 1901), 383; Sansing, "Congressional Reconstruction," 1:586–587; Ringold, "Some Liberal Aspects," 15.

5. W. Calvin Wells, "Reconstruction in Hinds County," in Riley, *Publications of the Mississippi Historical Society*, 9:102; E. H. Anderson, "A Memoir on Reconstruction in Yazoo City," *Journal of Mississippi History* 4, no. 4 (October 1942): 191; Garner, *Reconstruction in Mississippi*, 375, 378; *The Legislation of 1865 Concerning Freedmen: A Letter*, 1875, Special Collections Department, UM; "*Decrease of the Wealth of Mississippi under Radical Misrule*," Jackson Weekly Clarion, October 13, 1875; *The Clinton Riot: A True Statement, Showing Who Originated It*, 1875, MDAH; *Issues of the Canvass—Compiled From the Clarion, and Presented to the Democratic-Conservative Canvassers*, 1875, Special Collections Department, UM; "The Appointment of Election Supervisors," *Jackson Weekly Clarion*, October 13, 1875; "The Panola Fraud," *Jackson Weekly Clarion*, October 27, 1875; *Mississippi in 1875*, 1:385, 393–394.

6. Sansing, "Congressional Reconstruction," 1:586; Garner, *Reconstruction in Mississippi*, 374.

7. F. Z. Browne, "Reconstruction in Oktibbeha County," in Riley, *Publications of the Mississippi Historical Society*, 13:281; Julia Kendel, "Reconstruction in Lafayette County," in Riley, *Publications of the Mississippi Historical Society*, 13:244; "Montgomery County—Grand Rally of the People at Duck Hill," *Jackson Weekly Clarion*, October 27, 1875.

8. *Mississippi in 1875*, 2:1803.

9. Ibid., 1802; Johnston, "Conference of October 15, 1875," 69–70, 74.

10. Johnston, "Conference of October 15, 1875," 70.

11. Ibid., 71; *Mississippi in 1875*, 1:351. For a modern account of the meeting, see Nicholas Lemann, *Redemption: The Last Battle of the Civil War* (New York: Farrar, Straus and Giroux, 2007), 127–131.

12. *Mississippi in 1875*, 2:1803; Johnston, "Conference of October 15, 1875," 72, 76.

13. *Mississippi in 1875*, 1:387, 391, 394, 396–399.

14. J. Z. George to Adelbert Ames, October 19, 21, and 29, 1875, Governor Adelbert Ames Correspondence and Papers, 1874–1876, MDAH; Sansing, "Congressional Reconstruction," 1:588; *Mississippi in 1875*, 2:1804; Johnston, "Conference of October 15, 1875," 72–73, 76.

15. *Mississippi in 1875*, 2:1805; *Mississippi in 1875*, 1:xxvi, 91, 99.

16. *Mississippi in 1875*, 1:387, 391, 394, 396–399.

17. *Mississippi in 1875*, 2:1802, 1808.

18. Ibid., 1804, 1807; *Mississippi in 1875*, 2: Documentary Evidence, 65; *Mississippi in 1875*, 1:967; Stephen Cresswell, *Multi-party Politics in Mississippi, 1877–1902* (Jackson: University Press of Mississippi, 1995), 14.

19. "The Last Card of the Defeated and Desperate Office-seekers," *Jackson Weekly Clarion*, November 3, 1875; *Mississippi in 1875*, 2:1819.

20. *Mississippi in 1875*, 2:1819; Harris, *Day of the Carpetbagger*, 703.

21. *Mississippi in 1875*, 1:403, 406; "Mississippi," *New York Times*, November 3, 1875.

22. Sansing, "Congressional Reconstruction," 1:588–589; Johnston, "Conference of October 15, 1875," 75; *Mississippi in 1875*, 2:1806, 1809; *Mississippi in 1875*, 1:403; Harris, *Day of the Carpetbagger*, 692. Rumor had it that George had even stopped an assassination attempt on Ames's life. George denied it. Whether he did or not is unknown. He could have in order to keep violence down and thus federal troops out of the state, but he perhaps needed to deny it to keep support among militant Democrats. See "Card from Gen. J. Z. George," J. Z. George Scrapbook, Vol. 1, Box 2, James Z. George Papers, MDAH.

23. *Mississippi in 1875*, 2:1805; *Mississippi in 1875*, 1:xxvi, 91, 99; McNeily, "Climax and Collapse," 423–424.

24. *Mississippi in 1875*, 1:lvi–lvii.

25. J. Z. George Family Bible, Cotesworth; J. Z. George to L. Q. C. Lamar, September 11, 1876, L. Q. C. Lamar and Edward Mayes Papers, MDAH; Philip Dray, *Capitol Men: The Epic Story of Reconstruction through the Lives of the First Black Congressmen* (Boston: Houghton Mifflin Harcourt, 2008), 249.

26. J. Z. George to L. Q. C. Lamar, September 11 and October 19, 1876, L. Q. C. Lamar and Edward Mayes Papers, MDAH.

27. *Address of the State Executive Committee*, 1875, and *Radical Extravagance Contrasted with Democratic Economy*, 1875, together as *Issues of the Canvass, of 1876—The Committee*, 1875, UM; "Issues of the Canvass of 1876—No. 2," J. Z. George Scrapbook, Vol. 2, Box 2, James Z. George Papers, MDAH.

28. *Mississippi in 1875*, 1:15, 350.

29. Harris, *Day of the Carpetbagger*, 679; Albert D. Kirwan, *Revolt of the Rednecks: Mississippi Politics: 1876–1925* (New York: Harper and Row, 1965), 11–12; Willie D. Halsell, "James R. Chalmers and 'Mahoneism' in Mississippi," *Journal of Southern History* 10, no. 1 (February 1944): 42; C. Vann Woodward, *The Strange Career of Jim Crow*, 3rd ed. (New York: Oxford University Press, 1974), 57–58.

30. M. D. Leggett to Rutherford B. Hayes, March 12, 1877, Rutherford B. Hayes Papers, RBHPC; "Senator J. Z. George of Mississippi," undated, Rare Book and Special Collections, LC; "Kemper County Affair," *Mississippi Republican*, June 1876; "The Kemper County Affair," J. Z. George Scrapbook, Vol. 1, Box 2, James Z. George Papers, MDAH.

31. "Originator of the Mississippi Plan," *New York Times*, February 14, 1881; *Memorial Addresses on the Life and Character of James Z. George*, 96; J. S. McNeily, "War and Reconstruction in Mississippi, 1863–1890," in *Publications of the Mississippi Historical Society, Centenary Series*, 5 vols. (Jackson: Mississippi Historical Society, 1918), 2:532; Lemann, *Redemption*, 170.

Chapter 14

1. See Lexis Nexis legal database for George's cases during this period. Mississippi's high court was now called the supreme court instead of the High Court of Errors and Appeals.

2. "Senator J. Z. George," undated newspaper clipping, J. Z. George Scrapbook, Cotesworth; J. Z. George to L. Q. C. Lamar, June 1, 1883, L. C. Q. Lamar and Edward Mayes Papers, MDAH.

3. J. Z. George to Robert Lowry, August 7, 1877, Robert Lowry Papers, MDAH; J. Z. George to John M. Stone, September 13, 1878, Governor John M. Stone Correspondence and Papers, 1876–1882, MDAH; "Rewarded for Infamous Work," *New York Times*, January 24, 1880.

4. J. Z. George State University Board of Trustees Appointment, February 14, 1878, Register of Commissions, 1878–1881, MDAH, 11; J. Z. George Agricultural and Mechanical College Board of Trustees Appointment, May 8, 1879, Register of Commissions, 1878–1881, MDAH, 40; J. Z. George Agricultural and Mechanical College Board of Trustees Appointment, March 11, 1890, Register of Commissions, 1887–1891, MDAH, 13.

5. University of Mississippi Board of Trustee Reports and Minutes, Book 2, 1860–1882, Box 2, UM, 355, 358–359, 370, 372.

6. Ibid., 405, 439; J. Z. George to John M. Stone, May 7, 1879, Governor John M. Stone Correspondence and Papers, 1876–1882, MDAH.

7. Dunbar Rowland, *The Official and Statistical Register of the State of Mississippi, 1904* (Nashville, Tenn.: Brandon Printing, 1904), 271; *First Annual Catalogue of the Officers and Students of the Mississippi Agricultural and Mechanical College of Mississippi, 1880-'81* (Jackson, Miss.: Clarion Steam Publishing House, 1881), list of trustees in front; *Seventeenth Annual Catalogue of the Mississippi Agricultural and Mechanical College, 1896-'97* (Starkville, Miss.: E. L. Reid's Steam Printing Office, 1897), list of trustees in front; "Address of Hon. J. Z. George," September 22, 1879, newspaper clipping in J. Z. George Scrapbook, Vol. 4, Box 3, James Z. George Papers, MDAH. For a history of Mississippi State University, see Michael B. Ballard, *Maroon and White: Mississippi State University, 1878–2003* (Jackson: University Press of Mississippi, 2008).

8. J. Z. George and G. H. Peets to Board of Trustees, June 19, 1889, Mississippi State University Board of Trustees Correspondence, Box 1, Folder 1, Mississippi State University (hereafter cited as MSU); Mississippi State University Board of Trustee Minutes, Vol. 1, June 11 and 12, 1879, MSU, 41; Mississippi State University Board of Trustee Minutes, Vol. 2, June 1896 and June 1897, MSU, 36, 47; J. Z. George to John M. Stone, August 1, 1878, and July 28, 1879, Governor John M. Stone Correspondence and Papers, 1876–1882, MDAH.

9. Edward Mayes, *The State University: Reply of Prof. Edward Mayes to Senator J. Z. George* (University, Miss.: Edward Mayes, 1887), copy in MDAH; David G. Sansing, *The University of Mississippi: A Sesquicentennial History* (Jackson: University Press of Mississippi, 1999), 150–152; Roger D. Tate, "Franklin L. Riley and the University of Mississippi," *Journal of Mississippi History* 42, no. 2 (May 1980): 102; "The Oxford University," *Vicksburg Post*, October 19, 1887; "Senator George and State University," *Chickasaw Messenger*, October 13, 1887; "Senator George and State University," *Holly*

Springs Sentinel, October 19, 1887; "The Colleges Again," *Shubuta Mississippian*, October 22, 1887; "Another George Letter," *Natchez Banner*, October 20, 1887.

10. L. Q. C. Lamar to Rutherford B. Hayes, October 8, 1877, Rutherford B. Hayes Papers, RBHPC; *Jackson Weekly Clarion*, February 7, 1877.

11. "General Notes," *New York Times*, March 1, 1878.

12. "Famous Mississippians"; Rowland, *Mississippi*, 2:668; Skates, *History of the Mississippi Supreme Court*, 39.

13. J. Z. George Supreme Court Appointment, February 22, 1878, Register of Commissions, 1878–1881, MDAH, 3; May 10, 1879, entry, Supreme Court Minute Book F, 1879–1882, MDAH; J. B. H. Hemingway, *Reports of Cases in the Supreme Court for the State of Mississippi, Vol. LVI, Containing Cases Decided at the April Term, 1878, the January Special Terms, 1879, and the April Term, 1879* (St. Louis: G. I. Jones, 1880); "James Z. George, 1879–1881," *Jackson Daily Clarion Ledger*, December 31, 1937. A copy of this last article can be found in the Supreme Court, 1817–1913, Subject File, MDAH. For court-related biographical sketches, see "Mississippi Supreme Court Justice Biographical Project," Mississippi Supreme Court, n.p.; Clover S. Pitts, "James Z. George: Lawyer, Soldier, Judge, Statesman," *Mississippi Lawyer* (July–September 2000): 22–24; and "James Zachariah George," undated, Series 2, Box 3, Folder 21, John Ray Skates Papers, University of Southern Mississippi (hereafter cited as USM).

14. Rowland, *Mississippi*, 1:349–350, 390.

15. *Memorial Addresses on the Life and Character of James Z. George*, 13; May 12, 1879 entry, Supreme Court Minute Book F, 1879–1882, MDAH; J. A. Brown and J. B. H. Hemingway, *Reports of Cases in the Supreme Court for the State of Mississippi, Vol. LVII, Containing Cases Decided at the April and October Terms, 1879, and the April Terms, 1880* (Boston: Little, Brown, 1880).

16. May 10, 1879, entry, Supreme Court Minute Book F, 1879–1882, MDAH.

17. J. Z. George to Chambers, July 30, 1879, J. Z. George Letters, Cotesworth; George Opinion, 1881, Box 6, Folder 8, Barksdale Family Papers, MDAH; *Memorial Addresses on the Life and Character of James Z. George*, 66. See Lexis Nexis legal database for summary of cases during George's tenure.

18. 1880 Mississippi Census, Hinds County, NARA, 17; Thomas Gore Manuscript, 1882, Thomas Pryor Gore Papers, MDAH; "Mrs. Lizzie George Henderson," *Confederate Veteran* 13, no. 12 (December 1905): 532a.

19. July 6, 1880, entry, Supreme Court Minute Book F, 1879–1882, MDAH.

20. James W. Garner, "The Senatorial Career of J. Z. George," in Riley, *Publications of the Mississippi Historical Society*, 7:245; Bradley G. Bond, "Edward C. Walthall and the 1880 Senatorial Nomination: Politics of Balance in the Redeemer Era," *Journal of Mississippi History* 50 (February 1988): 2–3; Willie D. Halsell, "Democratic Dissensions in Mississippi, 1878–1882," *Journal of Mississippi History* 2 (July 1940): 125–129. For Walthall, see Bradley G. Bond, "Edward Cary Walthall, 1865–1890: A Redeemer Reappraisal" (master's thesis, University of Southern Mississippi, 1987).

21. Bond, "Edward C. Walthall," 6, 10; Halsell, "Democratic Dissensions," 126. Various historians differ on the definition of a Bourbon. Some include the economic and industrial supporters in the Bourbon wing because of their adherence to antebellum white supremacy, but I have sided with C. Vann Woodward, who defines Bourbons as those who looked backward with allegiance to the old Confederacy and

abhorred the new collusion with the Northern economy. See C. Vann Woodward, *Origins of the New South: 1877–1913* (Baton Rouge: Louisiana State University Press, 1951), 14, 75. See also Halsell, "Bourbon Period," 519–521.

22. Halsell, "Democratic Dissensions," 127–128; Bond, "Edward C. Walthall," 14–15.

23. Cresswell, *Multi-party Politics in Mississippi*, 37; *Journal of the House of Representatives of the State of Mississippi at a Regular Session Thereof, Convened in the City of Jackson, January 6, 1880* (Jackson, Miss.: J. L. Power, 1880), 142–143, 148–149; "Senatorial Ballotings," *Washington Post*, January 20, 1880; J. Z. George United States Senator Appointment, February 22, 1880, Register of Commissions, 1878–1881, MDAH, 2; E. V. Murphy, *Congressional Directory, 1st Session, 47th Congress* (Washington, D.C.: Government Printing Office, 1881), 39; Bond, "Edward C. Walthall," 15–16; Garner, "Senatorial Career of J. Z. George," 246; Halsell, "Democratic Dissensions," 128.

24. *Memorial Addresses on the Life and Character of James Z. George*, 17; James H. Stone, ed., "L. Q. C. Lamar's Letters to Edward Donelson Clark, 1868–1885: Part III, 1879–1885," *Journal of Mississippi History*, 43, no. 2 (May 1981): 150; Bond, "Edward C. Walthall," 9, 16–17; Woodward, *Origins of the New South*, 18; Halsell, "Bourbon Period," 524; "Books and School," *Tupelo Journal*, October 21, 1887. An early Lamar biographer mistakenly wrote that George and Lamar were "warm friends." See Wirt Armistead Cate, *Lucius Q. C. Lamar: Secession and Reunion* (Chapel Hill: University of North Carolina Press, 1935), 235.

25. July 6, 1880, entry, Supreme Court Minute Book F, 1879–1882, MDAH; J. B. H. Hemingway, *Reports of Cases in the Supreme Court for the State of Mississippi, Vol. LVIII, Containing Cases Decided at the October Term, 1880, and the April Term, 1881* (St. Louis: G. I. Jones, 1881), frontispiece; February 2, 1881, entry, Supreme Court Minute Book F, 1879–1882, MDAH; James D. Lynch, *The Bench and the Bar of Mississippi* (New York: E. J. Hale and Son, 1881), 534.

26. *Statistics of the Population of the United States at the Tenth Census (June 1, 1880)*, 22 vols. (Washington, D.C.: Government Printing Office, 1881), 1:234.

27. J. Z. George to L. Q. C. Lamar, June 1, 1883, L. C. Q. Lamar and Edward Mayes Papers, MDAH; Murphy, *Congressional Directory*, l70; Mrs. O. K. Gee, *Marriage Records in the Carroll County Courthouse* (Carrollton, Miss.: n.p., 1964), n.p.; Garner, "Senatorial Career of J. Z. George," 245.

Chapter 15

1. *Congressional Record*, Vol. 12, Part 1, 1 (hereafter cited as *CR*).

2. J. Z. George to L. Q. C. Lamar, April 29, 1881, L. C. Q. Lamar and Edward Mayes Papers, MDAH; J. Z. George to Mr. Buford, May 26, 1882, James Z. George Papers, MDAH; Murphy, *Congressional Directory*, 166.

3. *CR*, 12, 1:1; Garner, "Senatorial Career of J. Z. George," 246.

4. "A Bow Legged Statesman," *Jackson State Ledger*, December 24, 1887; Ringold, "Some Liberal Aspects," 18; "Old Rough and Ready," J. Z. George Scrapbook, Vol. 3, Box 3, James Z. George Papers, MDAH.

5. *CR*, 12, 1:33.
6. Ibid., 505; "The Senate's Work Ended," *New York Times*, October 30, 1881.
7. Mayes, *Lucius Q. C. Lamar*, 426; *CR*, 12, 1:161–164. For a printed copy, see *Remarks of Hon. J. Z. George of Mississippi, in the Senate of the United States, Friday April 1, 1881, on the Resolution Submitted by Mr. Dawes in Relation to the Election of Officers of the Senate* (Washington, D.C.: Government Printing Office, 1881).
8. *CR*, 12, 1:161–167.
9. Ibid., 164–165.
10. "City Talk and Chatter," *Washington Post*, April 30, 1881.
11. Ben Perley Poore, *Congressional Directory, 49th Congress, 1st Session* (Washington, D.C.: Government Printing Office, 1886), 47; *CR*, 17, 1:855.
12. *CR*, 17, 4:3538.
13. Poore, *Congressional Directory*, 188–189, 197.
14. "Personal Intelligence," *New York Times*, August 1, 1883; "Personal Intelligence," *New York Times*, August 12, 1883; "Personal Intelligence," *New York Times*, September 21, 1888. See the various *Congressional Directories* for his street addresses. See Seaborn J. Durham and Mary C. Durham tombstones in the Kosciusko, Mississippi, City Cemetery for death dates. See William Cothran's tombstone in Evergreen Cemetery, Carrollton, for his death date.
15. J. Z. George to Bettie, March 9, 1886, James Z. George Papers, MDAH.
16. J. Z. George Family Bible, Cotesworth; "Mrs. Lizzie George Henderson," 532a; J. Z. George to Bettie, December 16 and 28, 1884, April 2, 1885, March 4 and 9, 1886, and February 3, 1887, James Z. George Papers, MDAH; J. Z. George to Lizzie, December 2, 1886, J. Z. George Letters, Cotesworth.
17. Bettie George to Lizzie, April 28, 1883, Bettie George Letters, Cotesworth.
18. J. Z. George to Lizzie, February 29, April 12, and December 10, 1883, and undated except 1885, J. Z. George Letters, Cotesworth; Bettie George to Lizzie, April 28, 1883, Bettie George Letters, Cotesworth.
19. J. Z. George to Bettie, December 16, 1884, March 20, 1885, and February 24, 1887, James Z. George Papers, MDAH; J. Z. George to Lizzie, January 9, 1885, and October 9, 1887, J. Z. George Letters, Cotesworth; J. Z. George to Bettie, February 10, 1883, J. Z. George Letters, Cotesworth; J. Z. George to Winfield S. Featherston, January 15, 1888, Folder 5.33, Winfield S. Featherston Collection, UM.
20. J. Z. George to Bettie, December 16, 1884, March 20 and 24, 1885, and February 3, 1887, James Z. George Papers, MDAH.
21. Bettie George to Lizzie, April 28, 1883, Bettie George Letters, Cotesworth.
22. J. Z. George to Bettie, December 28, 1884, April 2, 1885, and February 3, 1887, James Z. George Papers, MDAH; *CR*, 15, 4:3057; *Report of the Committee of the Senate upon the Relations between Labor and Capital, and Testimony Taken by the Committee*, 5 vols. (Washington, D.C.: Government Printing Office, 1885). For an index of bills, motions, and amendments, see the indexes accompanying the various volumes of the *Congressional Record*. For an example of George's correspondence regarding an office seeker, see W. S. Featherston to J. Z. George, February 13, 1885, J. M. Stone to J. Z. George, February 14, 1885, J. Z. George and Edward C. Walthall to Grover Cleveland, March 25, 1885, and J. Z. George et al. to Grover Cleveland, April 7, 1885, all in William H. McCardle Papers, MDAH.

23. "The Courts," *Washington Post*, January 18, 1882; "The Courts," *Washington Post*, March 17, 1882; "The Courts," *Washington Post*, April 23, 1884; "The Courts," *Washington Post*, April 25, 1884; "United States Supreme Court," *New York Times*, October 16, 1884; "National Capital Topics," *New York Times*, November 24, 1885; "The Courts," *Washington Post*, November 24, 1885. See Lexis Nexis legal database for George's Supreme Court cases.

24. *CR*, 12, 1:161–167; *CR*, 13, 4:3463; *CR*, 16, 1:624, 684.

25. *CR*, 15, 3:2245, 2708; *CR*, 17, 2:1734–1739; Peck, "Life and Times of James Z. George," 81–82; Ringold, "Some Liberal Aspects," 22; Armstrong, "James Zachariah George," 44; *Northern Pacific Railroad Lands—Speech of Hon. James Z. George, of Mississippi, in the Senate of the United States, Friday, June 11, 1886* (Washington, D.C.: Government Printing Office, 1886); Allen J. Going, "The South and the Blair Education Bill," *Mississippi Valley Historical Review*, 44, no. 2 (September 1957), 280.

26. *CR*, 14, 4:3404; *CR*, 15, 6:5486–5488; *CR*, 17, 1:179; 17, 5:4681; Garner, "Senatorial Career of J. Z. George," 247; J. Z. George to Lizzie, October 9, 1887, J. Z. George Letters, Cotesworth; *Memorial Addresses on the Life and Character of James Z. George*, 33; "A Generous Pensioner," J. Z. George Scrapbook, Vol. 3, Box 3, James Z. George Papers, MDAH.

27. *CR*, 13, 1:579; *CR*, 15, 1:17, 342, 879; *CR*, 13, 6:6131; *CR*, 18, 2:1039, 1083; *CR*, 18, 3:2282; *Memorial Addresses on the Life and Character of James Z. George*, 35; Garner, "Senatorial Career of J. Z. George," 247, 257; May Spencer Ringold, "Senator James Zachariah George of Mississippi: Bourbon or Liberal?" *Journal of Mississippi History* 16, no. 3 (July 1954): 168; Peck, "Life and Times of James Z. George," 79, 81; Ringold, "Some Liberal Aspects," 72; Armstrong, "James Zachariah George," 61; "Begun the Inquiry," *Washington Post*, May 24, 1893; *Dealings in "Options" and "Futures"—Speech of Hon. James Z. George, of Mississippi, in the Senate of the United States, December 13, 14, and 15, 1892* (Washington, D.C.: Government Printing Office, 1892); Undated newspaper clipping, J. Z. George Subject File, MDAH; J. Z. George Scrapbook, Vol. 1, Box 2, James Z. George Papers, MDAH; William Lincoln Giles, "Agricultural Revolution: 1890–1970," in McLemore, *History of Mississippi*, 2:186; *Agriculture Department—Speech of Hon. James Z. George of Mississippi in the Senate of the United States, January 13, 1883* (Washington, D.C.: Government Printing Office, 1883). The Hatch Act, originally offered in the House, passed the Senate on January 27, 1887.

28. J. Z. George to Grover Cleveland, April 2, 1886, Grover Cleveland Papers, LC; *Mr. George, from the Committee on Woman Suffrage, Submitted the Following Views of the Minority, to Accompany Joint Resolution S.R. 60* (Washington, D.C.: Government Printing Office, 1882); Elizabeth Cady Stanton, Susan B. Anthony, and Matilda Joslyn Gage, eds., *History of Woman Suffrage*, 3 vols. (Rochester: Charles Mann, 1876–1885), 3:237–240; J. Z. George to Grover Cleveland, April 7, 1885, and W. S. Featherston to J. Z. George, February 13, 1885, both in William H. McCardle Papers, MDAH; *CR*, l3, 1:348; *CR*, 13, 6:5531; *CR*, 15, 2:1341.

29. *Issue of Circulating Notes—Speech of Hon. James Z. George of Mississippi in the Senate of the United States, Monday February 25, 1884* (Washington, D.C.: Government Printing Office, 1884).

30. *CR*, 13, 1:471; *CR*, 14, 1:112; *CR*, 15, 2:1346; *CR*, 17, 5:5103–5106; *Interstate Commerce: Speeches of Hon. Z. B. Vance, of N.C., and Hon. J. Z. George, of Miss., in the*

Senate of the United States, January 9, 1885 (Washington, D.C.: Government Printing Office, 1885), 6–14; J. Z. George to Robert Lowry, February 23 and March 7, 15, and 17, 1882, Governor Robert Lowry Correspondence and Papers, 1882–1890, MDAH.

31. *CR*, 15, 4:3057; *CR*, 16, 2:1248.

32. *CR*, 18, 2:1704; May Spencer Ringold, "Senator James Zachariah George and Federal Aid to Common Schools," *Journal of Mississippi History* 20, no. 1 (January 1958): 32.

33. *CR*, 13, 2:1637, 1673; *Chinese Immigration—Speech of Hon. James Z. George, of Mississippi, in the United States Senate, Wednesday, September 5, 1888* (Washington, D.C.: Government Printing Office, 1888).

Chapter 16

1. J. Z. George to Micajah Berry, May 13, 1885, Micajah Berry Papers, MDAH.

2. *Journal of the House of Representatives of the State of Mississippi at a Regular Session Thereof, Convened in the City of Jackson, January 5, 1886* (Jackson, Miss.: R. H. Henry, 1886), 122–123; *Journal of the Senate of the State of Mississippi at a Regular Session Thereof, Convened in the City of Jackson, January 5, 1886* (Jackson, Miss.: R. H. Henry, 1886), 104–105, 115.

3. J. Z. George to Bettie, December 16 and 28, 1884, March 20 and April 2, 1885, and February 24, 1887, James Z. George Papers, MDAH.

4. J. Z. George to Bettie, December 16, 1884, and February 24, 1887, James Z. George Papers, MDAH; Bettie George to Lizzie, February 2, 1887, Bettie George Letters, Cotesworth.

5. J. Z. George to Bettie, December 28, 1884, and February 14, 1887, James Z. George Papers, MDAH.

6. Bettie George to Lizzie, February 3, 1886, Bettie George Letters, Cotesworth; J. Z. George to Bettie, December 28, 1884, and February 14, 1887, James Z. George Papers, MDAH; J. Z. George to Winfield S. Featherston, January 15, 1888, Folder 5.33, Winfield S. Featherston Collection, UM.

7. J. Z. George to Bettie, December 28, 1884, and February 24, 1887, James Z. George Papers, MDAH; Bettie George to Lizzie, December 27, 1893, and January 15, 1894, Bettie George Letters, Cotesworth.

8. Rowland, *Courts, Judges, and Lawyers*, 102.

9. J. Z. George to J. B. Harris, April 22, 1892, James Bowmar Harris and Family Papers, MDAH; Bettie George to Lizzie, June 21, 1892, Bettie George Letters, Cotesworth.

10. Bettie George to Lizzie, June 14 and 21, 1892, Bettie George Letters, Cotesworth.

11. Undated and untitled newspaper clipping, J. Z. George Scrapbook, Cotesworth.

12. "Carrollton in Gloom"; "Hurrah for Jim," J. Z. George Scrapbook, Vol. 3, Box 3, James Z. George Papers, MDAH; Carrollton Baptist Church Minutes, November 25, 1888, Book 2, 1862–1895, Carrollton Baptist Church, 192.

13. Carrollton Baptist Church Minutes, November 24, 1889, Book 2, 1862–1895, Carrollton Baptist Church, 200; "Tribute to Gen. George," undated newspaper clipping, J. Z. George Scrapbook, Cotesworth.

14. "National Register of Historic Places Inventory—Nomination Form," November 30, 1977, Cotesworth Subject File, MDAH; Shanks, "Early Career of James Z. George," 59.

15. *CR*, 21, 1:78; Bettie George to Lizzie, August 30, 1888, Bettie George Letters, Cotesworth; J. Z. George to W. S. Featherston, January 15, 1888, Series 5, Box 5, Folder 33, Winfield S. Featherston Collection, UM.

16. *CR*, 22, 1:586, 805; W. H. Michael, *Official Congressional Directory for the Use of the United States Congress, Fifty-second Congress, First Session* (Washington, D.C.: Government Printing Office, 1892), 4; Dunbar Rowland to John R. Ficklen, May 26, 1904, John R. Ficklen Papers, Louisiana State University; *Memorial Addresses on the Life and Character of James Z. George*, 50; Garner, "Senatorial Career of J. Z. George," 250–251, 253; Ringold, "Senator James Zachariah George of Mississippi," 177, 179; Armstrong, "James Zachariah George," 73; "Death of Albert Bial," *New York Times*, August 15, 1897; "Justice Woods Dead," *New York Times*, May 15, 1887; Gilbert J. Clarke to Rutherford B. Hayes, September 27, 1892, Rutherford B. Hayes Papers, RBHPC.

17. Michael, *Official Congressional Directory for the Use of the United States Congress*, 4; *CR*, 19, 1:16; *CR*, 21, 1:7, 175–176; *CR*, 23, 1:73.

18. *CR*, 19:10, 9514; *CR*, 21:9, 8202; *CR*, 22, 3:2395; *CR*, 23, 1:76; "Delighted with Their Trip," *Washington Post*, February 28, 1888.

19. J. Z. George to Grover Cleveland, January 24 and 25, 1888, Grover Cleveland Papers, LC; *CR*, 21, 3:2517; *CR*, 23, 2:1169; J. Z. George to Micajah Berry, April 18, 1886, Micajah Berry Papers, MDAH; J. Z. George to H. Pendleton, June 6, 1888, Stephen D. Lee Papers, UNC.

20. *CR*, 21, 3:2112; *CR*, 23, 2:1360; *CR*, 25, 2:1639; *Relations between the Senate and Executive Departments—Speech of Hon. J. Z. George of Mississippi, in the Senate of the United States, March 23, 1886* (Washington, D.C.: Government Printing Office, 1886).

21. Bettie George to Lizzie, August 30, 1888, and February 10, 1893, Bettie George Letters, Cotesworth; Henderson, "Wife of Gen. J. Z. George."

22. *CR*, 20, 2:1036.

23. Ibid., 1036–1037.

24. Ibid., 1036–1038.

25. Ibid., 1037–1038.

26. Christopher Grandy, "Original Intent and the Sherman Antitrust Act: A Re-examination of the Consumer-Welfare Hypothesis," *Journal of Economic History*, 53, no. 2 (June 1993): 359–376; Samuel Eliot Morison and Henry Steele Commager, *The Growth of the American Republic*, 2 vols. (New York: Oxford University Press, 1942), 2:143; Donald A. Frederick, *Antitrust Status of Farmer Cooperatives: The Story of the Capper-Volstead Act* (Washington, D.C.: U.S. Department of Agriculture, 2002), 24–26; Armstrong, "James Zachariah George," 57–58, 60; *Trusts and Combinations—Speech of Hon. James Z. George, of Mississippi, in the Senate of the United States, Monday, February 4, 1889* (Washington, D.C.: Government Printing Office, 1889). George's ideas would later be included in Progressive Era legislation.

27. See the many mentions of commoner variations in George's scrapbooks in MDAH and at Cotesworth. For Bryan, see Michael Kazin, *A Godly Hero: The Life of William Jennings Bryan* (New York: Knopf, 2006).

28. *CR*, 22, 1:279–284. For a published copy of George's speech, see *The Federal Election Bill—Speech of Hon. J. Z. George of Mississippi, in the Senate of the United States, December 10, 1890* (Washington, D.C.: Government Printing Office, 1890); "The Education Bill Shelved," *Greenville Times*, January 10, 1891.

29. *CR*, 22, 1:282, 285–286.

30. Ibid., 286–293.

31. "The Force Bill Buried," *New York Times*, January 6, 1891; Fred Wellborn, "The Influence of the Silver-Republican Senators, 1889–1891," *Mississippi Valley Historical Review* 14, no. 4 (March 1928): 476–477; Thomas Adams Upchurch, *Legislating Racism: The Billion Dollar Congress and the Birth of Jim Crow* (Lexington: University Press of Kentucky, 2004), 155–156, 165.

32. *CR*, 19, 8:7766; *CR*, 19, 3:2247.

33. *CR*, 12, 1:165; *CR*, 21, 8:7664; *CR*, 22, 4:50, 52, 74; *CR*, 23, 3:2818; *Inquest Under National Authority—Speech of Hon. James Z. George of Mississippi, in the United States Senate, Wednesday September 26, 1888* (Washington, D.C.: Government Printing Office, 1888); *The Power of the Senate to Make Inquisitions—Speech of Hon. J. Z. George of Mississippi, in the Senate of the United States, January 28, 1890* (Washington, D.C.: Government Printing Office, 1890). Making his racial stances even more ironic, George apparently took a different view of Native Americans than he did of African Americans, ribbing Northern senators about the same bias in their voting qualifications that they complained about in Mississippi in reference to blacks.

34. *CR*, 26, 3:2935; *CR*, 15, 3:2376; *CR*, 13, 4:3462; Mayes, *Lucius Q. C. Lamar*, 463.

Chapter 17

1. *CR*, 21, 9:8202.

2. James L. Power, "The Black and Tan Convention," in Riley, *Publications of the Mississippi Historical Society*, 3:73–83; Johnston, "Public Services of Senator James Z. George," 212–213.

3. J. Z. George to Robert Lowry, January 25, 1888, Governor Robert Lowry Correspondence and Papers, 1882–1890, MDAH; James P. Coleman, "The Mississippi Constitution of 1890 and the Final Decade of the Nineteenth Century," in McLemore, *History of Mississippi*, 2:6–7; Cresswell, *Rednecks, Redeemers, and Race*, 91, 113; Peck, "Life and Times of James Z. George," 54; Bradley G. Bond, *Political Culture in the Nineteenth-Century South: Mississippi, 1830–1890* (Baton Rouge: Louisiana State University Press, 1995), 245.

4. T. P. Guyton to Gene Holcomb, October 21, 1940, T. P. Guyton Letter, Samuel P. Guyton Private Collection, Lakewood, Colo.; Coleman, "Mississippi Constitution," 2:8; Peck, "Life and Times of James Z. George," 49.

5. J. Z. George to Stephen D. Lee, July 17, 1890, Stephen D. Lee Papers, UNC; Johnston, "Public Services of Senator James Z. George," 211–212.

6. J. Z. George to Stephen D. Lee, July 17, 1890, Stephen D. Lee Papers, UNC; Johnston, "Public Services of Senator James Z. George," 211–212.

7. J. Z. George to Robert Lowry, January 25, 1888, Governor Robert Lowry Correspondence and Papers, 1882–1890, MDAH; *CR*, 22, 4:73; Johnston, "Public Services of Senator James Z. George," 214; Peck, "Life and Times of James Z. George," 49–50, 55–56.

8. "The Great Problem," J. Z. George Scrapbook, Vol. 3, Box 3, James Z. George Papers, MDAH; Frank Johnston, "Suffrage and Reconstruction in Mississippi," in Riley, *Publications of the Mississippi Historical Society*, 6:208–209; J. S. McNeily, "History of the Measures Submitted to the Committee on Elective Franchise, Apportionment, and Elections in the Constitutional Convention of 1890," in Riley, *Publications of the Mississippi Historical Society*, 6:130.

9. Cresswell, *Multi-party Politics in Mississippi*, 102; "Senator George," J. Z. George Scrapbook, Vol. 3, Box 3, James Z. George Papers, MDAH; Peck, "Life and Times of James Z. George," 56.

10. "Vote for Delegates from State-At-Large," *Jackson Daily Clarion Ledger*, August 11, 1890; "Tabular View of Mississippi Constitutional Convention—1890," *Jackson Daily Clarion Ledger*, November 1, 1890; John Roy Lynch, *Reminiscences of an Active Life: The Autobiography of John Roy Lynch*, ed. John Hope Franklin (Chicago: University of Chicago Press, 1970), 340; J. Z. George Constitutional Convention Commission, Register of Commissions, 1887–1891, MDAH, 24; John K. Bettersworth, *Mississippi: A History* (Austin, Tex.: Steck, 1959), 378–379.

11. *Memorial Addresses on the Life and Character of James Z. George*, 26; Michael Perman, *Struggle for Mastery: Dis-franchisement in the South, 1888–1908* (Chapel Hill: University of North Carolina Press, 2001), 75.

12. "The George Plan," *Vicksburg Post*, July 1, 1890; "Senator George," *Vicksburg Post*, July 4, 1890; *Memorial Addresses on the Life and Character of James Z. George*, 26; "Senator George's Plan," J. Z. George Scrapbook, Vol. 3, Box 3, James Z. George Papers, MDAH.

13. *Memorial Addresses on the Life and Character of James Z. George*, 26.

14. *Journal of the Proceedings of the Constitutional Convention of the State of Mississippi, Begun at the City of Jackson on August 12, 1890, and Concluded November 1, 1890* (Jackson, Miss.: E. L. Martin, 1890), 5–7; Robert Lowry and William H. McCardle, *A History of Mississippi, From the Discovery of the Great River by Hernando DeSoto, Including the Earliest Settlement Made by the French, Under Iberville, to the Death of Jefferson Davis* (Jackson, Miss.: R. H. Henry, 1891), 344–345; T. P. Guyton to Gene Holcomb, October 21, 1940, T. P. Guyton Letter, Samuel Percy Guyton Private Collection, Lakewood, Colo. Lee was very much interested in the farmers' positions in the constitution. See State Farmers' Alliance Report, in Stephen D. Lee Papers, MDAH. For an overview of the convention, see Eric C. Clark, "The Mississippi Constitutional Convention of 1890: A Political Analysis" (master's thesis, University of Mississippi, 1975).

15. Eric C. Clark, "Regulation of Corporations in the Mississippi Constitutional Convention of 1890," *Journal of Mississippi History* 48, no. 1 (February 1986): 32; *Memorial Addresses on the Life and Character of James Z. George*, 26, 85; Ray M. Thompson, "The Father of Mississippi's Constitution," *Biloxi/Gulfport Daily Herald*, *Jackson Daily News*, and *Jackson Clarion Ledger*, January 2, 1962, copy found in Series 2, Box 4, Folder 1, Ray M. Thompson Papers, USM; Rowland, *Courts, Judges, and Lawyers*, 237; Johnston, "Public Services of Senator James Z. George," 216; Perman, *Struggle for Mastery*, 85–87.

16. *Journal of the Proceedings of the Constitutional Convention of the State of Mississippi*, 22; Clark, "Regulation of Corporations," 32. John R. Lynch, on the other hand, has written that George and Calhoon were partners in the convention. See Lynch, *Reminiscences*, 341–344.

17. *Journal of the Proceedings of the Constitutional Convention of the State of Mississippi*, 18–19, 22, 29, 49, 62, 104, 108, 127, 134, 191, 273, 313, 340, 430, 439, 449, 527, 535.

18. Ibid., 298, 344, 428, 450–451, 475, 483, 487; Clark, "Regulation of Corporations," 32, 40.

19. Cresswell, *Rednecks, Redeemers, and Race*, 119; Albert D. Kirwan, "Apportionment in the Mississippi Constitution of 1890," *Journal of Southern History* 14, no. 2 (May 1948): 235–236; Perman, *Struggle for Mastery*, 85–87.

20. *Memorial Addresses on the Life and Character of James Z. George*, 26, 74; Bettersworth, *Mississippi*, 380; *Journal of the Proceedings of the Constitutional Convention of the State of Mississippi*, 619; Frank B. Williams Jr., "Public Reaction to the Poll Tax as a Suffrage Requirement in Mississippi, 1890–1905," *Journal of Mississippi History* 17, no. 4 (October 1955): 229–248; Kirwan, *Revolt of the Rednecks*, 70; Perman, *Struggle for Mastery*, 85–87. For context, see Cresswell, *Rednecks, Redeemers, and Race*, 110–129. For insight into the committee's work, see the minute books of the franchise committee in the Charles K. Regan Papers, MDAH. One historian claims Wiley P. Harris wrote the understanding clause, but the weight of evidence points to George. See Frank B. Williams Jr., "The Poll Tax as a Suffrage Requirement in the South, 1870–1901," *Journal of Southern History* 18, no. 4 (November 1952): 487. Williams cites no evidence for his contention that Harris wrote the clause.

21. *Journal of the Proceedings of the Constitutional Convention of the State of Mississippi*, 230, 316, 431, 619; William Alexander Mabry, "Disfranchisement of the Negro in Mississippi," *Journal of Southern History* 4, no. 3 (August 1938): 318–333.

22. *Acceptance and Unveiling of the Statues*, 44; George Speech Article, J. Z. George Scrapbook, Vol. 3, Box 3, James Z. George Papers, MDAH; "Franchise," J. Z. George Scrapbook, Vol. 3, Box 3, James Z. George Papers, MDAH.

23. *CR*, 22, 4:57; Undated newspaper article copy, J. Z. George Subject File, Mississippi Supreme Court.

24. *Journal of the Proceedings of the Constitutional Convention of the State of Mississippi*, 703.

Chapter 18

1. "Source Material for Mississippi History: Carroll County, Volume 8, Part 1, Compiled by WPA State-wide Historical Research Project, Suzy V. Powell, Supervisor, 1936–38," Circuit Clerk's Office, Carroll County Courthouse, 81–82.

2. J. Z. George Family Bible, Cotesworth; *CR*, 22, 1:730, 865.

3. *CR*, 22, 4:46–47. *Congressional Record* pages will be cited here. For a self-contained copy of the speech, see *Speech by Hon. J. Z. George of Mississippi, in the Senate of the United States, December 31, 1890, January 19 and 20, 1891—Defense of*

the Constitution of Mississippi (Washington, D.C.: Government Printing Office, 1891); "Gen. George's Able Defense of the Constitution," *Byhalia Journal*, February 13, 1891; Perman, *Struggle for Mastery*, 42–43.

4. *CR*, 22, 4:46–47.
5. Ibid., 47–53.
6. Ibid., 47, 49, 72; Upchurch, *Legislating Racism*, 155.
7. *CR*, 22, 4:49, 51.
8. Ibid., 52–53.
9. Ibid., 52, 54–56, 60.
10. Ibid., 57–58; Johnston, "Public Services of Senator James Z. George," 218.
11. *CR*, 22, 4:58–59; Bettie George to Lizzie, January 7, 1891, Bettie George Letters, Cotesworth.
12. *CR*, 22, 4:60.
13. Ibid., 60–64.
14. Ibid., 65–71.
15. Ibid., 72–74; Perman, *Struggle for Mastery*, 42.
16. *CR*, 22, 4:74–78.
17. Ibid., 78–81.
18. Ibid., 74, 82–83.
19. *Memorial Addresses on the Life and Character of James Z. George*, 27, 72, 115; Upchurch, *Legislating Racism*, 119; Bettersworth, *Mississippi*, 378; Rowland, *Political and Parliamentary Orators*, 394.
20. *CR*, 22, 4:47, 73, 83; James P. Coleman, "The Origin of the Constitution of 1890," *Journal of Mississippi History* 19, no. 2 (April 1957). 85.
21. Woodward, *Strange Career of Jim Crow*, 83–84; *The Constitution of the State of Mississippi* (Jackson, Miss.: Secretary of State, 1988), 44.

Chapter 19

1. "In Hotel Lobbies," *Washington Post*, July 8, 1891; "Hon. J. Z. George Endorsed by the Farmers," J. Z. George Scrapbook, Vol. 2, Box 2, James Z. George Papers, MDAH.
2. Cresswell, *Multi-party Politics in Mississippi*, 110–111; "Senator J. Z. George," undated newspaper clipping, J. Z. George Scrapbook, Cotesworth; Handwritten subtreasury speech, undated, J. Z. George Folder, Congressmen's Files, MDAH; Rowland, *Political and Parliamentary Orators*, 395; "Senator George's Great Speech," *Jackson Mississippian*, April 19, 1891.
3. "Famous Mississippians"; Garner, "Senatorial Career of J. Z. George," 258; Cresswell, *Multi-party Politics in Mississippi*, 111; Peck, "Life and Times of James Z. George," 88–89; Edward L. Ayers, *The Promise of the New South: Life After Reconstruction* (New York: Oxford University Press, 1992), 254–255; "Senator George Last Night," *West Point Forum*, July 1, 1891; *Journal of the House of Representatives of the State of Mississippi at a Regular Session Thereof, Convened in the City of Jackson, January 5, 1892* (Jackson, Miss.: R. H. Henry, 1892), 178–181, 187–189; *Journal of the Senate of the State of Mississippi at a Regular Session Thereof, Convened in the City*

of *Jackson, January 5, 1892* (Jackson, Miss.: R. H. Henry, 1892), 163; James Z. George Senate Commission, January 19, 1892, Register of Commissions, 1892–1895, MDAH, 2.

4. *CR*, 23, 3:2243; *CR*, 25, 1:2, 197.

5. *CR*, 28, 1:421; *CR*, 30, 1:942; J. Z. George to J. G. Carlisle, July 20, 1894, John M. Stone Papers, MDAH; "Clerks of Senate Committees," *New York Times*, January 2, 1896.

6. *CR*, 26, 4:3492.

7. *CR*, 27, 2:1527.

8. *Report of the Committee on Agriculture and Forestry on Condition of Cotton Growers in the United States, the Present Prices of Cotton, and the Remedy; and on Cotton Consumption and Production*, 2 vols. (Washington, D.C.: Government Printing Office, 1895); J. Z. George to John M. Stone, May 9, 1893, Governor John M. Stone Correspondence and Papers, 1889–1896, MDAH.

9. *CR*, 25, 2:1678–1679, 1681, 1683–1684; *Demonetization of Silver—Speech of Hon. James Z. George of Mississippi, in the Senate of the United States, Wednesday and Friday September 20 and 22, 1893* (Washington, D.C.: Government Printing Office, 1893); "James Z. George: The Great Commoner of Mississippi," George Family File, Monroe County Historical Society; Ringold, "Senator James Zachariah George of Mississippi," 179–181; Armstrong, "James Zachariah George," 67–68; "Withdrawing Small Notes," *Mobile Daily Register*, October 21, 1885.

10. *CR*, 27, 2:975, 978, 980; "Senator George on the Ocala Platform—Supplement," undated, Series 14, Box 16, Folder 15, Winfield S. Featherston Collection, UM.

11. Mayes, *Lucius Q. C. Lamar*, 584–590; J. Z. George to J. G. Carlisle, July 20 and 25 and August 1, 1894, and J. Z. George to John M. Stone, July 25, 1894, all in John M. Stone Papers, MDAH.

12. *CR*, 19, 7:6241–6243; *Hawaiian Affairs—Speech of Hon. James Z. George of Mississippi, in the Senate of the United States, March 20, 1894* (Washington, D.C.: Government Printing Office, 1894); *Etiquette and Diplomacy—Speech of Hon. James Z. George of Mississippi, in the Senate of the United States, January 29, 1889* (Washington, D.C.: Government Printing Office, 1889); Armstrong, "James Zachariah George," 80, 84; J. Z. George to Grover Cleveland, August 27, 1888, Grover Cleveland Papers, LC.

13. J. Z. George to W. T. Martin, May 8, 1894, W. T. Walthall Papers, MDAH; J. Z. George to Bettie, December 28, 1884, James Z. George Papers, MDAH; T. P. Guyton to Gene Holcomb, October 21, 1940, T. P. Guyton Letter, Samuel P. Guyton Private Collection, Lakewood, Colo.; J. Z. George to L. P. Reynolds, [no month], 26, 1893, L. P. Reynolds Papers, MDAH; "Miss McCardle's Application," *Washington Post*, February 9, 1889; J. Z. George to Grover Cleveland, March 24, 1893, and April 14, 1894, R. H. Taylor to J. Z. George, August 11, 1894, and unknown to J. Z. George, August 11, 1894, all in Grover Cleveland Papers, LC.

14. Bettie George to Lizzie, February 6 and 14 and July 15, 1892, March 1, 1893, and February 3, 1894, Bettie George Letters, Cotesworth. Lamar biographer W. A. Cate made the assertion that the Georges and Lamars also enjoyed one another's social company. See Cate, *Lucious Q. C. Lamar*, 454.

15. Bettie George to Lizzie, March 14, 1892, April 7, 1893, and January 26, 1894, Bettie George Letters, Cotesworth.

16. J. Z. George to Dear Sir, October 25, 1894, Robert Lowry Papers, MDAH; Bettie George to Lizzie, February 11, 1891, and December 5, 1893, Bettie George Letters, Cotesworth; *Speech of Hon. J. Z. George on the Financial Question, Delivered at Winona, Mississippi, Saturday July 13, 1895* (n.p.: n.p., n.d.); Carrollton Baptist Church Minutes, February 26, 1893, September 9 and 23 and October 4 and 28, 1894, and April 4 and August 25, 1895, Book 2, 1862–1895, Carrollton Baptist Church, 223, 232–233, 236, 238–239; Carrollton Baptist Church Minutes, June 28 and August 23, 1896, Book 3, 1895–1916, Carrollton Baptist Church, n.p.; "Source Material for Mississippi History," 245; *Memorial Addresses on the Life and Character of James Z. George*, 35–36.

17. J. Z. George Family Bible, Cotesworth; Frank Johnston to J. Z. George, November 20, 1890, J. Z. George Letters, Cotesworth; J. Z. George to son, February 11, 1895, J. Z. George Letters, Cotesworth.

18. G. D. Shands to J. Z. George, March 11, 1895, J. Z. George Letters, Cotesworth; J. Z. George to son, December 13, 1895, J. Z. George Letters, Cotesworth; "J. Z. George for President," undated newspaper clipping, J. Z. George Scrapbook, Cotesworth; "The Mississippi Senatorship," *New York Times*, October 12, 1897; "Senator J. Z. George," *New Orleans Times Democrat*, August 1, 1895; "Famous Mississippians"; "His Age," *Vicksburg Commercial Herald*, January 8, 1891.

19. "Stories and Comments Regarding . . . Senator George," undated and torn newspaper clipping, J. Z. George Scrapbook, Cotesworth; J. Z. George to W. W. Woodson, January 26, 1894, Grover Cleveland Papers, LC.

20. J. Z. George to Winfield S. Featherston, January 15, 1888, Folder 5.33, Winfield S. Featherston Collection, UM.

21. "Senator J. Z. George," *New Orleans Times Democrat*, August 1, 1895.

22. J. Z. George to A. J. McLaurin, September 16 and 29, 1895, Governor Anselm J. McLaurin Correspondence and Papers, 1895–1900, MDAH.

23. "Mississippi Senatorship"; *CR*, 25, 2:1639; *CR*, 26, 3:2940, 2942; *CR*, 29, 1:2; *CR*, 30, 1:12.

24. *Memorial Addresses on the Life and Character of James Z. George*, 30.

25. *CR*, 15: 4:3057; *CR*, 16, 2:1248; Armstrong, "James Zachariah George," 16. See each Congress's index for George's bills and amendments. At one point when George could not attend the Senate, he even had a fellow senator offer an amendment for him.

26. "Death of Albert Bial"; Garner, "Senatorial Career of J. Z. George," 261–262; Rowland, *Political and Parliamentary Orators*, 393, 395.

27. J. Z. George to W. W. Woodson, January 26, 1894, Grover Cleveland Papers, LC; *Memorial Addresses on the Life and Character of James Z. George*, 29; Garner, "Senatorial Career of J. Z. George," 249; Rowland, *Mississippi*, 1:771. Hoke was the secretary of the interior.

28. *CR*, 15, 3:2376; "Senator George on Supervision," *Aberdeen Weekly Examiner*, August 2, 1883; *Speech of Hon. J. Z. George on the Financial Question*; Kirwan, *Revolt of the Rednecks*, 48; Ringold, "Some Liberal Aspects," 36; "The Old and the New," *New York Times*, January 31, 1881; Ringold, "Senator James Zachariah George," 164–164, 181–182; Thomas Adams Upchurch, "Why Populism Failed in Mississippi," *Journal of Mississippi History* 65, no. 3 (Fall 2003): 265; Woodward, *Origins of the New South*,

18; *Supervision of Railroads in Interstate Commerce—Speech of Hon. J. Z. George, of Mississippi, in the Senate of the United States, Friday, December 19, 1884* (Washington, D.C.: Government Printing Office, 1885); "Senator George's Reply," J. Z. George Scrapbook, Vol. 3, Box 3, James Z. George Papers, MDAH; Collection Description, Mississippi Central Railroad Company Records, MDAH.

29. *CR*, 26, 3:2941; *CR*, 27, 2:975, 978–979; *CR*, 21, 3:2154–2157; Rowland, *Political and Parliamentary Orators*, 395.

30. "Death of Albert Bial"; Garner "Senatorial Career of J. Z. George," 261–262.

31. Upchurch, *Legislating Racism*, 140.

32. *Memorial Addresses on the Life and Character of James Z. George*, 15.

Chapter 20

1. E. C. Walthall to sister, August 11, 1897, Kate Freeman Clark Collection, MDAH; *Memorial Addresses on the Life and Character of James Z. George*, 17.

2. Mississippi State University Board of Trustee Minutes, Vol. 2, June 1896, MSU, 36; "The Committees," *New York Times*, July 8, 1896; "Grown of the Season," *Washington Post*, February 9, 1896; "Fair Maids En Masque," *Washington Post*, February 14, 1896; *Memorial Addresses on the Life and Character of James Z. George*, 93; Bettie George to Lizzie, March 16, 1894, Bettie George Letters, Cotesworth; Bettie George to Cottie, February 19, 1894, Bettie George Letters, Cotesworth.

3. *Memorial Addresses on the Life and Character of James Z. George*, 15; "Senator George's Health Improving," *Washington Post*, September 13, 1896; "Senator George Ill," *New York Times*, October 18, 1896; "Senator George Very Ill," *New York Times*, January 25, 1897.

4. *Memorial Addresses on the Life and Character of James Z. George*, 15–16; "Senator George Very Sick," *Washington Post*, January 25, 1897; "Senator George's Illness," *Washington Post*, January 26, 1897; "Senator George's Relapse," *Washington Post*, January 30, 1897.

5. J. Z. George Will, January 28, 1897, Will Book B, Carroll County Courthouse, 52–54.

6. "Senator George May Resign," *New York Times*, March 2, 1897; *Memorial Addresses on the Life and Character of James Z. George*, 15, 123; "Famous Mississippians."

7. "Senator and Mrs. George," undated newspaper clipping, J. Z. George Scrapbook, Cotesworth.

8. Undated and untitled newspaper clipping, J. Z. George Scrapbook, Cotesworth;

9. Coleman, "Mississippi Constitution," 21.

10. "Good Woman at Rest," undated newspaper clipping, J. Z. George Scrapbook, Cotesworth; "Senator James Z. George," undated newspaper clipping, J. Z. George Scrapbook, Cotesworth; "Topics of the Times," *New York Times*, August 12, 1897; "Obituary Record of a Day," *Washington Post*, July 30, 1897; "Famous Mississippians."

11. Elizabeth Brooks Young George Funeral Announcement, July 30, 1897, J. Z. George Collection, Cotesworth; "Topics of the Times"; "Obituary Record of a Day"; "Carrollton in Gloom"; "Famous Mississippians."

12. Undated and untitled newspaper clipping, J. Z. George Scrapbook, Cotesworth.
13. J. Z. George Will, July 31, 1897, Will Book B, Carroll County Courthouse, 54–55. See also J. Z. George Will, undated, James Z. George Collection, Cotesworth.
14. "Senator James Z. George," undated newspaper clipping, J. Z. George Scrapbook, Cotesworth; *Memorial Addresses on the Life and Character of James Z. George*, 16; "Topics of the Times."
15. "As to Senator George," *Jackson Weekly Clarion Ledger*, August 5, 1897.
16. "Mississippi in Mourning," undated newspaper clipping, J. Z. George Scrapbook, Cotesworth; "Senator George Dead," *Washington Post*, August 15, 1897.
17. "Senator George Dead," undated newspaper clipping, J. Z. George Scrapbook, Cotesworth; "Leader among Men," *Jackson Weekly Clarion Ledger*, August 19, 1897; "Senator George Dead, *Washington Post*, August 15, 1897. For newspaper coverage of George's death, see J. Z. George Scrapbooks, Cotesworth.
18. "Leader among Men."
19. "The Trip to Carrollton," *Jackson Weekly Clarion Ledger*, August 19, 1897; "Mississippi's Dead Senator," *New York Times*, August 16, 1897; "Leader among Men."
20. "Mississippi's Dead Senator"; "Honor for Dead Senator," *Washington Post*, August 16, 1897.
21. "Leader among Men"; Coleman, "Mississippi Constitution," 2:22; *Memorial Addresses on the Life and Character of James Z. George*, 16; "Honor for Dead Senator."
22. "Trip to Carrollton"; "Citizens Meeting," undated newspaper clipping, J. Z. George Scrapbook, Cotesworth; "Famous Mississippians"; "The Funeral Services," *Jackson Weekly Clarion Ledger*, August 19, 1897; Coleman, "Mississippi Constitution," 22.
23. "Funeral Party Passes Through," undated newspaper clipping, J. Z. George Scrapbook, Cotesworth; "Trip to Carrollton"; "Funeral of Senator George," undated newspaper clipping, J. Z. George Scrapbook, Cotesworth; Undated and untitled newspaper clipping, J. Z. George Scrapbook, Cotesworth; "Funeral Services"; "Senator George Dead," *Washington Post*, August 15, 1897; *Memorial Addresses on the Life and Character of James Z. George*, 87–88, 108.
24. *Memorial Addresses on the Life and Character of James Z. George*, 128.
25. Ibid., 136.
26. Ibid., 16.
27. "Senator George Dead," *Washington Post*, August 15, 1897; "Mississippi Senatorship."
28. *CR*, 31, 1:9, 11; "Meeting of the Senate," *New York Times*, December 7, 1897.
29. "A Distinguished Southerner," *Middleville (Mich.) Sun*, September 16, 1897; "Senator James Z. George, of Mississippi," *Chautauquan: A Monthly Magazine* 26 (October 1897–March 1898): 103.
30. Carrollton Baptist Church Minutes, January 13 and February 27, 1898, and March 9, 1902, Book 3, 1895–1916, Carrollton Baptist Church, n.p.; *Nineteenth Annual Catalogue of the Mississippi Agricultural and Mechanical College, 1898–1889* (Meridian, Miss.: Meridian News, 1898), 8; "Memorial at Greenwood," undated newspaper clipping, J. Z. George Scrapbook, Cotesworth.
31. *CR*, 31, 2:1952; *Memorial Addresses on the Life and Character of James Z. George*, 56–58; "Minutes of the Bar Association," undated, J. Z. George Subject File, Mississippi Supreme Court.

32. "War Talk in the Senate," *New York Times*, April 8, 1898. The Mississippi legislature also had eulogies. See *Memorial Addresses on the Life and Character of James Z. George*, 117–124. A copy of Cox's eulogy is also in the J. Z. George Subject File, Mississippi Supreme Court.

33. *Memorial Addresses on the Life and Character of James Z. George*, 17, 81, 97, 127.

34. Ibid., 35, 38, 41–42, 48, 52, 54, 116.

35. Ibid., 32, 35, 38, 41–42, 48, 52, 54, 75, 80, 94, 97, 101–102, 108, 115–116, 127, 133.

36. Ibid., 22–23, 38.

37. Ibid., 41–42, 64–65, 99, 114–115, 118, 125; "Famous Mississippians."

38. *Memorial Addresses on the Life and Character of James Z. George*, 43–44, 47.

Conclusion

1. See the works by Garner, Johnston, McNeily, and Rowland for examples.

2. George, *Political History of Slavery*, vii–viii; James W. Garner, review of *The Political History of Slavery in the United States*, by James Z. George, *Mississippi Valley Historical Review* 2, no. 4 (March 1916): 585–586; J. O. Burke, review of *The Political History of Slavery in the United States*, by James Z. George, *Journal of Negro History* 1, no. 3 (June 1916): 340–341.

3. "Speech by Hon. John Sharp Williams on James Z. George, The Man and Speech by Dr. Dunbar Rowland on James Z. George, the Statesman," copy in J. Z. George File, Greenwood-Leflore Public Library; *Steeljacket* (Starkville, Miss.: Agricultural and Mechanical College, 1918), 9; "George Hall," Vertical File, MSU; "Mrs. Lizzie George Henderson," 532a.

4. Rowland, *Official and Statistical Register of the State of Mississippi, 1904*, 163, 204, 572; Dunbar Rowland, *The Official and Statistical Register of the State of Mississippi, 1908* (Nashville, Tenn.: Brandon Printing, 1908), 285, 294; Horton, *Family History*, 140.

5. William D. McCain, "The Triumph of Democracy: 1916–1932," in McLemore, *History of Mississippi*, 2:82. For an account of the statues, see *Acceptance and Unveiling of the Statues*.

6. *Acceptance and Unveiling of the Statues*, 48.

7. Ibid.

8. Rowland, *Political and Parliamentary Orators*, 393.

9. Cresswell, *Rednecks, Redeemers, and Race*, 89.

10. Clayton Rand, *Men of Spine in Mississippi* (Gulfport, Miss.: Dixie Press, 1940), 211–213.

Bibliography

Primary Sources

Manuscripts

Carroll County Courthouse, Carrollton, Mississippi
  Chancery Court Minute Book, 1872–1888
  Circuit Court Minute Book, 1855–1857
  Circuit Court Minute Book K, 1871–1881
  Circuit Court Record Book D, 1845–1848
  Deed Books B, E, J, L–M, P, R–W, Y–Z, 1, 3, 5
  Marriage Book A
  Police Court Minutes, 1853
  Probate Court Minute Book, 1862–1866
  Probate Court Minute Book, 1867–1870
  Probate Court Record Book A, 1834–1841
  Probate Court Record Book B, 1841–1845
  Probate Court Record Book C, 1845–1848
  "Source Material for Mississippi History: Carroll County, Volume 8, Part 1, Compiled by WPA State-wide Historical Research Project, Suzy V. Powell, Supervisor, 1936–38"
  Will Book B

Carrollton Baptist Church, Carrollton, Mississippi
  Carrollton Baptist Church 175th Anniversary Program
  Church Minutes, Book 1, 1833–1861
  Church Minutes, Book 2, 1862–1895
  Church Minutes, Book 3, 1895–1916

Carrollton–North Carrollton Public Library, Carrollton, Mississippi
  Hamilton, William Franklin. "History of Carroll County." Undated

Cotesworth, James Z. George Home, Carrollton, Mississippi
  Elizabeth Young George Letters
  James Z. George Collection
  James Z. George Family Bible
  James Z. George Letters
  James Z. George Photographic Album

James Z. George Receipt Book, 1869–1870
James Z. George Scrapbooks

Duke University, Durham, North Carolina
  W. A. Rorer Letters
  James Bull Smith Dimitry Papers

Greenwood-Leflore Public Library, Greenwood, Mississippi
  J. Z. George File

Samuel Percy Guyton Private Collection, Lakewood, Colorado
  T. P. Guyton Letter

Jones County Courthouse, Gray, Georgia
  Probate Court Records
  Administrators and Guardians Bonds Book A
  Ordinary Annual Returns Book J

Leflore County Courthouse, Greenwood, Mississippi
  Deed Books E, 2, 8, 10

Library of Congress, Manuscripts Department, Washington, D.C.
  Grover Cleveland Papers

Library of Congress, Rare Book and Special Collections, Washington, D.C.
  Senator J. Z. George of Mississippi

Louisiana State University, Baton Rouge
  John R. Ficklen Papers
  James Z. George Biographical Vertical File

Mississippi Department of Archives and History, Jackson
  Amnesty Roll, Johnson's Island
  Barksdale Family Papers
  William R. Barksdale Papers
  Francis Marion Baxter Papers
  Micajah Berry Papers
  James C. Browning Diary
  Kate Freeman Clark Collection
  "The Clinton Riot," Campaign Document No. 2, Democratic Executive Committee, 1875
  Confederate States Army Casualties: Lists and Narrative Reports, 1861–1865
  Congressmen's Files
  Correspondence of Various Mississippi Officers and Military Staff Members, 1861–1865

General Registers of Prisoners, Johnson's Island, 1862–1864
James Z. George Papers
Thomas Pryor Gore Papers
James Bowmar Harris and Family Papers
L. Q. C. Lamar and Edward Mayes Papers
Stephen D. Lee Papers
List of Mississippians in First and Second Regiments of Mississippi Riflemen
Lockhart-Weir Family Papers
Robert Lowry Papers
William H. McCardle Papers
Mexican War Documents
Miller Family Papers
Mississippi Central Rail Road Company Records
Noble, Lawrence E. "The Georgia Background of James Zachariah George." Unpublished essay, April 1999
Official State Papers
    Adelbert Ames Correspondence and Papers, 1874–1876
    Fifth Regiment Cavalry Records
    Robert Lowry Correspondence and Papers, 1882–1890
    Anselm J. McLaurin Correspondence and Papers, 1895–1900
    John J. Pettus Correspondence and Papers, 1859–1863
    John J. Pettus Military Telegrams, 1860–1863
    Ridgely C. Powers Correspondence and Papers, 1871–1874
    Register of Commissions, 1858–1864
    Register of Commissions, 1878–1881
    Register of Commissions, 1887–1891
    Register of Commissions, 1892–1895
    John M. Stone Correspondence and Papers, 1876–1882
    John M. Stone Correspondence and Papers, 1889–1896
    Supreme Court Minute Book F, 1879–1882
    Third Regiment Cavalry, Mississippi State Troops Records
    Third Regiment Minute Men Records
    Twentieth Mississippi Infantry Regiment Records
J. A. Orr Papers
Carnot Posey and Family Letters
Power Family Papers
Register of Express Packages Received for Prisoners and Examined, Johnson's Island, 1865
L. P. Reynolds Papers
W. A. Rorer Letters
John M. Stone Papers
Subject Files
    Cotesworth
    James Z. George
    Runnymede

    Supreme Court, 1817–1913
    Robert W. Williamson
W. T. Walthall Papers
Watkins-Walton Family Papers

Mississippi State University, Starkville
  George Hall Vertical File
  Mississippi State University Board of Trustees Correspondence
  Mississippi State University Board of Trustee Minutes, Vol. 1
  Mississippi State University Board of Trustee Minutes, Vol. 2

Mississippi Supreme Court, Jackson
  J. Z. George Subject File
  Justice Biographical Project, Mississippi Supreme Court

Monroe County Courthouse, Forsyth, Georgia
  Probate Court Records
    Marriage Book A
    Ordinary Annual Returns Book B
    Record of Bonds, Book A, 1825–1854
  Probate Judge's Office
    Joseph W. George File
  Superior Court Records
    Deed Books D, G, and I

Monroe County Historical Society, Forsyth, Georgia
  George Family File

National Archives and Records Administration, Washington, D.C.
  1830 Georgia Census, Monroe County, Slave Schedules
  1840 Mississippi Census, Carroll County, Slave Schedules
  1850 Mississippi Census, Carroll County
  1850 Mississippi Census, Carroll County, Agricultural Census
  1850 Mississippi Census, Carroll County, Slave Schedules
  1860 Mississippi Census, Carroll County
  1860 Mississippi Census, Carroll County, Agricultural Census
  1860 Mississippi Census, Carroll County, Slave Schedules
  1870 Mississippi Census, Carroll County
  1880 Mississippi Census, Hinds County
  J. Z. George Civil War Compiled Service Record, Fifth Mississippi Cavalry
  J. Z. George Mexican War Compiled Service Record, First Mississippi Infantry
  J. Z. George Civil War Compiled Service Record, Twentieth Mississippi Infantry

Rutherford B. Hayes Presidential Center, Fremont, Ohio
  Rutherford B. Hayes Papers

Tennessee State Library and Archives, Nashville
  Annie E. Cody Papers

University of Mississippi, Oxford
  Winfield S. Featherston Collection
  J. Z. George Prisoner of War Autograph Book
  Issues of the Canvass—Compiled From the Clarion, and Presented to the Democratic-Conservative Canvassers
  Issues of the Canvass, of 1876–The Committee
  The Legislation of 1865 Concerning Freedmen: A Letter
  University of Mississippi Board of Trustee Reports and Minutes, Book 2, 1860–1882

University of North Carolina, Chapel Hill
  J. F. H. Claiborne Papers
  Stephen D. Lee Papers

University of Southern Mississippi, Hattiesburg
  John Ray Skates Papers
  Ray M. Thompson Papers

Newspapers

Aberdeen Weekly Examiner, August 2, 1883
Biloxi/Gulfport Daily Herald, January 2, 1962
Byhalia Journal, February 13, 1891
Canton American Citizen, April 4, 1868
Carrollton Democrat, June 10, 1846
Carrollton Mississippi Democrat, October 21, 1846
Chickasaw Messenger, October 13, 1887
Greenville Times, January 10, 1891
Holly Springs Sentinel, October 19, 1887
Jackson Clarion Ledger, April 16, 1908
Jackson Daily Clarion Ledger, August 11, 1890; November 1, 1890; December 31, 1937; January 2, 1962
Jackson Daily Mississippi Pilot, May 22, 1875
Jackson Daily News, January 2, 1962
Jackson Mississippian, April 19, 1891
Jackson State Ledger, December 24, 1887
Jackson Weekly Clarion, September 26, 1872; October 17, 1872; October 31, 1872; January 16, 1873; August 4, 1875; October 13, 1875; October 27, 1875; November 3, 1875; February 7, 1877
Jackson Weekly Clarion Ledger, August 5, 1897; August 19, 1897
Jackson Weekly Journal, October 10, 1872
Memphis Commercial Appeal, October 5, 1902
Middleville Sun, September 16, 1897

Mississippi Republican, June 1876
Mobile Daily Register, October 21, 1885
Monroe Advertiser, September 3, 1931
Natchez Banner, October 20, 1887
New Orleans Times Democrat, August 1, 1895
New Orleans Times Picayune, January 30, 1944
New York Times, November 3, 1875; March 1, 1878; January 24, 1880; January 31, 1881; February 14, 1881; October 30, 1881; August 1, 1883; August 12, 1883; October 16, 1884; November 24, 1885; May 15, 1887; September 21, 1888; January 6, 1891; January 2, 1896; July 8, 1896; October 18, 1896; January 25, 1897; March 2, 1897; August 12, 1897; August 15, 1897; August 16, 1897; October 12, 1897; December 7, 1897; April 8, 1898
New York Tribune, August 23, 1897; August 24, 1897
Shubuta Mississippian, October 22, 1887
Tupelo Journal, October 21, 1887
Vicksburg Commercial Herald, January 8, 1891
Vicksburg Post, October 19, 1887; July 1, 1890; July 4, 1890,
Washington Post, January 20, 1880; April 30, 1881; January 18, 1882; March 17, 1882; April 23, 1884; April 25, 1884; November 24, 1885; February 28, 1888; February 9, 1889; July 8, 1891; May 24, 1893; February 9, 1896; February 14, 1896; September 13, 1896; January 25, 1897; January 26, 1897; January 30, 1897; July 30, 1897; August 15, 1897; August 16, 1897
West Point Forum, July 1, 1891

Published Primary Sources

Acceptance and Unveiling of the Statues of Jefferson Davis and James Z. George. Washington, D.C.: Government Printing Office, 1932.
Agriculture Department—Speech of Hon. James Z. George of Mississippi in the Senate of the United States, January 13, 1883. Washington, D.C.: Government Printing Office, 1883.
Anderson, E. H. "A Memoir on Reconstruction in Yazoo City." *Journal of Mississippi History* 4, no. 4 (October 1942): 187–194.
Brown, J. A., and J. B. H. Hemingway. *Reports of Cases in the Supreme Court for the State of Mississippi.* Vol. 57, *Containing Cases Decided at the April and October Terms, 1879, and the April Terms, 1880.* Boston: Little, Brown, 1880.
Burke, J. O. Review of *The Political History of Slavery in the United States*, by James Z. George. *Journal of Negro History* 1, no. 3 (June 1916): 340–341.
Cabell, W. L. "Living Generals of the Confederate States Army." *Southern Historical Society Papers* 20 (1892): 39.
———. "Confederate Generals Yet Living." *Confederate Veteran* 2, no. 1 (January 1894): 28.
Causey, Jerry, ed. "Selected Correspondence of the Adjutant General of Confederate Mississippi." *Journal of Mississippi History* 43, no. 1 (February 1981): 31–58.
Chinese Immigration—Speech of Hon. James Z. George, of Mississippi, in the United States Senate, Wednesday, September 5, 1888. Washington, D.C.: Government Printing Office, 1888.

Congressional Record, 1881–1898.
The Constitution of the State of Mississippi. Jackson, Miss.: Secretary of State, 1988.
Dealings in "Options" and "Futures"—Speech of Hon. James Z. George, of Mississippi, in the Senate of the United States, December 13, 14, and 15, 1892. Washington, D.C.: Government Printing Office, 1892.
Demonetization of Silver—Speech of Hon. James Z. George of Mississippi, in the Senate of the United States, Wednesday and Friday September 20 and 22, 1893. Washington, D.C.: Government Printing Office, 1893.
Etiquette and Diplomacy—Speech of Hon. James Z. George of Mississippi, in the Senate of the United States, January 29, 1889. Washington, D.C.: Government Printing Office, 1889.
The Federal Election Bill—Speech of Hon. J. Z. George of Mississippi, in the Senate of the United States, December 10, 1890. Washington, D.C.: Government Printing Office, 1890.
First Annual Catalogue of the Officers and Students of the Mississippi Agricultural and Mechanical College of Mississippi, 1880-'81. Jackson, Miss.: Clarion Steam Publishing House, 1881.
Garner, James W. Review of *The Political History of Slavery in the United States*, by James Z. George. *Mississippi Valley Historical Review* 2, no. 4 (March 1916): 585–586.
George, James Z. *Reports of Cases Argued and Determined in the High Court of Errors and Appeals for the State of Mississippi—Volume XXX—Volume I, Containing Cases Determined at the December Special Term, 1855, and a Part of the April Term, 1856*. Philadelphia: T. & J. W. Johnson, 1857.
———. *Reports of Cases Argued and Determined in the High Court of Errors and Appeals for the State of Mississippi—Volume XXXI—Volume II, Containing Cases Determined at a Part of the April Term, 1856, and a Part of the October Term*. Philadelphia: T. & J. W. Johnson, 1858.
———. *Reports of Cases Argued and Determined in the High Court of Errors and Appeals for the State of Mississippi—Volume XXXII—Volume III, Containing Cases Determined at a Part of the October Term, 1856*. Philadelphia: T. & J. W. Johnson, 1858.
———. *Reports of Cases Argued and Determined in the High Court of Errors and Appeals for the State of Mississippi—Volume XXXIII—Volume IV, Containing Cases Determined at the April Term, 1857, and a Part of the October Term, 1857*. Philadelphia: T. & J. W. Johnson, 1859.
———. *Reports of Cases Argued and Determined in the High Court of Errors and Appeals for the State of Mississippi—Volume XXXIV—Volume V, Containing Cases Determined at a Part of the October Term, 1857, and a Part of the April Term, 1858*. Philadelphia: T. & J .W. Johnson, 1859.
———. *Reports of Cases Argued and Determined in the High Court of Errors and Appeals for the State of Mississippi—Volume XXXV—Volume VI, Containing Cases Determined at the April Term, 1858, and a Part of the October Term, 1858*. Philadelphia: T. & J. W. Johnson, 1860.
———. *Reports of Cases Argued and Determined in the High Court of Errors and Appeals for the State of Mississippi—Volume XXXVI—Volume VII, Containing Cases*

Determined at a Part of the October Term, 1858, and a Part of the April Term, 1859. Philadelphia: T. & J. W. Johnson, 1860.

———. *Reports of Cases Argued and Determined in the High Court of Errors and Appeals for the State of Mississippi—Volume XXXVII—Volume VIII, Containing Cases Determined at a Part of the April Term, 1859, and a Part of the October Term, 1859.* Philadelphia: T. & J. W. Johnson, 1860.

———. *Reports of Cases Argued and Determined in the High Court of Errors and Appeals for the State of Mississippi—Volume XXXVIII—Volume IX, Containing Cases Determined at a Part of the October Term, 1859, and a Part of the April Term, 1860.* Philadelphia: T. & J. W. Johnson, 1861.

———. *Reports of Cases Argued and Determined in the High Court of Errors and Appeals for the State of Mississippi—Volume XXXIX—Volume X, Containing Cases Determined at February and October Terms, 1860, April and October Terms, 1861, and April Term, 1863.* Philadelphia: T. & J. W. Johnson, 1867.

———. *A Digest of the Reports of the Decisions of the Supreme Court and of the High Court of Errors and Appeals of the State of Mississippi, From the Organization of the State, to the Present Time.* Philadelphia: T. and J. W. Johnson, 1872.

———. *The Political History of Slavery in the United States.* New York: Neale, 1915.

Hardee, W. J. *Rifle and Light Infantry Tactics; For the Exercise and Manoeuvres of Troops When Acting as Light Infantry or Riflemen*, 2 vols. Philadelphia: J. B. Lippincott, 1861.

Hawaiian Affairs—Speech of Hon. James Z. George of Mississippi, in the Senate of the United States, March 20, 1894. Washington, D.C.: Government Printing Office, 1894.

Hemingway, J. B. H. *Reports of Cases in the Supreme Court for the State of Mississippi, Vol. LVI, Containing Cases Decided at the April Term, 1878, the January Special Terms, 1879, and the April Term, 1879.* St. Louis: G. I. Jones, 1880.

———. *Reports of Cases in the Supreme Court for the State of Mississippi, Vol. LVIII, Containing Cases Decided at the October Term, 1880, and the April Term, 1881.* St. Louis: G. I. Jones, 1881.

Inquest Under National Authority—Speech of Hon. James Z. George of Mississippi, in the United States Senate, Wednesday September 26, 1888. Washington, D.C.: Government Printing Office, 1888.

Interstate Commerce: Speeches of Hon. Z. B. Vance, of N.C., and Hon. J. Z. George, of Miss., in the Senate of the United States, January 9, 1885. Washington, D.C.: Government Printing Office, 1885.

Issue of Circulating Notes—Speech of Hon. James Z. George of Mississippi in the Senate of the United States, Monday February 25, 1884. Washington, D.C.: Government Printing Office, 1884.

Johnston, Frank. "The Conference of October 15, 1875, Between General George and Governor Ames." In *Publications of the Mississippi Historical Society*, 13 vols., ed. Franklin L. Riley, 6:65–77. Oxford: Mississippi Historical Society, 1902.

Journal of the House of Representatives of the State of Mississippi. Jackson, Miss.: E. Barksdale, 1859.

Journal of the House of Representatives of the State of Mississippi: Called Session. Jackson, Miss.: Ethelbert Barksdale, 1860.

Journal of the House of Representatives of the State of Mississippi at a Regular Session Thereof, Held in the City of Jackson. Jackson, Miss.: Price and Fall, 1846.
Journal of the House of Representatives of the State of Mississippi at a Regular Session Thereof, Held in the City of Jackson, 1854. Jackson, Miss.: Barksdale and Jones, 1854.
Journal of the House of Representatives of the State of Mississippi: December Session of 1862, and November Session of 1863. Jackson, Miss.: Cooper and Kimball, 1864.
Journal of the House of Representatives of the State of Mississippi at a Regular Session Thereof, Convened in the City of Jackson, January 6, 1880. Jackson, Miss.: J. L. Power, 1880.
Journal of the House of Representatives of the State of Mississippi at a Regular Session Thereof, Convened in the City of Jackson, January 5, 1886. Jackson, Miss.: R. H. Henry, 1886.
Journal of the House of Representatives of the State of Mississippi at a Regular Session Thereof, Convened in the City of Jackson, January 5, 1892. Jackson, Miss.: R. H. Henry, 1892.
Journal of the Proceedings of the Constitutional Convention of the State of Mississippi, Begun at the City of Jackson on August 12, 1890, and Concluded November 1, 1890. Jackson, Miss.: E. L. Martin, 1890.
Journal of the Senate of the State of Mississippi at a Regular Session Held in the City of Jackson, 1856. Jackson, Miss.: E. Barksdale, 1856.
Journal of the Senate of the State of Mississippi at a Regular Session Thereof, Convened in the City of Jackson, January 5, 1886. Jackson, Miss.: R. H. Henry, 1886.
Journal of the Senate of the State of Mississippi at a Regular Session Thereof, Convened in the City of Jackson, January 5, 1892. Jackson, Miss.: R. H. Henry, 1892.
Journal of the Senate of the State of Mississippi at a Regular Session Thereof Held in the City of Jackson. Jackson, Miss.: Price and Fall, 1846.
Journal of the State Convention and Ordinances and Resolutions Adopted in January, 1861, With an Appendix. Jackson, Miss.: E. Barksdale, 1861.
Journal of the State Convention and Ordinances and Resolutions Adopted in March, 1861. Jackson, Miss.: E. Barksdale, 1861.
Laws of the State of Mississippi Passed at a Regular Biennial Session of the Legislature Held in the City of Jackson in January, February and March, A.D. 1846. Jackson, Miss.: C. M. Price and G. R. Fall, 1846.
Laws of the State of Mississippi Passed at a Regular Session of the Mississippi Legislature Held in the City of Jackson January, February, and March, 1850. Jackson, Miss.: Fall and Marshall, 1850.
Lynch, James D. *The Bench and the Bar of Mississippi.* New York: E. J. Hale and Son, 1881.
Lynch, John Roy. *Reminiscences of an Active Life: The Autobiography of John Roy Lynch.* Ed. John Hope Franklin. Chicago: University of Chicago Press, 1970.
Macaulay, Thomas Babington. *Critical and Historical Essays Contributed to the Edinburgh Review.* Vol. 3. Leipzig: Bernhard Tauchnitz, 1850.
Mayes, Edward. *The State University: Reply of Prof. Edward Mayes to Senator J. Z. George.* University, Miss.: Edward Mayes, 1887.

Memorial Addresses on the Life and Character of James Z. George (Late a Senator from Mississippi) Delivered in the Senate and House of Representatives. Washington, D.C.: Government Printing Office, 1898.

Michael, W. H. *Official Congressional Directory for the Use of the United States Congress, Fifty-second Congress, First Session.* Washington, D.C.: Government Printing Office, 1892.

Mississippi in 1875: Report of the Select Committee to Inquire into the Mississippi Election of 1875, With the Testimony and Documentary Evidence, 2 vols. Washington, D.C.: Government Printing Office, 1876.

Mr. George, from the Committee on Woman Suffrage, Submitted the Following Views of the Minority, to Accompany Joint Resolution S.R. 60. Washington, D.C.: Government Printing Office, 1882.

"Mrs. Lizzie George Henderson." *Confederate Veteran* 13, no. 12 (December 1905): 532a.

Murphy, E. V. *Congressional Directory, 1st Session, 47th Congress.* Washington, D.C.: Government Printing Office, 1881.

Nineteenth Annual Catalogue of the Mississippi Agricultural and Mechanical College, 1898–1889. Meridian, Miss.: Meridian News, 1898.

Northern Pacific Railroad Lands—Speech of Hon. James Z. George, of Mississippi, in the Senate of the United States, Friday, June 11, 1886. Washington, D.C.: Government Printing Office, 1886.

The Official Records of the Union and Confederate Navies in the War of the Rebellion. 30 vols. Washington, D.C.: Government Printing Office, 1894–1922.

Poore, Ben Perley. *Congressional Directory, 49th Congress, 1st Session.* Washington, D.C.: Government Printing Office, 1886.

Power, J. L. *Proceedings of the Mississippi State Convention, Held January 7th to 26th, A.D. 1861. Including the Ordinances, as Finally Adopted, Important Speeches, and a List of Members, Showing the Postoffice, Profession, Nativity, Politics, Age, Religious Preference, and Social Relations of Each.* Jackson, Miss.: Power and Cadwallader, Book and Job Printers, 1861.

The Power of the Senate to Make Inquisitions—Speech of Hon. J. Z. George of Mississippi, in the Senate of the United States, January 28, 1890. Washington, D.C.: Government Printing Office, 1890.

Proceedings of the Grand Royal Arch Chapter of the State of Mississippi at Its Thirty-third Annual Convocation, Held at Jackson, February 7th and 8th, 1881. Jackson, Miss.: Clarion Steam Book Publishing House, 1881.

Relations between the Senate and Executive Departments—Speech of Hon. J. Z. George of Mississippi, in the Senate of the United States, March 23, 1886. Washington, D.C.: Government Printing Office, 1886.

Remarks of Hon. J. Z. George of Mississippi, in the Senate of the United States, Friday April 1, 1881, on the Resolution Submitted by Mr. Dawes in Relation to the Election of Officers of the Senate. Washington, D.C.: Government Printing Office, 1881.

Report of the Committee of the Senate upon the Relations between Labor and Capital, and Testimony Taken by the Committee. 5 vols. Washington, D.C.: Government Printing Office, 1885.

Report of the Committee on Agriculture and Forestry on Condition of Cotton Growers in the United States, the Present Prices of Cotton, and the Remedy; and on Cotton

Consumption and Production. 2 vols. Washington, D.C.: Government Printing Office, 1895.

Rowland, Dunbar, ed. *Jefferson Davis, Constitutionalist: His Letters, Papers and Speeches.* 10 vols. Jackson: Mississippi Department of Archives and History, 1923.

"Senator James Z. George, of Mississippi." *Chautauquan: A Monthly Magazine* 26 (October 1897–March 1898): 103.

Seventeenth Annual Catalogue of the Mississippi Agricultural and Mechanical College, 1896-'97. Starkville, Miss.: E. L. Reid's Steam Printing Office, 1897.

Speech by Hon. J. Z. George of Mississippi, in the Senate of the United States, December 31, 1890, January 19 and 20, 1891—Defense of the Constitution of Mississippi. Washington, D.C.: Government Printing Office, 1891.

Speech of Hon. J. Z. George on the Financial Question, Delivered at Winona, Mississippi, Saturday July 13, 1895. N.p.: n.p., n.d.

Stanton, Elizabeth Cady, Susan B. Anthony, and Matilda Joslyn Gage, eds., *History of Woman Suffrage.* 3 vols. Rochester, N.Y.: Charles Mann, 1876–1885.

Statistics of the Population of the United States at the Tenth Census (June 1, 1880). 22 vols. Washington, D.C.: Government Printing Office, 1881.

Steeljacket. Starkville, Miss.: Agricultural and Mechanical College, 1918.

Stone, James H., ed. "L. Q. C. Lamar's Letters to Edward Donelson Clark, 1868–1885: Part III, 1879–1885." *Journal of Mississippi History* 43, no. 2 (May 1981): 135–164.

Supervision of Railroads in Interstate Commerce—Speech of Hon. J. Z. George, of Mississippi, in the Senate of the United States, Friday, December 19, 1884. Washington, D.C.: Government Printing Office, 1885.

A Thousand American Men of Mark of To-day. Chicago: American Men of Mark, 1917.

Trusts and Combinations—Speech of Hon. James Z. George, of Mississippi, in the Senate of the United States, Monday, February 4, 1889. Washington, D.C.: Government Printing Office, 1889.

Walton, William Martin. *An Epitome of My Life: Civil War Reminiscences.* Austin, Tex.: Waterloo Press, 1956.

War of the Rebellion: A Compilation of the Official Records of the Union and Confederate Armies. 128 vols. Washington D.C., 1880–1901.

Woods, Thomas H. "A Sketch of the Mississippi Secession Convention of 1861—Its Membership and Work." In *Publications of the Mississippi Historical Society*, 13 vols., ed. Franklin L. Riley, 6:91–104. Oxford: Mississippi Historical Society, 1902.

Secondary Sources

Allardice, Bruce S. *More Generals in Gray.* Baton Rouge: Louisiana State University Press, 1995.

———. *Confederate Colonels: A Biographical Register.* Columbia: University of Missouri Press, 2008.

Armstrong, Margaret. "James Zachariah George: Champion of White Supremacy." Master's thesis, University of Alabama, 1938.

Ayers, Edward L. *The Promise of the New South: Life After Reconstruction.* New York: Oxford University Press, 1992.

Ballard, Michael B. *Maroon and White: Mississippi State University, 1878–2003*. Jackson: University Press of Mississippi, 2008.
Bauer, K. Jack. *The Mexican War: 1846–1848*. New York: Macmillan, 1974.
Bearss, Edwin C. *The Vicksburg Campaign*. 3 vols. Dayton, Ohio: Morningside House, 1986.
Bettersworth, John K. *Mississippi: A History*. Austin, Tex.: Steck, 1959.
Bond, Bradley G. "Edward Cary Walthall, 1865–1890: A Redeemer Reappraisal." Master's thesis, University of Southern Mississippi, 1987.
———. "Edward C. Walthall and the 1880 Senatorial Nomination: Politics of Balance in the Redeemer Era." *Journal of Mississippi History* 50 (February 1988): 1–20.
———. *Political Culture in the Nineteenth-Century South: Mississippi, 1830–1890*. Baton Rouge: Louisiana State University Press, 1995.
Browne, F. Z. "Reconstruction in Oktibbeha County." In *Publications of the Mississippi Historical Society*, 13 vols., ed. Franklin L. Riley, 13:273–298. Oxford: Mississippi Historical Society, 1913.
Cate, Wirt Armistead. *Lucius Q. C. Lamar: Secession and Reunion*. Chapel Hill: University of North Carolina Press, 1935.
Chance, Joseph E. *Jefferson Davis's Mexican War Regiment*. Jackson: University Press of Mississippi, 1991.
Clark, Eric C. "The Mississippi Constitutional Convention of 1890: A Political Analysis." Master's thesis, University of Mississippi, 1975.
———. "Regulation of Corporations in the Mississippi Constitutional Convention of 1890." *Journal of Mississippi History* 48, no. 1 (February 1986): 31–41.
Coleman, James P. "The Origin of the Constitution of 1890." *Journal of Mississippi History* 19, no. 2 (April 1957): 69–92.
———. "The Mississippi Constitution of 1890 and the Final Decade of the Nineteenth Century." In *A History of Mississippi*, 2 vols., ed. Richard A. McLemore, 2:3–28. Hattiesburg: University and College Press of Mississippi, 1973.
Cooling, Benjamin F. *Forts Henry and Donelson: The Key to the Confederate Heartland*. Knoxville: University of Tennessee Press, 1987.
Cresswell, Stephen. *Multi-party Politics in Mississippi, 1877–1902*. Jackson: University Press of Mississippi, 1995.
———. *Rednecks, Redeemers, and Race: Mississippi After Reconstruction, 1877–1917*. Jackson: University Press of Mississippi, 2006.
Davis, William C. *Jefferson Davis: The Man and His Hour, a Biography*. New York: Harper Collins, 1991.
Dictionary of American Biography. New York: Scribners, 1932.
Dray, Philip. *Capitol Men: The Epic Story of Reconstruction Through the Lives of the First Black Congressmen*. Boston: Houghton Mifflin Harcourt, 2008.
Dubay, Robert W. *John Jones Pettus, Mississippi Fire-eater: His Life and Times, 1813–1867*. Jackson: University Press of Mississippi, 1975.
Duncan, Bingham. "A History of Carroll County from 1871." Master's thesis, University of Mississippi, 1933.
Foner, Eric. *Reconstruction: America's Unfinished Revolution, 1863–1877*. New York: Harper Collins, 1989.

Foote, Shelby. *The Civil War: A Narrative.* 3 vols. New York: Random House, 1958–1974.
Frank, Joseph Allan, and George A. Reaves. *Seeing the Elephant: Raw Recruits at the Battle of Shiloh.* Westport, Conn.: Greenwood Press, 1989.
Frederick, Donald A. *Antitrust Status of Farmer Cooperatives: The Story of the Capper-Volstead Act.* Washington, D.C.: U.S. Department of Agriculture, 2002.
Freehling, William W. *The Road to Disunion: Secessionists at Bay, 1776–1854.* New York: Oxford University Press, 1990.
———. *The Road to Disunion: Secessionists Triumphant, 1854–1861.* New York: Oxford University Press, 2007.
Freemen, Douglas Southall. *R. E. Lee: A Biography*, 4 vols. New York: Charles Scribner's Sons, 1934.
Garner, James W. *Reconstruction in Mississippi.* New York: Macmillan, 1901.
———. "The Senatorial Career of J. Z. George." In *Publications of the Mississippi Historical Society*, 13 vols., ed. Franklin L. Riley, 7:245–262. Oxford: Mississippi Historical Society, 1903.
Gee, Mrs. O. K. *Marriage Records in the Carroll County Courthouse.* Carrollton, Miss.: n.p., 1964.
Giles, William Lincoln. "Agricultural Revolution: 1890–1970." In *A History of Mississippi*, 2 vols., ed. Richard A. McLemore, 2:177–211. Hattiesburg: University and College Press of Mississippi, 1973.
Going, Allen J. "The South and the Blair Education Bill." *Mississippi Valley Historical Review* 44, no. 2 (September 1957): 267–290.
Grandy, Christopher. "Original Intent and the Sherman Antitrust Act: A Re-examination of the Consumer-Welfare Hypothesis." *Journal of Economic History* 53, no. 2 (June 1993): 359–376.
Griffith, V. A. "Mississippi Reports and Reporters." *Mississippi Law Journal* 22, no. 1 (December 1950): 37–58.
Halsell, Willie D. "Democratic Dissensions in Mississippi, 1878–1882." *Journal of Mississippi History* 2 (July 1940): 123–135.
———. "James R. Chalmers and 'Mahoneism' in Mississippi." *Journal of Southern History* 10, no. 1 (February 1944), 37–58.
———. "The Bourbon Period in Mississippi Politics, 1875–1890." *Journal of Southern History* 11, no. 4 (November 1945): 519–537.
Hamilton, W. F. and Betty Wiltshire. *Military Annals of Carroll County, MS, Expanded.* Carrollton, Miss.: Pioneer, 2004.
Harris, J. William. *Deep Souths: Delta, Piedmont, and Sea Island Society in the Age of Segregation.* Baltimore: Johns Hopkins University Press, 2001.
Harris, William C. *Presidential Reconstruction in Mississippi.* Baton Rouge: Louisiana State University Press, 1967.
———. "The Reconstruction of the Commonwealth, 1865–1870." In *A History of Mississippi*, 2 vols., ed. Richard A. McLemore, 1:542–570. Hattiesburg: University and College Press of Mississippi, 1973.
———. *Day of the Carpetbagger: Republican Reconstruction in Mississippi.* Baton Rouge: Louisiana State University Press, 1979.

Heidler, David S., and Jeanne T. Heidler, eds. *Encyclopedia of the American Civil War: A Political, Social, and Military History*, 5 vols. Santa Barbara, Calif.: ABC-CLIO, 2000.

Hesseltine, William B. *Civil War Prisons*. Kent, Ohio: Kent State University Press, 1997.

Horton, Lucy Henderson. *Family History*. Franklin, Tenn.: Press of the News, 1922.

Johnston, Frank. "The Public Services of Senator James Z. George." In *Publications of the Mississippi Historical Society*, 13 vols., ed. Franklin L. Riley, 8:201–226. University: Mississippi Historical Society, 1904.

———. "Suffrage and Reconstruction in Mississippi." In *Publications of the Mississippi Historical Society*, 13 vols., ed. Franklin L. Riley, 6:141–244. Oxford: Mississippi Historical Society, 1902.

Kazin, Michael. *A Godly Hero: The Life of William Jennings Bryan*. New York: Knopf, 2006.

Kendel, Julia. "Reconstruction in Lafayette County." In *Publications of the Mississippi Historical Society*, 13 vols., ed. Franklin L. Riley, 13:223–271. Oxford: Mississippi Historical Society, 1913.

Kirwan, Albert D. "Apportionment in the Mississippi Constitution of 1890." *Journal of Southern History* 14, no. 2 (May 1948): 234–246.

———. *Revolt of the Rednecks: Mississippi Politics: 1876–1925*. New York: Harper and Row, 1965.

Lemann, Nicholas. *Redemption: The Last Battle of the Civil War*. New York: Farrar, Straus and Giroux, 2007.

Lowry, Robert, and William H. McCardle. *A History of Mississippi, From the Discovery of the Great River by Hernando DeSoto, Including the Earliest Settlement Made by the French, Under Iberville, to the Death of Jefferson Davis*. Jackson, Miss.: R. H. Henry, 1891.

Mabry, William Alexander. "Disfranchisement of the Negro in Mississippi." *Journal of Southern History* 4, no. 3 (August 1938): 318–333.

Mayes, Edward. *Lucius Q. C. Lamar: His Life, Times, and Speeches, 1825–1893*. Nashville, Tenn.: Publishing House of the Methodist Episcopal Church, South, 1896.

McCain, William D. "The Triumph of Democracy: 1916–1932." In *A History of Mississippi*, 2 vols, ed. Richard A. McLemore, 2:59–96. Hattiesburg: University and College Press of Mississippi, 1973.

McLemore, Richard A., ed. A History of Mississippi. 2 vols. Hattiesburg: University and College Press of Mississippi, 1973.

McMurry, Richard M. *Two Great Rebel Armies: An Essay in Confederate Military History*. Chapel Hill: University of North Carolina Press, 1989.

McNeily, J. S. "History of the Measures Submitted to the Committee on Elective Franchise, Apportionment, and Elections in the Constitutional Convention of 1890" In *Publications of the Mississippi Historical Society*, 13 vols., ed. Franklin L. Riley, 6:129–140. Oxford: Mississippi Historical Society, 1902.

———. "Climax and Collapse of Reconstruction in Mississippi, 1874–1876." In *Publications of the Mississippi Historical Society*, 13 vols., ed. Franklin L. Riley, 12:283–474. University: Mississippi Historical Society, 1912.

———. "War and Reconstruction in Mississippi, 1863–1890." In *Publications of the Mississippi Historical Society, Centenary Series*, 2:165–535. Jackson: Mississippi Historical Society, 1918.

Morison, Samuel Eliot, and Henry Steele Commager. *The Growth of the American Republic*, 2 vols. New York: Oxford University Press, 1942.

Murphy, James B. *L. Q. C. Lamar: Pragmatic Patriot*. Baton Rouge: Louisiana State University Press, 1973.

Perman, Michael. *Struggle for Mastery: Dis-franchisement in the South, 1888–1908*. Chapel Hill: University of North Carolina Press, 2001.

Rainwater, Percy L. *Mississippi: Storm Center of Secession, 1856–1861*. Baton Rouge: Louisiana State University Press, 1938.

Pitts, Clover S. "James Z. George: Lawyer, Soldier, Judge, Statesman." *Mississippi Lawyer* (July–September 2000): 22–24.

Power, James L. "The Black and Tan Convention." In *Publications of the Mississippi Historical Society*, 13 vols., ed. Franklin L. Riley, 3:73–83. Oxford: Mississippi Historical Society, 1900.

Ranck, James Byrne. *Albert Gallatin Brown: Radical Southern Nationalist*. New York: Appleton-Century, 1937.

Rand, Clayton. *Men of Spine in Mississippi*. Gulfport, Miss.: Dixie Press, 1940.

Riley, Franklin L., ed. *Publications of the Mississippi Historical Society*. 13 vols. Oxford: Mississippi Historical Society, 1898–1914.

Ringold, May Spencer. "Some Liberal Aspects in the Senatorial Policies of James Zachariah George during the Period 1881–1890." Master's thesis, University of Mississippi, 1950.

———. "Senator James Zachariah George: Bourbon or Liberal?" *Journal of Mississippi History* 16, no. 3 (July 1954): 164–182.

———. "Senator James Zachariah George and Federal Aid to Common Schools." *Journal of Mississippi History* 20, no. 1 (January 1958): 30–36.

Rowland, Dunbar. "Rise and Fall of Negro Rule in Mississippi." In *Publications of the Mississippi Historical Society*, 13 vols., ed. Franklin L. Riley, 2:189–199. Oxford: Mississippi Historical Society, 1899.

———. *Political and Parliamentary Orators and Oratory of Mississippi*. Harrisburg, Pa.: Press of Harrisburg, 1901.

———. *The Official and Statistical Register of the State of Mississippi, 1904*. Nashville, Tenn.: Brandon Printing, 1904.

———. *Mississippi; Comprising Sketches of Counties, Towns, Events, Institutions and Persons, Arranged in Cyclopedic Form*. 3 vols. Atlanta: Southern Historical Printing Association, 1907.

———. *The Official and Statistical Register of the State of Mississippi, 1908*. Nashville, Tenn.: Brandon Printing, 1908.

———. *Courts, Judges, and Lawyers of Mississippi, 1798–1935*. Jackson, Miss.: Harderman Bros., 1935.

Rowland, Dunbar, and H. Grady Howell Jr. *Military History of Mississippi: 1803–1898, Including a Listing of All Known Mississippi Confederate Military Units*. Madison, Miss.: Chickasaw Bayou Press, 2003.

Sansing, David G. "Congressional Reconstruction." In *A History of Mississippi*, 2 vols., ed. Richard A. McLemore, 1:571–589. Hattiesburg: University and College Press of Mississippi, 1973.

———. *The University of Mississippi: A Sesquicentennial History*. Jackson: University Press of Mississippi, 1999.

Seigenthaler, John. *James K. Polk*. New York: Times Books, 2003.

Shanks, John Hal. "The Early Career of James Z. George." Master's thesis, University of Mississippi, 1938.

Skates, John Ray. *A History of the Mississippi Supreme Court, 1817–1948*. Jackson: Mississippi Bar Foundation, 1973.

Smith, Allene De Shazo. *Greenwood Leflore and the Choctaw Indians of the Mississippi Valley*. Memphis, Tenn.: C. A. Davis Printing, 1951.

Smith, Timothy B. *Mississippi in the Civil War: The Home Front*. Jackson: University Press of Mississippi, 2010.

Sword, Wiley. *Shiloh: Bloody April*. Dayton, Ohio: Morningside Bookshop Press, 1988.

Tate, Roger D. "Franklin L. Riley and the University of Mississippi." *Journal of Mississippi History* 42, no. 2 (May 1980): 99–111.

Upchurch, Thomas Adams. "Why Populism Failed in Mississippi." *Journal of Mississippi History* 65, no. 3 (Fall 2003): 249–276.

———. *Legislating Racism: The Billion Dollar Congress and the Birth of Jim Crow*. Lexington: University Press of Kentucky, 2004.

Wade, John William. "Lands of the Liquidating Levee Board Through Litigation and Legislation." In *Publications of the Mississippi Historical Society*, 13 vols., ed. Franklin L. Riley, 9:273–313. Oxford: Mississippi Historical Society, 1906.

Wellborn, Fred. "The Influence of the Silver-Republican Senators, 1889–1891." *Mississippi Valley Historical Review* 14, no. 4 (March 1928): 462–480.

Wells, W. Calvin. "Reconstruction in Hinds County." In *Publications of the Mississippi Historical Society*, 13 vols., ed. Franklin L. Riley, 9:85–108. Oxford: Mississippi Historical Society, 1906.

Williams, Frank B. Jr. "The Poll Tax as a Suffrage Requirement in the South, 1870–1901." *Journal of Southern History* 18, no. 4 (November 1952): 469–496.

———. "Public Reaction to the Poll Tax as a Suffrage Requirement in Mississippi, 1890–1905." *Journal of Mississippi History* 17, no. 4 (October 1955): 229–248.

Witty, Fred M. "Reconstruction in Carroll-Montgomery Counties." In *Publications of the Mississippi Historical Society*, 13 vols., ed. Franklin L. Riley, 10:115–134. Oxford: Mississippi Historical Society, 1909.

Woodward, C. Vann. *Origins of the New South: 1877–1913*. Baton Rouge: Louisiana State University Press, 1951.

———. *The Strange Career of Jim Crow*. 3rd ed. New York: Oxford University Press, 1974.

Wooster, Ralph A. "The Membership of the Mississippi Secession Convention of 1861." *Journal of Mississippi History* 16, no. 4 (October 1954): 242–257.

Index

Abbeville, Mississippi, 60, 72
Aberdeen, Mississippi, 108, 112
Adair, John, 4
Adair, Mary, 4
Address of the State Executive Committee, 112
African Americans, ix, xii, 86–88, 95–96, 98–100, 102–9, 111–13, 119–20, 125, 131, 133, 140, 144, 146–53, 156–57, 159, 161–62, 181–82, 188, 218n33
Agricultural Experiment Stations, 131
Alabama, 56, 112, 130, 181
Alcorn, James L., 37–39, 95, 97, 99, 117, 150, 152, 164
Aldridge, Francis Marion, 20, 89, 92
Aldridge, Francis Minter, 89
Aldridge v. Grider, 20
Aleck (slave), 61, 69, 77
Allen, John M., 183
Allen, William V., 166
Ames, Adelbert, 95, 99–100, 102–7, 109, 112, 210n22
Amite County, Mississippi, 107
Anderson, Fulton, 20, 95
Angelo's Hall, 106
Arkansas, 2nd Cavalry, 73
Army of the Tennessee, 66
Arthur, Chester A., 123–24
Articles of Confederation, 142
Antioption Bill, 131
Attala County, 190n15
Ayers, T. S., 77

Baldwin, William E., 50, 53
Baldwin County, Georgia, 4
Bankruptcy, 88, 133, 165

Barksdale, Ethelbert, 99, 101, 108, 114, 119–20, 164
Barksdale, William R., 38, 40, 89, 127
Barry, William S., 23, 37–38, 42
Baptists, 17, 30, 37, 89–90, 137, 168, 179, 181–83
Bate, William B., 181, 184
Batesville, Mississippi, 59
Baton Rouge, Louisiana, 66
Beasley Creek, 43
Beck, James B., 126
Benton, Thomas Hart, 185
Berry, Micajah F., 135
Bible, 90, 183, 199n11
Big Sand Creek, 90, 182
Black and Tan Convention, 95, 146
Black Codes, 87
Blackstone, William, 56
Blair, John A., 150
Blair Education Bill, 130
Blythe, Green L., 61, 64
Boles, W. P., 21
Boonshill, Tennessee, 203n12
Booth, William, 37
Boston, Massachusetts, 127
Bourbons, 119, 144, 173, 212n21
Bowling Green, Kentucky, 49
Bowman House, 29
Brazos Santiago, 13
Brooke, Walker, 37–38
Brown, Albert Gallatin, 16, 24, 97, 208n6
Brown, John, 19
Brown, William N., 50–53, 199n24
Bruce, Blanche K., 98, 119–20, 161
Bryan, William Jennings, 142
Buckner, Simon B., 52–53

243

INDEX

Buena Vista, Battle of, 15
Burkitt, Frank, 164

Cairo, USS, 59
Calhoon, Solomon S., 151, 220n16
Calhoun, John C., 171, 185
California, 11–12, 19, 140
Call, Wilkinson, 126
Camargo, Mexico, 14
Camden, Johnson N., 123
Cameron, Angus, 125
Camp Allen, 15
Camp Chase, 53, 81
Camp Davis, 46
Camp Defiance, 46
Camp Independence, 13
Campbell, Josiah A. P., 99, 101, 118, 150, 181
Canada, 93
Canton, Mississippi, 120
Carpetbaggers, 95, 99, 146
Carroll County, Mississippi, 6–10, 12, 14–16, 19–20, 23–24, 36–37, 44–45, 92, 94, 100, 163, 188; Board of Police, 21, 23; Courthouse, 16, 96, 181
Carroll County Farmer's Alliance, 163
Carroll County Volunteers, 12
Carroll Guards, 44–45, 51, 198n2, 200n11
Carroll Rangers, 44
Carrollton, Mississippi, x, xi, xiii, xv, 6, 9, 12–13, 15–17, 20–21, 23–24, 27, 30–32, 36–37, 42–44, 46, 48, 56, 65, 78–79, 82, 85, 87–88, 90, 92–94, 96, 121, 137–38, 155, 167–70, 177, 179–84
Carrollton Baptist Church, 17, 30, 90, 137, 168, 179, 181–83
Carrollton Ladies Association, 46
Carrollton-Grenada Road, 23, 43
Carlisle, J. G., 167
Catchings, Thomas C., 94, 167
Cate, W. A., 222n14
Chalmers, Hamilton H., 118, 121
Chalmers, James R., 65–72, 74, 118
Chambliss, Edmund S., 5–7

Chambliss, Mary (grandmother), 4
Chambliss, Mary (mother), 4
Chambliss, Zachariah, 4, 190n12
Chase, George K., 107–9, 125
Chattanooga, Tennessee, 72, 129
Chicago, Illinois, 55, 77, 81
Chickasaw Indians, 6
Chickasaw Messenger, 164
China, 133
Chinese Exclusion Act, 133
Christmas, 31, 60–61, 75, 129, 136
Choctaw County, Mississippi, 88
Choctaw Indians, 6–7, 46
Civil Rights Era, ix, 162
Civil Service, 144, 172
Civil War, ix, x, xv, 12, 34, 44–84, 98, 112, 126, 128, 144, 151, 179, 186
Clark, Charles, 99, 115
Clay, Henry, 171, 185
Cleveland, Grover, 140, 164, 166, 169, 172
Clinton, Mississippi, 103
Clinton, Parson, 30
Clinton Riot, 103
Clinton Riot, The, 104
Coldwater River, 64–65, 72
Collierville, Tennessee, 72–74, 76, 90
Colorado, 184
Columbia County, Georgia, 4
Columbus, Mississippi, 37, 112
Columbus, Ohio, 53, 183
Commager, Henry S., 142
Compromise of 1850, 19
Compromise of 1877, 112
Confederate States of America, 42, 44, 59, 63, 70, 85, 94; Congress, 42, 97, 101, 118; Constitution, 42, 78; War Department, 46, 58
Congressional Record, x
Connecticut, 156–58, 160, 185
Conscription, 58–59, 66
Constitutional Convention (1890), 139, 146–55, 161; Elective Franchise, Apportionment, and Elections Committee, 151; Judiciary Committee, 153
Cooper, Timothy E., 121

INDEX

Corinth, Mississippi, 112
Cotesworth, x, xiv, 43, 77, 82, 83, 86, 89–90, 92–94, 121, 137–38, 155, 168–70, 177–79, 182, 188, 198n21
Cothran, Francis Elizabeth, 18
Cothran, Francis M. Young, 9, 18
Cothran, William, 9–11, 16, 18–20, 29, 31, 33, 56, 76, 79, 82, 86, 97, 126, 129, 193n18, 214n14
Cotton Mountain, (West) Virginia, 47
Cresswell, Stephen, xii, 40, 147
Critical and Historical Essays Contributed to the Edinburgh Review, 56
Crosby, Peter, 102
Crow, Jim, 142, 161
Crowder v. Nelson, 20
Cumberland River, 53
Cushman, J. F., 24

Davis, Alexander K., 109
Davis, Jefferson, 12–15, 30, 58, 71, 130, 187
Davis, Reuben, 15, 89
Davy (apprentice), 96
Dawes, Henry L., 125, 129
Deas, George, 48
Deavours, Stone, 187
Declaration of Immediate Causes, 41
Declaration of Independence, 142
Decrease of the Wealth of Mississippi under Radical Misrule, 104
Delaware, 184
Delta, 93
Democratic Party, 23, 95, 99, 101–3, 105, 110–11, 119–20, 163–64, 166, 169, 172, 176; Resolutions Committee, 176
Department Number 2, Confederate, 45
DeSoto County, Mississippi, 106
District Number 5, Confederate, 65, 68
Dolph, Joseph N., 157
Drake, Joseph, 51
Duck Hill, Mississippi, 105
Dunning, William A., ix
Durham, Fannie, 5

Durham, Fayette, 48
Durham, Matthew, 5–6
Durham, Seaborn, 5–10, 17, 126, 179, 214n14
Dutch, 83

Ebenezer Church, 4
Edmunds, George F., 157–58
Egypt, 37
Elections Bill (Force Bill), 142–43, 147–48, 155, 159–60
Ellett, Henry T., 26
England, 41, 92
Enterprise, Mississippi, 112
Ethiopian Eunuch, 90
Evergreen Cemetery, 36, 56, 179, 182, 214n14

Fair, James G., 123
Fair Lawn Institute, 119
Farmer's Alliance, 132, 163
Featherston, Winfield S., 99, 120, 151–52, 169
Fewell, J. W., 153
Fifteenth Amendment, 146, 148, 156–57, 159
Florida, 112, 126, 139
Floyd, John B., 46–50, 52–53
Fontaine, Charles D., 64
Forsyth, Georgia, 4
Fort Donelson, 49–53, 62, 77, 84
Fort Henry, 62
Fort Pemberton, 65
Fort Sumter, 44
Fortress Monroe, 81
Fourteenth Amendment, 159
Freedmen, 92, 96–97, 104, 125
Fullerton (overseer), 82
Furloughs, 58–59, 61–62, 66, 201n14

Garfield, James A., 123–24
Garfield Hospital, 177
Garner, James W., 186
Gee, Jo, 79
George, Alfred, 33, 79, 89, 111, 179, 183, 187

George, Elizabeth (daughter), 69, 119, 127–28, 136–37, 139, 155, 159, 167–68, 176, 186
George, Elizabeth Brooks Young (wife): antebellum years, 17–36; during Civil War, 42–84; death, 179; family background, 9; in Jackson, 94–122; marriage, 11, 16–17; paralysis, 169, 177; during Reconstruction, 85–113; during Senate years, 123–75
George, Emma (daughter), 17, 34, 79, 89
George, Francis (Fannie), 17, 89, 127
George, Frank (son), 47–48, 56, 182
George, James (grandfather), 3–4, 6, 9
George, James Z.: 1875 election, 102–12; 1876 election, 111–12; at 1890 Constitutional Convention, 146–54; ambition of, xi, 8, 11, 15, 18, 21–22, 32, 33, 187; Battle of Collierville, 72–75; at Battle of Fort Donelson, 49–53; on board of trustees, Agricultural and Mechanical College, 115–16; on board of trustees, University of Mississippi, 115; captain, 20th Mississippi infantry, 44–58; childhood, 5–10; and children, 17, 21, 32–34, 36, 45, 47–48, 56, 61, 69, 82, 89, 111, 119, 121, 127, 155, 167; colonel, 5th Mississippi Cavalry, 71–84; and Cotesworth, 23–24, 42–43, 92–93, 137–38, 168–69, 177, 179, 198n21; court reporter, 24–28, 91; death of, 180; defense of Mississippi Constitution, 155–62; education, 7; Executive Committee Chairman, 99–113; family background, 3–5; and finances, 19, 34, 45, 86–87, 94, 128; first Senate term, 123–34; funeral, 180–82; and health issues, 49, 80, 128–29, 137, 170–71, 176–80; independence of, xi, 8, 12, 30, 40–41, 53, 62–63, 66–67, 71, 90, 124, 147, 169, 172–74; land, 17–18, 22–23, 42–43, 82, 92; and the law, 8–9, 16, 19–21, 56, 88, 91–92, 94, 100, 114, 129, 153; and loneliness, 21–22, 28, 31–32, 47, 49, 55, 61, 78–79, 89, 121, 127, 135, 179; marriage of, 16–17; meeting with Ames, 105–6; memorials, 182–88; in Mexican War, 11–16, 91; and Mississippi Plan, 111, 113, 161; as Mississippi Senate engrossing clerk, 24; on Mississippi Supreme Court, 117–19, 121; move to Jackson, 93–94; personality of, xi, 20, 22, 32, 37, 63, 67, 90–91, 124–25, 127, 171–75, 188; potential U.S. Supreme Court seat, 116–17; prisoner of war, 53–57, 76–84; racial views of, xi–xii, 83, 86, 96, 112, 133, 152–53, 161, 218n33; at Reconstruction, 85–112; and religion, 17, 30, 76, 89–91, 136–37, 168, 182; retirement of, 169–71; as road overseer, 23; Secession Convention delegate, 36–42; second Senate term, 135–45; and slaves, 34, 40–41, 61, 69, 77, 86, 96–97, 138, 155, 179, 182; and society, xi, 28–30, 94, 123–24, 136, 167, 174; State Brigadier General, 58–71; third Senate term, 163–71
George, James Z., Jr. (grandson), 164, 177
George, James Z., Jr. (son), 36, 56, 182
George, Joseph W. (father), 3–5, 89
George, Joseph W. (son), 89, 127, 168, 177, 187
George, Kate (daughter), 21, 79, 89, 92, 111
George, Katy Boyd (granddaughter), 187
George, Mary (daughter), 21, 48, 79, 89
George, Mary (mother), 3–8, 17, 21, 56, 82, 87, 126, 179, 190n15, 214n14
George, Pinckney (son), 89, 127, 168
George, Thomas J. (son-in-law), 127
George, William Cothran (son), 33, 47, 119, 127, 177, 179, 183, 187
George County, 187
George Rifles, 187
George School, 186

Georgia, xiv, 3–4, 6–7, 9, 17, 22–23, 43, 77, 112, 187; Legislature, 9
Gerrymandering, 152, 158–59
Gilded Age, ix, xiv, 147, 173
Gildy, Charles, 93
Giles, William L., 132
Graham, Robert, 16
Grand Junction, Tennessee, 49
Grant, Ulysses S., 52, 59–60, 66, 72, 76, 96, 100, 103, 109, 130
Gray, George, 184
Greeley, Horace, 96
Greenback Party, 120
Greenwood, Mississippi, 12, 27, 65, 183, 186
Grenada, Mississippi, 23, 43, 60–69, 71
Grierson, Benjamin, 65–66
Grubbs, Mollie, 34
Guatemala, 89
Guyton, David T., 151

Hardee's Tactics, 199n24
Hardin County, Tennessee, 191n23
Harper, A. Y., 78
Harper's Ferry, (West) Virginia, 19
Harris, Isham G., 130, 143
Harris, Wiley P., 37–39, 41, 76, 93–94, 97, 99–100, 108, 114, 150, 220n20
Hatch, Edward, 76
Hatch Act, 131–32, 215n27
Hawaiian Islands, 167
Hawk, Robert M. A., 132
Hawley, Joseph R., 156–59
Hayes, Rutherford B., 111–12, 116–17
Helm, W. B., 24
Hemingway, J. B. H., 89, 114, 121
Henderson, Thomas R., 155
Herod, 37
Hinds County, Mississippi, 102–3; Democratic Party, 103
Hoar, George F., 125, 129, 133, 142–43, 157, 160
Holly Springs, Mississippi, 60
Holman, Daniel W., 203n12
Holt, Alfred C., 40
Hooker, Charles E., 167

Howard, Bainbridge D., 12–14
Hughes School, 7
Humphreys, Benjamin, 87
Hurlbut, Stephen A., 76

Idaho, 159–60
Illinois, 132
Iowa, 157
Iowa, 2nd Cavalry, 76
Ireland, 93
Isom, Thomas D., 150
Issues of the Canvas, 104
Iuka, Mississippi, 45

J. Z. George Chapter, UDC, 186
J. Z. George High School, 188
J. Z. George Scholarship, 183
Jackson, Andrew, 7, 9
Jackson, Mississippi, 20–21, 24–32, 34, 36, 38, 42, 64–66, 71, 88–89, 91, 93–97, 99–101, 104–5, 107, 114, 119–21, 137, 147, 149–50, 167, 179–81, 186
Jackson, Tennessee, 49
Jackson Weekly Clarion Ledger, 180
Jake (slave), 86, 138, 155, 179, 182
James Z. George Club, 104
Jasper County, Mississippi, 135
Johnson, Andrew, 87
Johnson, John L., 180–82
Johnson and Company (publisher), 27, 82, 91
Johnson's Island, 52–57, 76–85, 151
Johnston, Albert Sidney, 48
Johnston, Joseph E., 67
Jones County, Georgia, 4
Journal of Negro History, 186
Judea, 37

Kanawha River, 46–47
Kansas, 19, 141
Kansas Nebraska Act, 19
Keirn, Walter L., 150
Kemper County Tragedy, 113
Kennedy, Benjamin, 9
Kentucky, 4, 48–49, 81, 126
Kincannon, Andrew A., 187

King, Preston, 159
Kosciusko, Mississippi, 82, 190n15, 214n14
Kosciusko City Cemetery, 214n14
Ku Klux Klan, 88

La Grange, Tennessee, 68
La Teneria, 14
Lafayette County, Mississippi, 104–5
Lake Erie, 54–55
Lamar, L. Q. C., 37–39, 88, 98, 100–101, 111–12, 114–17, 119–21, 123, 125–26, 147–48, 150, 163, 166, 213n24, 222n14
Lamkin, Edward O., 74
Leavell, William H., 89, 186
Lee, Robert E., 46–48
Lee, Stephen D., 115, 147–48, 151–52, 219n14
LeFlore, Greenwood, 7, 46
LeFlore County, Mississippi, 92
Leggett, Mortimer D., 101
Legislation of 1865 Concerning Freedmen, The, 104
Lexington, Mississippi, 32
Liberia, 133
Lincoln, Abraham, 34–35, 67, 85, 159, 173
Liquidating Levee Board, 93
Loring, William W., 64–65
Lost Cause, 119
Louisiana, 66, 112
Louisiana State University, ix
Lowry, Robert, 99, 147–48, 181
Lukeman, Augustus, 187
Lynch, James S., 97
Lynch, John R., 113, 149
Lynchburg, Virginia, 46

MacAfee, Mrs. Mat, 29
Macaulay, Thomas B., 56
Macon, Mississippi, 112
Madison, Mississippi, 108
Magna Carta, 92
Malmaison Plantation, 7
Manassas, Battle of First, 47
Manor, John I., 56

Mardi Gras, 127
Martin, William, 9
Martin, William T., 151–52
Masons, 19
Massachusetts, 95, 98, 109, 125, 129, 133, 142–43, 157, 159
Massachusetts, USS, 13
May (apprentice), 96
Mayes, Edward, 116, 150
McCullough, Robert, 69
McLaurin, Anselm, 170
McMillan, Samuel, 125
McMurry, Richard M., 67
McRae, John J., 23, 29–30
Meek, John E., 108
Memphis, Tennessee, 65, 68, 71–72, 76–77, 87, 165
Memphis and Charleston Railroad, 72
Memphis Appeal, 109
Mexican War, 11–16, 44, 91, 131
Mexico, 11, 15, 18, 23, 48
Michigan, 115
Middleton, Mississippi, 7
Millsaps College, 181
Minnesota, 125, 157–58
Mississippi: Agricultural and Mechanical College, 115–16, 130–31, 147, 173, 176, 183, 187; Baptist Convention, 168; Capitol, 20, 25–26, 36, 38, 99, 106, 147, 154, 181, 188; Department of Archives and History, x, xiv, 186; governor, 10, 16, 23–24, 29–30, 36–37, 58–59, 61–66, 71, 87–88, 95, 97–100, 102–6, 108–9, 112, 115, 117–18, 147–50, 166, 169–70, 181–82; Hall of Fame, 186, 188; High Court of Errors and Appeals, 20–21, 24, 26, 28, 30, 41, 43, 78, 88–89, 91, 93–94, 114, 121; House of Representatives, 10, 24, 78, 98–99, 118, 120, 147–48, 150, 164; governor's mansion, 104–5; Legislature, 9–10, 19, 24–25, 28, 31, 34, 36, 39–42, 78, 88, 95, 98–99, 109, 111, 117, 119–20, 135, 147, 149, 152, 162, 164, 170, 178, 182–83, 187,

INDEX 249

192n25, 226n32; militia, 58–61, 65, 67, 70, 100, 103, 105–7, 151, 159, 181; Senate, 10, 19, 24, 78, 97, 109, 115, 117, 120, 164; State Conservative Democratic Executive Committee, 95; Supreme Court, ix, 20, 36, 91, 93, 117–19, 121, 126, 129, 152–53, 180, 183, 188, 211n1. *See also* Constitutional Convention; Secession Convention
Mississippi Central Railroad, 23, 174
Mississippi City, Mississippi, 179
Mississippi Plan, 111, 113, 161
Mississippi Rifle, 12
Mississippi River, 66
Mississippi State University, ix, 115
Mississippi troops
   Civil War Confederate: 1st Cavalry, 44; 2nd Partisan Rangers, 68; 3rd State Cavalry, 73; 4th Infantry, 51; 5th Cavalry, 72–74, 78, 203n12; 11th Infantry, 87; 15th Infantry, 92; 19th Cavalry Battalion, 71; 20th Infantry, 45–53; 24th Infantry, 87; 29th Infantry, 87; Dunn's Battalion Partisan Rangers, 68; McGuirks Battalion Partisan Rangers, 68
   Mexican War: 1st Infantry, 12–15; 2nd Infantry, 15
Mississippi Valley Historical Review, 186
Missouri, 44, 185
Mizner, John K., 69
Money, Hernando D., 167, 170, 177, 181–82, 184, 186
Monroe County, Georgia, 4–5
Monterrey, Mexico, 14–15, 44
Montgomery, Alabama, Convention, 42, 94
Morgan, John T., 130
Morison, Samuel E., 142
Murrah, W. B., 181

Natchez Democrat, 180
Native Americans, 6, 218n33. *See also* Chickasaw Indians; Choctaw Indians

Neal, John A., 16
Neal Building, 100
Neale Publishing Company, 186
Nebraska, 19, 166
Nero, 81
Nevada, 123
New England, 141, 157
New Jersey, 159
New Orleans, Battle of, 33
New Orleans, Louisiana, 13, 33, 87, 89, 165
New Orleans Times Democrat, 170
New York, 96, 156, 159, 186
New York, USS, 13
New York Hotel, 126
New York Times, 113–14, 117, 139, 143, 173–74, 177, 179–80
New York Tribune, 124
Newton, Mississippi, 66
North Carolina, 4–5, 126
Noxubee County, Mississippi, 6, 43

Oakwood Cemetery, 193n25
Odd Fellows College, 94
Ohio, 53, 183; 123rd Infantry, 56
Ohio State Journal, 183
Oktibbeha County, Mississippi, 104
Old Capitol Museum, 188
Oregon, 157
Oxford, Mississippi, 37, 60, 88, 115

Panola, Mississippi, 65, 68–69, 71
Pearson, James M., 56
Pemberton, John C., 60, 64–65
Pettus, Edmund W., 181
Pettus, John J., 37, 58–67, 71, 76
Phelan, James, 89
Philadelphia, Pennsylvania, 27, 82, 91
Philip the Evangelist, 90
Pierrepont, Edward, 102
Pillow, Gideon, 50–52
Pittman, Henry, 90, 138
Platt, Orville H., 185
Plumb, Preston B., 141
Political History of Slavery, The, 169, 186
Polk, James K., 11–12, 23

Polk, Leonidas, 45
Populist Party, 164, 166
Posey, Carnot, 13
Proctor, Redfield, 185
Progressive Era, 217n26
Puritans, 83

Quitman, John A., 14

Radical Extravagance Contrasted with Democratic Economy, 112
Railroads, 23, 69, 72–73, 130, 139, 163, 167, 173, 181
Ratliff Place, 6
Reconstruction, ix, 85–113, 117, 119, 125, 130, 133, 139, 142, 146, 148–50, 159–61, 163, 169, 185–86, 205n8; Presidential Reconstruction, 87, 96; Radical Reconstruction, 87, 96
Resaca, Battle of, 87
Revels, Hiram, 98, 140
Revolutionary War, 4
Richardson, R. V., 72
Richmond, Virginia, 76, 81
Ringold, May Spencer, 173
Rio Grande River, 11, 13–14
Rome, Italy, 22, 81
Rorer, W. A., 53
Rosecrans, William S., 46
Rowland, Dunbar, ix, 136, 139, 151, 172, 188
Runnymede, 92, 168, 177
Russell, Daniel R., 12, 14–15, 44–45, 47, 50
Russellville, Georgia, 5
Ryne, James, 93

Sandusky, Ohio, 53–54
Scalawags, 95, 99, 146
Scales, William N., 73–74, 77, 81
Scot, Dred, 19, 144
Scott, Mary, 77
Secession Convention (1861), 36–42, 44, 64, 67, 89, 92, 94, 97, 112, 133, 150, 180; Committee on Federal Jurisdiction and Property, 39; Committee on Postal, Financial, and Commercial Affairs, 40
Senate, United States, x, 19, 27, 30, 100, 110–11, 115, 117, 119–21, 123–47, 150–52, 155–76, 178–80, 183–87; Agriculture and Forestry Committee, 124, 131–32, 134, 139, 163–65, 168; Claims Committee, 124, 132; Commerce Committee, 142; Education and Labor Committee, 124, 130, 139, 164; Immigration Committee, 139; Judiciary Committee, 124, 126, 134, 139, 142, 164; Military Affairs Committee, 124; Potomac River Front Committee, 164; Railroad Committee, 139; Select Committee on Women's Suffrage, 132, 139, 164; Transportation Routes to the Seaboard Committee, 139, 164
Sessions, J. F., 80
Seward, William, 159
Sewell Mountain, (West) Virginia, 46–47
Shanty (plantation), 92
Sharkey, William L., 87, 95
Sharp, John, 12
Sherman, John, 141–42
Sherman, William T., 72, 130
Sherman Anti Trust Act, 141, 152
Shiloh, Battle of, 92
Shongalo, Mississippi, 7, 9, 17, 45, 92
Short (apprentice), 96
Shuqualak, Mississippi, 6
Sidney (apprentice), 96
Silver Issue, 143, 165–66, 172
Simrall, Horatio F., 117
Singleton, Otho R., 119–20, 167
Slavery, 4–8, 11, 17–19, 22–23, 34, 36, 39–41, 43, 55, 59, 61, 69, 77, 83, 86–87, 96–97, 112, 119, 131, 133, 138, 155, 157, 169, 173, 179, 182, 186; slave trade, 40, 157
Slemons, W. F., 72–74
Smith, Cotesworth Pinckney, 24, 28, 43, 89

Smith, Hoke, 172, 223n27
South Carolina, 4, 9, 35, 47–48, 112; Legislature, 9
Spooner, John C., 157
St. James Hotel, 126
St. Louis, Missouri, 165–66
St. Nicholas Hotel, 126
Starkville, Mississippi, 115, 130–31, 168
State Street, Jackson, 119
States' Rights, 19, 140, 142, 144, 166, 183, 186
Statuary Hall, 187
Stephens, Hubert D., 187
Stevens, Thaddeus, 159
Stone, John M., 99, 109, 115, 117–18, 149, 166, 181
Stone Mountain, Georgia, 187
Stones River, Battle of, 87
Subtreasury Plan, 163, 166, 172
Sumner, Charles, 100
Sunflower County, Mississippi, 88, 92

Tallahatchie County, Mississippi, 88
Tallahatchie River, 59, 64, 68, 72
Taney, Roger B., 144
Tariff, 130, 140–42, 163
Taylor, Zachary, 11, 13–14
Teller, Henry M., 184
Tennessee, 9, 14, 20, 48–50, 60, 66, 68, 70, 72, 130, 181, 191n23, 203n12
Texas, 11, 13, 50; 7th Infantry, 50
Tilden, Samuel, 111–12, 116
Tilghman, Lloyd, 62–64
Treaty of Dancing Rabbit Creek, 7
Tupper, Tullius C., 61
Turley, Thomas B., 181
Turpie, David B., 150, 161, 173, 184

United Daughters of the Confederacy, 186
United States: Agriculture Department, 132; Army, 11–12, 60, 66, 87, 131; Capitol, xi, 123–24, 129, 136, 167, 169, 187–88; Constitution, 96, 118, 124, 132, 139, 141–44, 148, 150, 153, 156, 158, 165, 183, 185; Court of Appeals, 88; District Courts, 39, 88; government, 100, 106, 113, 144, 148–50, 166; House of Representatives, 99, 111, 132, 140, 164, 183–84; Justice Department, 107; Secretary of the Interior, 126, 223n27; Secretary of the Treasury, 124, 167; Supreme Court, 115–17, 147, 149, 154, 161, 166, 169; War Department, 133
University of Alabama, ix
University of Mississippi, ix, 115–16, 130, 187
University of Virginia, 19

Vaiden, C. M., 46
Vaiden, Mississippi, 6–7, 17, 43–44, 65, 71, 82, 88, 92, 109, 181
Van Dorn, Earl, 60, 64
Vance, Zebulon, 126
Vardaman, James K., 183
Vermont, 157–58, 160, 185
Vicksburg, Mississippi, 12–13, 27, 57, 59, 64–66, 68–70, 102, 117, 148; Campaign, 59, 68–69
Vicksburg Herald, 117, 148
Virginia, 19, 46, 48, 52–53, 56

Walthall, Edward C., 27, 88, 99, 101, 118–21, 126, 147–48, 152, 159, 163–64, 166–67, 169–71, 176–77, 179–81, 183–84
Walton, William M., 19
Warner, Alexander, 108
Warren County, Georgia, 4
Washington, D.C., xi, 13, 23, 39, 99, 101, 105, 120–21, 123, 126–29, 131, 135–36, 138–39, 149–50, 154–55, 164, 167–69, 171, 173, 176–81, 183–84, 187–88
Washington Post, 139, 180–81
Washington Street, Carrollton, 16–17, 24
Water Valley, Mississippi, 72
Webster, Daniel, 171, 185
West, Absalom M., 120
West Virginia, 123

Wharton, Thomas J., 24, 26, 106
Wheeler, Joseph, 203n12
Whig Party, 37, 101, 113, 150
White House, 111, 164, 169
White Supremacy, xii, 41, 98, 113, 119, 133, 144, 147, 173, 180, 186
Williams, John Sharp, 113, 186
Williams v. Mississippi, 161
Williamson, Robert W., 20, 87–88, 93, 183
Wilson, James F., 157
Wilson, Mary, 8
Winchester, Tennessee, 203n12
Winona, Mississippi, 23, 48, 65, 91, 93, 181
Winter, Richard H., 62
Wisconsin, 125, 157
Woodward, C. Vann, 112, 121, 212n21
World War I, 187
Wyatt, Mississippi, 72

Yalobusha County, Mississippi, 20, 88, 92
Yazoo Baptist Association, 168
Yazoo City, Mississippi, 12, 64
Yazoo County, Mississippi, 12, 102, 104–6
Yazoo Pass, 64–65
Yazoo River, 8, 12, 27, 59, 64–65
Yerger, Jacob S., 37–38
Yocona River, 69
Young, J. T., 56
Young, Sarah, 9, 36, 56
Young, Thomas, 9

www.ingramcontent.com/pod-product-compliance
Lightning Source LLC
Chambersburg PA
CBHW022003220426
43663CB00007B/939